The Pen, Not The Sword

The Pen, Not The Sword

BY MARY AND GORDON CAMPBELL

AURORA PUBLISHERS INCORPORATED
NASHVILLE / LONDON

Dedicated to Ronnie Stewart

CONTENTS

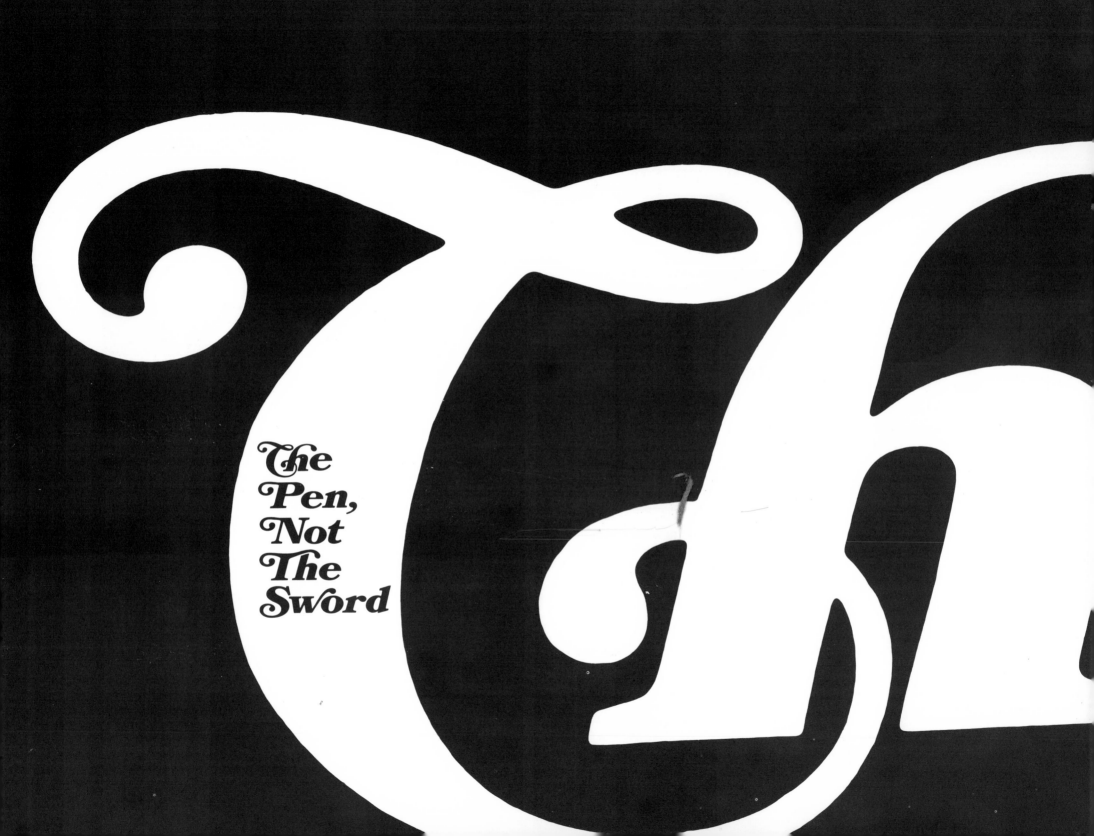

The
Pen,
Not
The
Sword

INTRODUCTION

There can be no more delightful way of studying history than through the eyes of the cartoonist. Cartoons have been records of major events since the days of James Gillray, William Hogarth, Thomas Rowlandson and John Leech. Following in the footsteps of these early satirists were John Tenniel, who recorded Britain's political and social history for thirty years, and Raven Hill, Bernard Partridge, and F. H. Townsend, foremost artists of England's *Punch* magazine.

It might be said that cartooning had its origin in the caricature and cartooning of Honore Daumier (1808-1879). He created more than a hundred lithographs for *La Caricature*, a political weekly founded by Philipon, which reflected the history of French caricature. Daumier has been called the "Historian of the Bourgeois Government," a merciless satirist because of his mastery of portraiture.

After the suspension of *La Caricature*, a daily paper called *Le Charivari* was formed and he became a contributor to it. With an association that lasted nearly forty years, Daumier took up painting in the last years of his life, but recognition of his genius came too late to be of any pleasure to him. In 1878, a friend, Durand Ruel, exhibited a collection of his paintings. Daumier's

eyesight was failing and he had entirely ceased work. A year later he died at Valmondois.

William Hogarth may be considered the father of cartooning and none of his many descendants has been his equal. From Hogarth's work, we can learn how he thought about "the live issues" and about the serious problems of his day. Hogarth's cartoons always focused on social issues, such as bribery, cruelty, prison abuses, the liquor business and child labor. Never did a cartoonist wield the pen with such inspired skill as did Hogarth. Never had vices a fiercer enemy or mankind a more sympathetic friend. This is why his cartoons have become "classic."

Another great early cartoonist was John Leech, born in London August 29, 1817. From his childhood, Leech showed a marked aptitude for drawing, inheriting some talent in this direction from his father, a scholarly man. Young Leech, at the age of seven, was sent off to Charterhouse School, where he was to make his lifelong acquaintance with Thackeray. Leaving Charterhouse, he entered Bartholomew's College in London to study medicine and managed to acquire a knowledge of anatomy that helped him greatly in his later work. He finally abandoned the idea of becoming a doctor and decided

to gain his living by drawing. He was eighteen when he published his first book entitled *Etchings and Sketchings, by A. Pen.* It was not until August 1841 that he entered upon a career that was to make him immortal.

Punch magazine was at that time about three weeks old. He contributed a drawing called "Foreign Affairs." The drawing, a woodcut, arrived late and by holding up the presses, the publishers disappointed many subscribers.

It might be interesting to know how the cartoons for *Punch* were determined. From the very beginning of the publication, it had been the custom to hold weekly dinners for the staff. These dinners fell on Wednesday, and the contents of the upcoming issue were discussed. The first question was, "What shall the cartoon be?" In Leech's time, Mark Lemon was the editor and Thackeray a leading contributor. Often the artist himself would suggest a subject; at other times, the combined staff suggested ideas for a cartoon. Leech died suddenly at work, October 29, 1864. Four days before the end came, he had dined at the usual staff dinner; his last sketch was never completed.

In 1855, a young man by the name of Thomas Nast walked into the office of *Leslie's Weekly* and landed a job on the art staff. At the time, he was fifteen years of age. Four years later he was working for the New York *Illustrated News*, covering a variety of news events. One assignment carried him to the British Isles to do sketches of the Heenan and Sayers heavyweight prize fight. On the same trip, he was assigned to cover Garibaldi's campaign that was to unite Italy.

Back from the Mediterranean, he found the United States on the verge of civil war. With art experience, Nast joined the staff of *Harper's Weekly*. By 1863, he began to draw the weekly cartoons that brought him world-wide fame for the next twenty-five years. Nast is still remembered as the architect of the political cartoon in America. When his popularity was waning, other men began laying the foundations for today's political cartoon builders.

Joseph Keppler, another artist of foreign birth, was born in Vienna in 1839, the year before Thomas Nast was born in Bavaria on September 27, 1840. Nast came to America at the age of six, while Keppler came at the age of twenty-nine. Joseph Keppler had received a good education; he was so skilled with the pencil that he decided to study art and enrolled at the Academy of Fine Arts in Vienna. He soon found a vein of humor creeping into his drawings. Keppler submitted several humor sketches and cartoons to a comic weekly in Vienna. In the meantime, he became interested in amateur theatricals and hesitated when the door to drawing was opening to him. Finally, he decided that the theatre was calling him. He joined an opera company and toured Italy and Austria.

Keppler had been engaged to sing in opera at St. Louis and sailed to America in 1868. While in St. Louis, Keppler became dissatisfied with his singing and again felt the urge to draw. In his spare time, he drew humorous sketches to contribute to the St. Louis papers. His drawings were accepted and he became more and more known as a humorist.

Joseph Keppler was a multitalented man, well edu-cated, a splendid singer, an able artist and above all, a keen businessman. Keppler felt that the Germans in St. Louis wanted a humorous weekly and he decided to attempt the publication of such a periodical. The Germans, however, did not respond; and without the circulation, the business folded for lack of funds. The failure in St. Louis did not discourage Keppler; instead, it convinced him that his next attempt at publishing should be national, not local. His next move was to New York City. Nothing destroyed his confidence in the belief that a humor weekly would be successful. In the beginning of his New York venture, he was compelled to postpone his career as a publisher.

In New York, he sought out Frank Leslie, publisher of Leslie's *Illustrated News*. Leslie hired him in 1872 and Keppler remained with the publication until 1877. During his years with Leslie's, Keppler was searching for ways to give the public a real humor magazine. At last he was able to interest Adolph Schwarzmann in establishing a German *Puck* magazine. The first edition appeared in March of 1877. From the very beginning it was a success. That was during President Rutherford B. Hayes's administration. Keppler was then convinced that the Americans would support a comic weekly, if given the opportunity. The English version started the following year.

Prior to the founding of *Puck*, Thomas Nast had the cartoon field to himself, and *Harper's Weekly* was regarded as the foremost cartoon periodical. A dozen other weeklies had come and gone during that period. Other than Matt Morgan, cartoonist on Leslie's *Weekly*, Keppler had little rivalry. *Life* Magazine started on January 4, 1883 and was printed in black and white. It was more sophisticated than *Puck* and *Judge*, which didn't gain momentum until the mid-eighties but was founded on October 21, 1881.

Puck at first was printed in black and one tint, but the colors were so distributed in the fountain of the lithographic press as to make it possible with one im-pression to obtain a blending of two or three tints.

Puck's early policy was a fearless one; it took an independent stand in politics, was the party organ of none and was free from the dictates of class or creed. It dealt alike with the Roman Catholic and Protestant churches, and it ridiculed the Jews unmercifully. *Puck* handled everything with gloves—boxing gloves, that is.

Keppler, too, had a remarkably keen insight in detecting new talent for his art staff. Many artists would not have gained prominence without the guiding hand of Keppler. He was a strenuous worker, and the demands of the publishing business did not interfere with his output of cartoons. Few issues of *Puck* failed to carry at least one of his cartoons.

James A. Wales, a former wood engraver from Ohio, was one of the first cartoonists on *Puck's* art staff. Starting in 1879 and remaining until 1881, Wales drew some very effective and remarkable cartoons. One of his most remembered was in the March 17, 1880 issue of *Puck*, representing Roscoe Conkling, the New York senator trying to work the 15, 14, 13 (The Great Presidential) puzzle. At that time, the puzzle in question was all the rage and its application to this cartoon was quite timely, inasmuch as Conkling was endeavoring to back Grant for a third term.

In 1881, Wales had a disagreement with Keppler and left his employer to found his own publication. Wales' *Judge* magazine didn't gain prominence nor circulation until after W. J. Arkell purchased the magazine and hired Bernhard Gillam away from *Puck* to make him art director, with a handsome salary and a block of the company's stock. Long before that time, Keppler had come into his own as a publisher with the help of Gillam. Keppler had shown he was not only an artistic genius, but also a sound businessman. He was always on the alert for the latest method and improvements in the printing business. Keppler was the first to publish cartoons in color from wood engravings and later by lithography. This made his publication the foremost periodical in the country during the latter part of the nineteenth century.

When Gillam took over his duties on *Judge*, Eugene Zimmerman tendered his resignation with *Puck* and joined Gillam's art staff. Zimmerman was born in Basel, Switzerland, May 26, 1862, but came to America as a youth. Zimmerman, when first noticed by Keppler, was a sign painter in New York and was doing some bulletin work on the east side. He was assigned to paint sketches for *Mulligan's Picnic*, then one of Harrigan and Hart's well-known plays. Keppler at once noted his unusual skill. He sought out Zimmerman and asked him if he had ever attempted comic drawings. The sign painter replied that he had a few at home and was requested to bring them to the *Puck* office. The next week he was hired and worked closely with Keppler and Gillam for the next three years on *Puck Weekly* and with Gillam on *Judge* until the time of Gillam's death in 1894.

Two men, Karl von Stur and F. Graetz, were imported from Germany to serve as staff artists on *Puck* in the early 1880s, but the European artists were too slow in grasping American politics. While their work was excellent, their technique was often so decidedly German that it did not fit the situation. Graetz spoke no English whatever, so all ideas had to be interpreted in German for his benefit. Graetz eventually returned to Germany and resumed his former position.

Among the many gifted and resourceful cartoonists in America, Frederick Opper was probably the most individualistic and prolific of all. Born in Madison, Ohio, in 1857, he left school at the age of fourteen and worked in one of the village stores for a time. For a few years he served as an apprentice printer on the local paper. He then came to New York to seek his fortune by setting type in some newspaper office. He found he had not served long enough at the printer's trade to get a job, and he finally secured a job in a large store making price labels. While here, he got up comic sketches and took them to *Wild Oats*, a humor publication. The fact that some of these were accepted encouraged him so that he gave up his position and supported himself by making humorous drawings.

He was offered a place on the staff of *Leslie's Weekly*. After three years he was hired by Keppler. Opper stayed with *Puck* from 1880 until 1898 and then severed his relations with *Puck* to accept a position with William Randolph Hearst.

Opper's work rarely caricatured individuals; he preferred to employ original figures to typify certain evil classes. His drawings usually created a smile while conveying some important truth. His range of work has been remarkably wide; he has done cartoons, social humor, satire, and character work and has illustrated books by such writers as Mark Twain, Bill Nye, Hobart, the author of *Dinkelspiel*, and F. P. Dunne. Opper continued to draw political cartoons for Hearst along with "Happy Hooligan," "Gloomy Gus," "Howson Lott," "Alphonse and Gaston," and "Maude the Mule."

When Bernhard Gillam died, it took from the world of satirical art one of its most capable workers. He combined in a marked degree the qualities most essential to the successful cartoonist—humor, originality, technique, and true artistic feeling. Gillam was a satirist of the English school on the order of Sir John Tenniel, of whom he was a great admirer. His drawings were always carefully and almost painfully drawn. He was a hard worker and availed himself of little relaxation or recreation, for he was always searching for ideas. Until his untimely death from typhoid fever, he had proved himself one of the ablest disciples of the school of political caricature founded by Joseph Keppler. Keppler's influence on his early work was considerable, and it was with *Puck* that he won his first honors. Some of *Puck*'s strongest cartoons during the first eight years of its life were Gillam's—either in inspiration or actual work. One of his creations was the famous Blaine cartoon entitled "The Tattooed Man," and it was introduced repeatedly in many of Keppler's cartoons.

The death of Bernhard Gillam, while it dealt a severe blow to *Judge*, did not find the publication unprepared. The art staff was well equipped for any emergency. Fred Gillam, who had worked under the name of F. Victor or Victor, had been with *Judge* for some time and his drawing technique resembled his brother Bernhard's very closely. The public, in general, didn't realize that Bernhard's death had wrought any great change. *Judge* had many capable artists at that time, and Grant E. Hamilton stepped in to fill Gillam's place.

Hamilton was born in Youngstown, Ohio. He never studied art but always took naturally to drawing. As a youth, he sold ideas to *Harper*'s, *Puck* and the New York *Daily Graphic*. His original sketches were so often used by the *Graphic* that it eventually became more economical for its editors to engage his services than to buy separate sketches, and they sent for him to join their art staff. Hamilton went from the *Graphic* to *Judge*, where he became a fixture on that comic journal.

Louis Dalrymple was always comprehensive and earnest about cartooning. From his earliest boyhood days he had been a keen observer and enthusiast. His ideas came at any time or place and immediately he reached in his pocket for a clean bit of paper on which to make a little rough pencil sketch. This he used to retain some action or expression to complete a cartoon. Dalrymple's years were all too few; born in 1865, he died December 27, 1905.

William Allen Rogers took up illustrating as a profession in 1872. A year later he became a member of the staff of the New York *Daily Graphic*, a publication that developed some of the outstanding artists of that period. Later he entered the employ of *Harper's Weekly* where he contributed a number of excellent drawings. In 1880 he drew a cartoon during the Hancock campaign. It made an instant hit. After that time, he found it impossible to devote his attention to illustrating. Rogers' cartoons are usually calculated to provoke a smile, even when they deal with the loathsome mass of corruption in politics.

Rogers was born in Springfield, Ohio. When he was fourteen years old, he drew a number of small cartoons on wood, and an engraver in Dayton, Ohio, engraved them for a syndicate. So far as is known, these were the first cartoons to be syndicated in the daily papers. They were drawn with a pen directly on the wood block. Rogers contributed cartoons to *Puck* magazine in the early 1890s, but he is best known for his newspaper cartoons directed against America's great gambling world and trust spawning-ground, Wall Street.

The lithographic cartoon of the latter part of the nineteenth century was driven out of business because the process was too slow to compete with the daily papers on timely subjects: the big dailies in New York, Boston, Philadelphia and other large metropolitan areas were hiring political cartoonists. The daily newspaper could produce a cartoon in twenty-four hours by the photoengraving process. They had a decided advantage over the colored lithographic cartoon that sometimes required several weeks to finish.

Of course, there was a certain charm about the lithographic cartoon which one doesn't experience in black and white cartoons. The cartoonist drew his cartoon directly onto the soft, gray stone surface, working with crayon, which required unusual care and an abundance of patience. The weight of a double page stone was at least sixty pounds, according to its thickness. Therefore, a lithographic cartoon was usually finished in the same position in which it was begun. In the earlier years of stone lithography, the artists drew three colored cartoons on one large stone, all at the same time, each laboring on his own cartoon. That was when the circulation was small and the editions were printed directly from the original stone. Later, however, duplicate stones were made from transfers. A transfer is made by means of an impression from the original stone upon coated paper; this in turn is transferred to another stone or metal plate and etched with acid in the same manner and by the same process as the original drawing on lithographic stone.

The death of Joseph Keppler on February 19, 1894 was a loss to periodical literature. He left more than a half million dollars. His fame was not only deserved but is a compliment to public judgment and to the courage which made him a pioneer in the branch of art that has remained most popular in this country. He died when he was best prepared to live. It was the verdict of more than one country that his summons came much too soon.

Joseph Keppler, Jr., followed in his father's footsteps. Although he was an excellent cartoonist in his own right, he didn't have the desire to continue in the publishing business. The properties were sold to Nathan Straus, Jr., who had been associated with the Kepplers. Hy (Henry) Mayer took over the duties of the art editor. *Puck* ceased publication during World War I.

The *Judge* comic weekly continued on through the twenties and through the depression years. *Judge* had a struggling existence in its latter years with competition from the *New Yorker, College Humor,* and *Esquire* magazines. In 1938 the October and November issues were never published, and the January 1939 issue was its final effort. Again in 1953 *Judge* reappeared in print, beginning on October 26, but published only four issues. The end came with the final magazine of November 16, 1953.

Mary and Gordon Campbell

Nashville, Tennessee

The Pen, Not The Sword

POLITICS

One of the candidates for the Republican nomination in 1880 was Ulysses S. Grant whom Roscoe Conkling of New York, John A. Logan of Illinois and Donald Cameron of Pennsylvania were backing for the Stalwart faction, for a third term. Among the other contenders were Senator Blaine of Maine, Senator Edmunds, and Secretary John Sherman of Ohio. Grant had made a world tour in 1877, after his retirement from high office. In the course of the tour he had been received with great acclaim. That was very flattering to the American people. The Republicans thought this sojourn gave him experience and would enable him to avoid many of the blunders he had committed during his earlier terms in office. His candidacy was greeted with much enthusiasm and much strong opposition.

The Republican convention, which met in Chicago on June 2, 1880, praised both the record of the Republican party and the presidential performance of Rutherford B. Hayes. The Republican platform denounced the Democratic party's "supreme and insatiable lust of office and patronage" and the methods it took to secure the solid South. Roscoe Conkling presented Grant's name in nomination in a resounding speech. James A. Garfield's speech in behalf of John Sherman was also a splendid effort, but it had unexpected results. On the first ballot Grant led with 304 votes, Blaine with 284, Sherman with 93, and Edmunds with 34, with a few scattered votes among the others. Grant's forces stuck with him to the end, but his vote never rose above 313, which was 65 short of a majority. Sherman controlled 120 votes on the thirtieth ballot, but could gain no more. Blaine's count never exceeded 285. On the second ballot one delegate voted for Garfield and on a few succeeding ballots he received one or two votes. On the thirty-fourth ballot Wisconsin gave him sixteen votes. To show his loyalty to Sherman, Garfield protested but the chairman, Senator George F. Hoar (Mass.), ruled Garfield out of order. On the following ballot Garfield received fifty votes and on the thirty-sixth ballot, after Blaine and Sherman threw their support to him, he received 399 votes and the nomination.

The Conkling faction was appeased by the nomination of Chester A. Arthur of New York for vice president. The Stalwarts had been defeated by the Half-Breeds, as they were contemptuously called by their opponents within the party. To them James Garfield was a representative of the Half-Breeds. Conkling had supported him in the campaign, despite his personal feeling. Friends of Conkling thought his influence could have been used to keep New York State in the Stalwart's camp. Garfield would not give Conkling any special privileges. Garfield was a man of integrity, giving equal patronage to both party factions. In an effort to discredit Garfield, Conkling tried to manipulate New York politics against Garfield. He failed, but his actions served to increase intra-party bitterness.

James A. Garfield, a darkhorse candidate, was born at Orange, Ohio, in 1831. His parents were poor, and as a boy he drove mules on the tow path of the Ohio canal. Garfield's childhood was marred by hardship; when he was only two years old his father died. He cheerfully helped his mother in supporting the family. After graduating from Williams College, he was a college professor for a time. Afterwards he studied law. During the Civil War he was promoted to the rank of major general. Garfield's term of service in the House from 1863 to 1880 was so successful that he was elected to the Senate in 1880. Before taking his seat in the Senate he was nominated by the Republicans for president. The story of his rise from poverty and obscurity gave him strong popular appeal.

The Democrats nominated Winfield Scott Hancock of Pennsylvania as their man. Many people felt that the Democrats would renominate Samuel J. Tilden and under his leadership try to right the wrong of the 1876 campaign. Tilden was far from popular with most of the party leaders. On the first ballot nearly a score of candidates received votes. Among them were Henry B. Payne of Ohio, Thomas F. Bayard of Delaware, Allen G. Thurman of Ohio, and Thomas A. Hendricks of Indiana. But Hancock led and on the second ballot was nominated. The ex-general was a veteran of both the Mexican and Civil Wars and had greatly distinguished himself. His fine appearance and soldierly bearing had won him the nickname of "The Superb." Although Hancock had fought against the South, he was opposed to measures taken during Reconstruction. His running mate was William H. English of Indiana, a former member of Congress.

In the campaign the Democrats dwelled constantly on the "Fraud of 1876," an issue which their platform declared paramount. The Republicans retaliated with many charges concerning suppression of the Negro vote in the South. The campaign of 1880 centered on the issue of the tariff and currency. Neither party fought for any great cause.

Hancock carried the South, but in the North and West he won only New Jersey, Nevada, and five of the six electoral votes in California. In all, his total electoral vote was 155. Garfield carried the same number of states but received 214 electoral votes and the presidency. The Republicans regained control of the House, and the Senate was balanced: thirty-seven Republicans and thirty-seven Democrats, with two independents and the vice president to tip the balance of power.

Garfield named as secretary of state James G. Blaine, one of Conkling's bitterest enemies. W. H. Robertson was selected for collector of the port of New York, a highly respectable position that carried great weight in politics. The collector had over a thousand subordinates under his command, all patronage positions. Robertson had repeatedly defied Conkling, the Stalwart boss, and had supported Blaine instead of Grant. Conkling believed that Robertson's appointment was a personal insult to him; and in retaliation, Conkling made public a letter written by Garfield to stir up the lagging collections of campaign contributions from government employees. The exposure discredited the president but it did not enable Conkling to persuade the Senate to reject Robertson's appointment. Conkling therefore resigned his seat in the Senate. Thomas C. Platt did likewise, thus earning the nickname of "Me Too." Both expected reelection as justification, but the legislature of New York elected two other men, Warner Miller and E. G. Lapham. Conkling's political career was ended; he never held public office again. Platt regained his power and became a familiar figure in both state and national political circles.

Garfield had written a letter to the chairman of the Republican Congressional Committee, J. A. Hubbell, during the campaign. Conkling made its contents public. This letter caught the attention of Assistant Postmaster General Brady. The assistant postmaster general and cronies had been involved in corrupt dealings in connection with the Star mail routes. When the new postmaster general, Thomas L. James, began an investigation of the malpractices, Brady tried to intimidate Garfield into firing Hubbell. Brady published Hubbell's letter, adding to the furor created by the Conkling exposure. The Star Route frauds involved several prominent men, including Senator Dorsey of Arkansas. The prosecution was hindered by many obstacles and only one minor offender was even brought to trial.

Numerous office seekers crowded into Garfield's waiting-room, and many were disappointed. Charles J. Guiteau, who had been at various times a preacher, editor and politician, had an insane notion that the death of Garfield would help heal the Republican party. On July 2, 1881, Garfield and Blaine were walking together on the platform of a railway station in Washington when Guiteau fired two bullets into Garfield's back. For eleven weeks the president lingered between life and death. He died on September 19 and was succeeded by Vice-President Chester A. Arthur.

Arthur was a Republican machine politician of New York who had been put on the national ticket in 1880. When Arthur ascended to the presidency, the Republican spoilsmen got the surprise of their lives. There was an unexpected and remarkable change in Arthur's personality. He repudiated machine politics and became an advocate of honesty, efficiency, and good government. He possessed good executive ability and went about his work efficiently. The presidency brought his finer qualities to light. His messages and state papers read like those of a man of unusual ability. He dealt with the bills sent to him by Congress in a way that lacked neither courage nor discrimination.

In accordance with custom, the members of Garfield's cabinet tendered their resignations. These were not accepted at once as Arthur insisted that each member retain his position. The secretary of the treasury was first to leave. He was succeeded by Charles J. Folger of New York. Wayne Mac Veagh of Pennsylvania, the attorney general, also resigned a short time later; his successor was Benjamin H. Brewster, also from Pennsylvania. The next to retire was James G. Blaine, secretary of state. It was not expected that Mr. Blaine would remain, though the president and the secretary had worked in harmony during the interim. Frederick T. Frelinghuysen of New Jersey was called to the State Department. He had served two terms in the United States Senate. Thomas L. James, one of the best postmaster generals was replaced by Timothy O. Howe of Wisconsin. Robert T. Lincoln, secretary of war, remained. Later, William E. Chandler of New Hampshire became secretary of the navy, and Henry M. Teller of Colorado became secretary of the interior. Two important men were later brought into the cabinet as death made changes necessary. Walter Q. Gresham of Indiana succeeded Timothy O. Howe as postmaster general and in 1884 was made secretary of the treasury, after the death of Judge Folger. The following month Gresham resigned to become a circuit judge. Hugh McCulloch of Indiana, who had entered Lincoln's second cabinet as secretary of the treasury and continued under President Johnson, held the position of postmaster general until March 4, 1885.

The change in the cabinet was so noticeable that it appeared as if another political party had come into office. This reveals the extent to which the Republicans were split. On one side was the Stalwart faction, the deep rooted followers of the party, and on the other side the Half-Breeds, the party members opposed to political machine domination. The division had its origin in the problems of civil service reform, office appointments, problems of reconstruction in the South, and conflicting personal ambitions.

President Arthur's courage in vetoing an inflated river and harbor bill won public acclaim. During that time the treasury showed a surplus of revenue and Congress was tempted to be extravagant. The measure of 1882 provided for an expenditure of over eighteen million dollars. Congress overrode the president's veto. The congressional elections of 1882 gave the Democrats a majority in the House. The Democrats won 196 seats and the Republicans retained only 118. The president's recommendations to Congress were well received, though few were acted upon. In the local elections in the following year the Republicans regained some of their losses. Both parties approached the election of 1884 with some degree of hope. President Arthur desired reelection. He would have been nominated if it had not been for Blaine's popularity. Blaine hesitated to enter the race but he was determined to defeat Arthur. In looking about for another candidate he selected General Sherman. Sherman refused, remembering the bitter experiences of his friend General Grant. Blaine did enter the race, along with George F. Edmunds of Vermont, John A. Logan of Illinois, and John Sherman of Ohio, a brother of the general.

The convention was held in Chicago, June 3, 1884. Many young politicians were assembled there as convention delegates. Among them were William McKinley, Mark Hanna, Benjamin Harrison, and Theodore Roosevelt. The Blaine supporters used every device to stampede the convention. They distributed Blaine symbols, a helmet and plume. On the first ballot Blaine led with 334½ votes, with Arthur second with 278; on each succeeding ballot Blaine gained support, and on the fourth ballot he received 541 votes and the nomination. John A. Logan of Illinois was selected as the vice-presidential candidate.

A bitter feud arose between Blaine and the reform element. The reformers had issued warnings months in advance aimed against Blaine, and his nomination caused a split in the party. Some reformers grudgingly gave him support while others refused to do so. A conference of reformers held in New York City on June 16 issued a statement declaring that Blaine and Logan represented principles and methods which they could

not tolerate. The reformers were labeled "mugwumps," a name the Indianapolis *Sentinel* newspaper had coined a few years before.

The Democratic presidential hopefuls in 1884 were Allen G. Thurman of Ohio, Thomas F. Bayard of Delaware, Samuel J. Randall of Pennsylvania, and Thomas A. Hendricks of Indiana. The convention was held in Chicago, July 8. Grover Cleveland, the man the "mugwumps" hoped would be named, received a majority on the first ballot and the necessary two-thirds on the second. The convention named Hendricks for the vice-presidency. Mr. Hendricks died eight months after taking office.

For the first time in a quarter of a century the United States had a Democratic president and cabinet. Cleveland was a newcomer to the national scene. He was born in 1837 at Caldwell, New Jersey, son of a Presbyterian minister. When he was four years old the family moved to Fayetteville, New York. In his boyhood he clerked for a time in a general store. Later he taught in a school for the blind. He set out on his own at an early age, worked in a law office in Buffalo, New York, and was admitted to the Bar. In 1881 he was elected mayor of Buffalo. By making efficiency rather than politics the theme of his administration he gained much popularity. Then in 1882 he was nominated by the Democrats for the governorship of New York. As governor he was honest and stood for clear convictions and forceful courage. While serving as mayor he had incurred the bitter hostility of Tammany Hall. Cleveland was not considered brilliant; his education had been limited and his views at times were narrow.

In the campaign of 1884 major issues were the tariff and the "solid South." The race soon degenerated into mud-slinging, and people became disgusted by the tactics of both parties.

Both sides realized the importance of New York as a key state. Blaine's colleagues knew that he would suffer from the antagonism of the mugwumps and hatred of Roscoe Conkling, who still carried a grudge. The "Plumed Knight" was popular with the Irish. His sister was the Superior of a Catholic convent. His mother was Irish, and he supported the cause of Ireland. It was hoped that he would gain enough Irish votes to offset the loss from Republican defections.

On the other hand, Cleveland, as governor, had offended the Catholics, the labor vote and Tammany Hall. The loyalty of Tammany Hall was restored by personal reconciliation with Hendricks, while the Irish Catholics were alienated from Blaine by unkind state-

bered his speeches and many commonplace phrases that he had used. Cleveland was also favored by the capitalist and banking interests because of his monetary policies during his administration. The Democratic Convention met in St. Louis on June 5 of 1888. President Cleveland had antagonized many members of his party, but he was renominated by acclamation, as no other name was placed in nomination. For his running mate, the convention selected ex-Senator Allen G. Thurman of Ohio. The platform praised the administration's record but devoted most of its attention to the tariff question.

In the Republican party, the popularity of the candidates changed from month to month. Sherman's increase in popularity was noticeable early in 1887, when he took a trip through the South and reconciled many prejudices caused by his previous denunciations of the suppression of the Negro vote. He referred to the kindly spirit of the Southern whites towards the Negro. He made an earnest plea to new industrialists of the South to support the tariff. Whatever gain Sherman made by this political tour was lost by a speech he made a few weeks later in Springfield, Illinois, when he called the Democratic party "the left wing of the new Confederate Army." Many of Blaine's friends insisted that if a unanimous nomination were offered to him he would accept it. However, Blaine again wrote from Europe stating that his withdrawal was final. Blaine supporters did not know which way to turn. Other presidential hopefuls were suggested, but there was no single favorite when the convention opened.

The Republican Convention met in Chicago on June 19, 1888. On the third day, nine candidates were placed in nomination. On the first ballot, Sherman received 229 votes; Gresham, 111; Depew, 99; Alger, 84; Harrison, 80; with a few scattered votes among the others. For five more ballots Sherman held the lead, but his total never exceeded 249 votes. At one critical time, an appeal was cabled to Blaine, who was visiting Andrew Carnegie in Scotland. In response, Carnegie replied: "Too late, Blaine immovable. Take Harrison and Phelps." This word had some influence, as did the course taken by boss Thomas Platt of New York, who offered his power on conditions, to Gresham, but finally cast it to Harrison. On the seventh ballot Harrison moved forward and on the eighth he won the nomination. Ignoring Blaine and Carnegie's suggestion, the delegates nominated Levi P. Morton, a New York banker, for vice-president. Morton had been a member of Congress and had also served as a Minister to France.

The National Prohibition party also ran a candidate for the presidency. Clinton B. Fisk of New Jersey was nominated. He was a successful businessman with an interest in education for Negro students, as evidenced by his establishment of Fisk University in Nashville, Tennessee. The prohibition platform was a comprehensive statement of principles. In 1884 it advocated temperance and the repeal of the whisky and tobacco taxes. It denounced polygamy and suggested that woman's suffrage be left to the discretion of the local party leaders. The 1888 platform endorsed a protective tariff. Its issues were directed mostly to social reform.

Both sides openly bought votes during the campaign. This practice was exposed in a letter said to have been written by W. W. Dudley, treasurer of the national Republican committee, to party leaders in Indiana. "Divide the floaters into blocks of five and put a trusted man with the necessary funds in charge of these five and make him responsible that none get away and that all vote our ticket." (*New York Times*, October 31, 1888). Large contributions had been secured from manufacturers who benefited from protective tariffs. Sen. Matthew S. Quay of Pennsylvania directed the campaign. He was later charged with misconduct during his terms as secretary of state and state treasurer of Pennsylvania.

The main contests centered in Indiana and New York. Both parties used all the money available and neither party was too scrupulous. Although the use of money for buying votes was not new in political elections, it was felt that at the close of the campaign political morality stood at its lowest ebb in both parties. Bribery of voters reached nearly every precinct in the country; even some members of both parties demanded pay for voting their own ticket. If their demands were ignored they remained away from the polls, or in revenge, voted for the opposing candidates. Voting was done openly; a party worker could place a ballot in a bribed man's hand, take him to the ballot box, and watch him deposit it. Voting laws were weak, and faulty or nonexistent registration laws made it easy for corrupt practices.

The Republicans again were back in office. Harrison received 233 electoral votes to 168 for Cleveland. The popular vote was won by Cleveland, who polled 5,540,329 votes. Harrison received 5,439,853. Fisk received 249,506 on the Prohibition ticket and Streeter, of the Union Labor party, polled 146,935. New York State again held the balance of power, giving Harrison a slight edge, 13,000 out of a total 1,315,000 votes cast. Harrison carried his own state with a margin of 2,248 votes. Governor David Hill was reelected. It was charged that some of his followers entered into agreement to cast votes for Harrison in return for Republican votes for Hill. Whatever the truth of these charges, Cleveland did not have the united support of the Democrats in his own state. Several factors contributed to Cleveland's defeat in New York—neither Hill or Tammany Hall liked him. Also, Abram S. Hewitt, mayor of New York, would not participate in the campaign.

President Harrison appointed his cabinet in March of 1889. Blaine was named secretary of state, the post the "Plumed Knight" had held during Garfield's administration and one that suited his tastes. The other men appointed were without national reputation. Perhaps the exception was John Wanamaker of Pennsylvania, who became postmaster general. Harrison named William Windom of Minnesota as secretary of the treasury. Thomas Platt was highly disappointed at that appointment, for he claimed that Harrison had offered him the post in return for convention support. Windom had formerly served in Garfield's cabinet. Ex-governor Jeremiah M. Rusk of Wisconsin was picked for the recently created Department of Agriculture. John W. Noble of Missouri became secretary of the interior; W. H. H. Miller became attorney general. He was from Indiana and was Harrison's law partner. Benjamin F. Tracy of New York served as secretary of the navy; Redfield Proctor of Vermont became secretary of the War Department.

During the first two years of Harrison's administration, the Republicans controlled both houses and were able to put through party legislation. Their majority was small in the House of Representatives and the minority frequently tried to block measures by filibustering. The Speaker at this time was Thomas B. Reed of Maine, a big boisterous man, gifted with the ability to utter incisive phrases. Reed repressed the Democratic measures to such an extent that he was nicknamed "Czar" Reed, and for a time the "tyranny of Czar Reed" overshadowed all other questions of public interest. The stringent rules adopted by the House were referred to as the "Reed Rules." The bitterness was more intense because there was reason to believe that the rules were manipulated during several election cases, for the purpose of increasing the small Republican majority in Congress. Many believed that Speaker Reed had no authority to set aside precedents which had governed the House for years. The Speaker was accused of leaving the House without rules in order to rule it himself. (The Democratic members, according to former practice, though present, refused to vote, so that the "yeas" and "nays" would not show a quorum. The chairman would then have the call repeated, and, to the names of those who answered, add a few names of Democrats whom he saw before him.) The quorum, thus made, proceeded to adopt a rule authorizing the Speaker to count the quorum. The Speaker thus obtained a quorum by counting members orally absent but physically present, and found a long needed means of preventing the minority from bringing government to a standstill. A more serious dispute arose over the rules which was finally settled by the committee. The Speaker was given two courses of action: first, to refuse to consider delaying motions; and, second, to count members present in making up a majority.

These innovations were challenged by the Democrats, who promoted the rights of minorities. They contested the legality of these procedures. The Republicans would not yield, and the new rules were passed by a vote of 161 to 144. Throughout his term as Speaker, Reed adopted a domineering attitude which led to continued charges of tyranny and dictatorship. The count of members as present extended even to those in the cloakroom and barbershop (*Congressional Record*, Fifty-first Congress, February 20, 1891).

The selection of candidates for the presidential campaign of 1892 was not marked by any unusual excitement. President Harrison had displayed integrity and ability, but he never succeeded in becoming the real master of his party. He antagonized many of the great Republican leaders, especially Matthew S. Quay of Pennsylvania and Thomas C. Platt of New York. He was abrupt and cold in manner; a strict party man, he did not awaken party enthusiasm. Blaine's followers believed that he was not receiving just recognition from the president. Harrison's enemies beseeched Blaine once more to enter the presidential race. As secretary of state, Blaine did not achieve the reputation which was expected, though this was not altogether his fault. Blaine will be chiefly remembered for his influence outside of the duties of the State Department in attempting to force the principles of reciprocity upon the financial policy of the treasury. In February of 1892, Blaine had declared that he was not a candidate for the high office, but three days before the Republican National Convention, June 4, 1892, he suddenly resigned from the cabinet. Harrison and Blaine had never been very cordial and their political differences had multiplied. A feud had even developed between their wives. Blaine did not explain the cause of his resignation in the formal letter which he sent to President Harrison. It was difficult to understand his action. Some interpreted the resignation as a sign that Blaine would accept the nomination. He would be unhampered by considerations of loyalty to his superior, and he could enter the convention as a free agent. But it was too late. The Harrison delegates controlled the convention, which was held in Minneapolis June 7, 1892. They renominated Harrison on the first ballot with 535 votes, 82 more than a majority. Blaine and McKinley received 182 votes each. Whitelaw Reid, editor of the *New York Tribune*, was selected for the vice-presidency. The magnetic Blaine retired to his home in Maine, sick and disillusioned, where he died the following year.

When Grover Cleveland retired from office in 1889, he returned to the practice of law in New York City. His enemies hoped that his political career was ended, but he was often called upon to make speeches to express his opinions on political questions. These speeches ultimately helped him; they created a widespread demand for his renomination. Between the followers of Cleveland and David B. Hill, who had become a United States Senator, there seemed to be a heated contest. Governor Hill had been supported by a record of success. For seven years he led his party to victory. However, his dependence upon Tammany Hall caused distrust and many thought that he was insincere. In February 1892, Hill used his political intrigue to call a state convention long before the usual time in order to pick convention delegates who were favorable to him. The Cleveland backers held an "anti packed" convention and sent a contesting delegation to the national convention in Chicago on June 21, 1892. Cleveland was renominated on the first ballot, receiving 617 votes; and Adlai E. Stevenson of Illinois was named for the vice-presidency. The course of events had helped Cleveland. Serious labor disturbances had taken place just prior to the campaign and many predicted that industries would cut wages of employees. The Carnegie Steel Company provoked a strike at Homestead, Pennsylvania, when it cut employee wages, causing bloody clashes in which many workers were killed and wounded. This and other events were detrimental to the Republicans.

The election was close. Cleveland carried the solid South and New York. His total electoral vote was 277. Harrison's total was 145, and James B. Weaver, running on the People's Ticket or Populist, received 22 electoral votes. Of the popular vote, Cleveland received 5,556,543; Harrison, 5,175,582 and Weaver 1,040,886. The Democrats also secured both branches of Congress. For the first time since 1859, the Democrats were in complete control.

It is too late, Mr. Arthur; you ought to have thought of it before. It will do a little temporary good, but it will not get you out of the trouble in which your Administration finds itself. Marshal Henry, Postmaster Ainger, Assistant-Postmaster Parker, Foreman Helm and ex-Senator Spencer made up a weighty parcel of ballast for a respectable party to carry, and it was as well to get rid of it; and the Cabinet air-ship will be little better off for the lightening. The Republican party has a pretty heavy task before it to regain the confidence of the people. It has lost it, and deservedly so, and he would be a bold man who would venture to fix the time when the sins of recreant Republicans are to be forgiven and the party is once more to direct affairs. Still, it is a good sign that the Administration has become ashamed of the company it keeps, and shows a disposition to put its house in order before retiring from the business for an indefinite period. Such acts will be placed to its credit, and will certainly not be forgotten for many years. It shows that the sense of decency is not wholly lost, and that the party is not willing to die without first endeavoring to make some little atonement for its crimes.

THE BALLOON IN DISTRESS.—THROWING OUT BALLAST.

We are heartily wearied of the daily exercises at Albany in connection with the election of Senators to succeed Messrs. Conkling and Platt. What Mr. Conkling's persistent supporters hope to gain by their childish and ridiculous proceedings is very hard to tell—although their action is really no worse than that of the friends of the other candidates. It is almost too much to hope that by the time this number of PUCK gets into the hands of our readers, a decision will be arrived at. But, to say the truth, we don't expect anything of the kind. Whatever may be the result, it will not surprise us. The members of both Houses have for so long a time been pursuing such an idiotic course, that any little common sense or judgement they may have possessed has long since been exhausted. So that it would seem nothing more than natural if Dr. Mary Walker, or Chang, or Tom Thumb, or even Iroquois were chosen; for which there is a precedent in that part of Roman history which treats of the Emperor Caligula's doings.

By his unwarrantable interference, General Grant is, to a great extent, responsible for the delay in the election. Some people are weak enough to be still guided by what he says in such a matter; although he has as much pretension to the title of statesman as has "his" Senator Conkling. Senator Conkling, for reasons which were obvious, moved heaven and earth to obtain the nomination of General Grant at Chicago for a third term. Although gratitude is not a very striking feature in Grant's character, still he would be scarcely human unless he had a little of it in his composition. This gratitude he exhibits by becoming Mr. Conkling's champion, and seeking to vindicate him in his silly and unjustifiable resignation. It is now Mr. Conkling's turn to find somebody of prominence to hang on to, and Grant turns up just in the nick of time. But, in the present state of public opinion, it is a mighty poor support.

The personal popularity of General Grant, which certainly at one time did exist to a great extent, is no longer what it once was. It has undergone too hard usage, and is useless for practical purposes. It is very hard for Grant to make up his mind to this—and still harder to admit it. If he had sense enough to appreciate the situation he would, if only for his own personal safety, think twice before permitting Mr. Conkling to hang on to his coat-tails over a dangerous precipice, when Grant himself has but that rotten reed of decayed popularity to cling to. We almost wish that the support would give way and carry both the clinger and clinger-on completely out of sight. The American people are nauseated with them and their political methods—they are nuisances that should be got rid of—men whose patriotism means patronage, whose politics mean place. No wonder the Mountaineer President and his companion from a place a safety view with satisfaction the perilous position of their enemies.

ANOTHER MATTERHORN CATASTROPHE.

17

And it came to pass that Democracy, the daughter of Secession, went down to the river; but not to wash herself; for such is not the custom in the land of the Bourbons.

And with her were her young men and her maidens; Lamar, which is, being interpreted, the Long-Haired, and Benjamin, surnamed Hill, the alleged fire-chewer; and Barnum, not he of the beasts; but that other Barnum which passeth round the hat; and Dana, the high-priest of the *Sun*, and likewise John of the Kellyites, and Samuel, the father of the pyramids, which the same was sore stricken in years.

And when they had come unto the river, they saw an ark, wherein was a child.

And he was a goodly kid.

And Democracy took him up, and said:

"Lo, now, this is a child of the Republicans, which have us in bondage these many years. Let us take him now unto ourselves, that in the end he may be to us for a leader out of the land of captivity."

And the children of the land of Bourbon saw that her words were good, and they took the child, and they did even so unto him as the Daughter of Secession had said; and they chose him for a leader, saying:

"Behold, now, these many years have we labored and had no rest, neither the fruit of our toil nor the good things of the earth. But this child is given unto us for a sign and a token of deliverance."

And they rejoiced with an exceeding joy.

But the Lord said unto Moses:

Thou shalt not enter into the Promised Land.

Forasmuch as being a righteous man, thou hast been a leader unto the hosts of unrighteousness; and being wise, thou hast had communion with folly.

For these people are not thy people, nor their gods thy gods. For behold, of old time thou didst wage war with them that rose up against the nation for to destroy it; thou didst buckle on thy sword, and thou smotest the enemies of the Lord, yea, thou didst grievously afflict them; and in that day was the judgement of righteousness fulfilled, and my people made whole, and as a glory among the nations unto all time.

And this thing shall be an honor unto thee, and unto thy house forever more. For they shall say of thee: He did battle with the hosts of oppression, and with them that held slaves; and them that spake for division of the nation.

But now thou hast gone over to the children of Secession, and thou hast given thy strength unto them who have been cast out from the high places of the land because they were false in the sight of the people.

Now therefore thou shalt not come into the place which thou seekest; but thou shalt gaze upon it from afar off. For this people is a jealous people, and it hath not forgotten those things that were done aforetime, in the hour of distress and in the season of adversity.

THE DEMOCRATS FINDING THEIR MOSES.

Constitutional law and common-sense alike make it incumbent upon the President of the United States to take the oath of office before he enters upon his official duties. But, to the best of our knowledge, there is nothing in the Constitution which requires him to turn that simple ceremony into a cheap circus. It is quite true that Mr. George Washington set the bad example of letting himself be inaugurated on a firework, Fourth-of-July basis, and went in for booming cannon and cheers from the populace.

But then, the example of antiquity is not at all times to be followed, as Artemus Ward pointed out when the primitive Christians came to his show at Oberlin, barefooted and unshaven, and wanted dead-head tickets on the ground that they were following in the footsteps of the original apostles. A good many things were permissible in Washington's day that will not do in 1881. Washington owned slaves, powdered his hair and wore knee-breeches. The fact of his having bought human flesh as he did porcine is a serious blot on his noble record. His taste for looking as if he had dived into a flour-barrel and his economy in the matter of trousers are both immaterial considerations in our estimate of his character. But no one will ask that in either of these three things Mr. Garfield should follow Washington's lead.

Not that it is necessary that Mr. Garfield should adopt Jefferson's style, and go and hunt up an old mare and come ambling into Washington, a touching picture of Spartan simplicity. But on the other hand, what is the use of all this absurd and expensive tomfoolery—soldiers and guns and music and a procession? That sort of thing is all very well for the coronation of a despot. The show amuses a servile people, and gives them a wholesome fear of the power that can get it up. But here in America we know—or ought to know—better than to take such nonsense seriously. However big the turn-out in honor of Mr. Garfield may be, it will mean nothing except that there are a great many foolish persons who like to show themselves off in any sort of public parade, and a great many more idle ones who like to see them do it.

It will not mean that Mr. Garfield is a man in whom the nation has a great and implicit confidence. As we had occasion to remark, several times in the course of last summer, Mr. Garfield's record is not absolutely stainless. And if the very first act of his official life should be one calculated to offend the majority of our citizens, he would be as unpopular as Buchanan was or as Johnson was. We mention this simply as a fact, not because the wish is father to the thought, or because we are anxious to refer up Mr. Garfield's record at a time when he has the chance of making a new one for himself. But it is something to be borne in mind, now and always, that the idea of personal loyalty is foreign to the true spirit of republicanism. All this henchman business, this blind following of the blind, which gives a poor vain trickster like Conkling a factitious power, or semblance of power, is not only a disgraceful thing in itself, but a bad sign for our future.

INAUGURATION.

JEFFERSON'S INAUGURATION 1801.

The quadrennial contest for Presidential Beauty approaches. The year, so far, is young: but the months soon slip round, and before we can realize that the summer is upon us, the nominations will be made and the contest for the prize will wax fierce. In the language of Confucius, it is so far a perfect *embarras du choix*. It is like the dog in the proverbial butcher-shop. Which is it to be? Are we to have a Free Trade or Protection Beauty? Is it to come from the East, West or South? And, above all, is a Democratic belle to fill the place now held by a Republican?

There is not space to go through the whole list, but a few of the more prominent entries may be mentioned. The pride of the Empire State, Arthur, has many admirers. "Golden opinions" have been won by him during his term of office, and if we are correctly informed, he is quite prepared to win as many more as may be permitted. The next entry in point of importance is our never-to-be-forgotten and beloved dear old Nunky Sammy. He is not much on physique; but, oh! how beautiful, how touching, how tender, how gentle is his expression! Shall we dwell on the charms of the other specimens of humanity in the show? No. Why should we? Our artist has placed them before you, and you can study them at your leisure.

We recently expressed hopes that Mr. Conkling's fight against the administration might not be successful. These hopes have been more than realized. Not only has Mr. Conkling been signally defeated in his attempt to interfere with the prerogatives of the President, but, like Marc Antony, he has fallen on his own sword after his discomfiture; thus committing political suicide. The parallel, however, is not complete, for the Roman hero knew that his act would end his career, while Mr. Conkling, in resigning his seat in the Senate, fondly hopes that his Stalwart supporters will triumphantly re-elect him, and show the world that he is, after all, "a bigger man" than old Garfield. As things look now the chances of Mr. Conkling retaining the title of ex-Senator for an indefinite period seem very favorable, indeed, and we think the country can stand it, if Mr. Conkling can.

This gentleman has so long been under the delusion that the Government could not be carried on without his assistance, that it will be quite a novel experience for him to find that the sun can actually rise and set, and that nominations can be made and confirmed without the intervention of his graceful fingers in the patronage pie. With all due respect to Mr. Conkling's greatness, we venture to believe that he can very well be spared from the councils of the nation. We believe that the political atmosphere will be clearer, brighter, healthier without him. Although not personally corrupt, he set a bad example to our younger citizens who take an interest in the politics of their native land. He lowered the dignity of the exalted office of Senator by making it little more than a means of jobbing offices out among those who flattered his vanity. There is no useful law, no patriotic measure, with which Roscoe Conkling's name has ever been associated. From first to last he has been a clever and powerful political huckster and intriguer.

At first sight it seemed a very terrible affair, this sudden resignation. Some of the papers, for the want of a better name, called it "a bombshell;" but it was not a bit like a bombshell. A bombshell explodes and deals death and destruction all round. Mr. Conkling has exploded, but with results that are perfectly harmless. He has hurt nobody but himself. We think it better to compare him to a windbag that has become, from excessive inflation, so distended that it explodes with a loud report, but destroys nothing but the bag that contains the wind. It will be noticed that there is a little baby balloon attached to the extreme end of the exploding Mr. Conkling's coat-tails. This is Mr. ex-Senator Platt, who is also enjoying his little explosion. But he is a very small satellite of the Conkling planet, and is scarcely worth mentioning. Yet he has to obey political astronomical laws, and to travel in the orbit permitted him by the overshadowing Conkling body—to travel, and quickly, we reckon, back to the obscurity whence he came.

A HARMLESS EXPLOSION.

Last week we spoke of the manner in which public business was conducted—or rather was not conducted—by that once dignified body, the Senate of the United States. We say once dignified advisedly, for surely no one, after watching its recent proceedings, can look at the Senate collectively as anything else than as one of the vulgarest and most corrupt assemblages that ever had the responsibility of assuming to legislate for a free people. What is the Senate going to do? What has become of its self-respect? For the past few weeks it has done little but neglect the business of the country, in order to fight about the appointment of its individual friends, toadies and hangers-on. The question of selecting a miserable door-keeper, a flunkey sergeant-at-arms or a scrubber is allowed to interfere with matters of the most vital importance to the community.

"But," say the Senators, "it is not these little offices in themselves that we care for; it is the patronage and control of the Senate for our party that we want, and we can only obtain them by fighting for these offices. There is a great principle involved." This is simply the most contemptible kind of sophistry. So long as competent persons are appointed to offices, the people do not care a red cent whether Democrats or Republicans get the places. But law-making and the interests of the people are entirely lost sight of while the unseemly bickering, quarreling and corrupt bargaining appear to be the sole object of the sittings. The Senate is no longer a legislative body. It resembles more a patronage exchange or a stock

26

"bucket-shop." "I'll give your man a Consulship in exchange for a Post-Office," cries one. "A Judgeship for sale," shouts another. "How much am I offered for best places in my State?" yells a third. It is not a pretty scene, and our artist has endeavored to make it as lifelike and as truthful as possible.

When the whole country is so disgracefully represented collectively in the Senate, we cannot hope to have a very choice style of representative in our own local legislature at Albany. We do not expect much, and we get rather less than we expect; for, after the recent vote on the Street-Cleaning bill, the Republican voters in our State may pride themselves on having the most worthless, the most corrupt, the most venal, the most rapacious set of rascals as representatives on record. Disease and Death are stalking through the city, among the festering heaps of offal, mud and filth of all kinds that are allowed to lie in the streets by the political knaves whose duty it was to cleanse them. Mayor Grace is a man of business. He says: "Give me authority and I will give you a clean city." Our best citizens prepare a bill for the purpose, which these graceless Republican Assemblymen throw out because they did not see any money or patronage in it, and they won't have the city relieved of its filth by a Democratic Mayor—as if wretched politics should have anything to do with a matter of this kind! We are prepared to pity and almost forgive the boorish, shallow-pated, clodhopping scamps who come from the rural districts and voted against the bill. Such men can always

be "seen." Besides, what can such ignorant yokels know of the requirements of the metropolis? But the guilty members from the City of New York must not be let off so easily. Here are their names: CHARLES E. BREHM, JOHN R. BRODSKY, R. R. HAMILTON, I. I. HAYES, WILLIAM R. TRIMBLE, A. W. WILLIAMS, all Republicans. Let their faithlessness be ever remembered. They have already, by their perfidy, forfeited the esteem of all honest men.

There is now nominally on the bench of the Superior court a gentleman who is, by the colleagues and associates whom the law compels to do the work for which his family is paid $15,000, pronounced to be insane. Governor Cornell, in a sensible and matter-of-fact message to the Legislature, has suggested as a measure for expediting public business that he be retired on pay for the remainder of his term, and that a new Judge be appointed. But the Bar Association, which seems to care far less for the public business than for the technicalities which usually constitute the trade of shysters, objects and says it cannot be done. "For," say these Solons: "to be removed he must be tried, and that a lunatic cannot be." As the lawyers never scruple to decide *ex parte* on the mental condition of anyone who may be so unfortunate as to fall into their clutches, Gov. Cornell will do a good thing if he ignores their advice and forces the substitution of some person of confessedly sane mind for this lunatic, who, according to the Bar Association, must continue to pronounce judgements on his less unfortunate fellow-citizens.

THIS IS NOT THE NEW YORK STOCK EXCHANGE, IT IS THE PATRONAGE EXCHANGE, CALLED U. S. SENATE.

The funeral of the remains of the Democratic party is about to take place, but the Milesian wake must be held over them—not exactly because such a ceremony is absolutely necessary, but simply out of deference to the nationality of Mr. John Kelly, who is ostensibly chief mourner, and to whom the Republican party is under considerable obligation for his kindness in presenting it with the electoral vote of New York State. But the Democratic party is dead—for the present, at any rate—and it is of no use wasting time in vain regrets. So dance, Mr. John Kelly, and flourish your shillelah. Kick up your heels, Mr. Ben Butler.

You thoroughly identified yourself with Democratic principles in the late campaign, doubtless thinking your support would insure success for the party; but it had not the desired effect, so you can tread a lively measure to Mr. Kelly's jig. Poor Mr. Hewitt, you too are overcome by the solemnity of the occasion. It might have been otherwise if the Chairmanship of the Democratic Committee had been entrusted this time to your tender care, as it was four years ago. Then there is the able but disappointed Senator Bayard, who had set his heart on being Hancock's Secretary of State.

He is swooning, and a friendly Democrat endeavors to revive him by pouring Bourbon whiskey down his throat. The death is bad for Mr. Bayard; It puts off to a remoter period than ever his chance for the Presidency; therefore it is not a matter of surprise that his feelings are too much for him. Mr. Dana, too, feels a little sorry. He was a staunch friend of the dead, provided things could go according to the *Sun's* wishes. But there is really no very good reason why Mr. Dana should be among these mourners. Although with Democratic proclivities, he has not been warm in his advocacy of the claims of the Superb. His idea of Democracy goes so far as it is represented in the person of Mr. Samuel J. Tilden and no further.

Well, what are these mourners going to do? Will they endeavor to galvanize their corpse into life, or bury it deep, and manufacture some new principles around which they can rally and become a new party? Or will they continue to stick to their old threadbare questions, and contest a Presidential canvass always on the same line? If they do, we fear that we shall be obliged to draw a similar cartoon at the end of another four years, and tell the Democratic party what its policy ought to be in 1888. Not that we think our advice or instruction will do it much good, but there is a good supply of years ahead, and by constantly pegging away, we may by the end of the next century see the results of our disinterested admonitions.

THE WAKE OVER THE REMAINS OF THE DEMOCRATIC PARTY.

The following verses, recently received at this office, may be deficient in genuine literary merit, and it is undeniable that they have rather a personal and individual than a general interest; but they are so unmistakably the sincere cry of a wounded spirit that we publish them for what they are worth, leaving it to our readers to imagine for themselves the deep painfulness of the situation, at which the poet can merely hint:

THE RAVEN.

Once upon a midnight dreary,
  While I pondered, weak and weary,
Over many an often-vetoed
    Bogus pension bill of yore—
  While I nodded, nearly napping,
  Suddenly there came a tapping,
  As of someone gently rapping,
    Rapping at my chamber door—
" 'Tis some visitor," I muttered,
    "Some durn statesman at my door—
      Only this and nothing more!"

But the sick'ning sad uncertain
  Thoughts of foes behind that curtain
Thrilled me, filled me with fantastic
    Terrors often felt before,
  So that now, to still the beating
  Of my heart, I stood repeating:
  " 'Tis some politician treating
    Who has 'tret' a half a score—
'Tret' too much, and now entreating
    Office at my chamber door—
      This it is and nothing more."

Presently my soul grew stronger;
  Hesitating then no longer,
Said I, "Is't the Soop'rintendent
    Of the school I taught of yore?
  Of the Sunday-school I taught in,
  In the town my votes were bought in,
  In the town my job was caught in—
    Job whereof I'd like some more?
If 'tis you, or even Dudley—"
    Here I opened wide the door—
      Nothing there, and nothing more.

Back into the chamber turning,
  (In the hall a light was burning—
I am quite a nervous party
    Since I cottaged by the shore—)
  Soon again I heard a tapping
  As of someone loudly rapping
  Fit to wake a dead man's napping—
    Rapping at my chamber door—
And I took a soda-tablet,
    (Soda-mint,) and ope'd the door,
      " 'Tis dyspepsia—nothing more!"

But I saw two bright eyes peering,
  And with calm assurance leering—
In there walked an ancient raven,
    Quite suggestive of a bore.
  Not the least obeisance made he,
  Not a minute stopped or staid he,
  But with mien of lord or lady,
    Flopped above my chamber door—
Flopped upon the bust of Gran'pa,
    Just above my chamber door—
      Perched and sat, and nothing more.

Then this ebony bird beguiling
  My sad fancy into smiling,
By its manner strange, suggesting
    Little Rock and Arkad*sor*,

"Though thy plumes are not Elysian,"
  Said I, "tell me with precision,
Art a jimblaine or a vision?
    Art thou here for peace or war?
Tell me, is it peace between us?
    Shall an end be made of war?"
      Quoth the Raven, "Nevermore!"

Much I marveled this confounded
  Fowl the question thus propounded
With veracity to answer—
    Which was not his wont of yore.
  "But," I thought, "he is but thinking
  Of his own hopes, shipwrecked, sinking,
  As he sits there blankly blinking,
    Dreaming still of '84,

Dreaming of his matchless tumble,
    In the year of '84—"
      Quoth the Raven, "Nevermore!"

"Prophet!" said I, "thing of evil!
  Prophet, if you are a *deevil*—
Whether Reed gets left or whether
    Poor McKinley goes ashore—
  Tell me, am I Fate's selection
  For a glorious reëlection—
  Shall I join a freak collection—
    Shall I serve my first term o'er—
Must I go to Injinap'lis?
    Can't I tide two termlets o'er?"
      Quoth the Raven, "Nevermore!"

"Be that word our sign of parting!
  Is it time that you were starting—
What's the matter with Augusta,
    Or Bar Harbor's rock-bound shore?
I have never been familiar
  With your old Crédit Mobilier,
  Get you gone, or I will kill yer!
    Quit that bust above my door—
Quit my gran'pa's cerebellum—
    Quit, oh quit my pious door!
      Quoth the Raven, "Nevermore!"

And the Raven, never flitting,
  Still is sitting, still is sitting,
On the plaster bust of Gran'pa,
    Just above my chamber door.
  And his eyes have all the seeming
  Of a jimblaine's that is scheming,
  And the lamplight o'er him streaming
    Throws his shadow on the floor
And my soul from out that shadow
    That lies floating on the floor
      Shall be lifted—Nevermore.
                                    B. H.

P. S.—[*by the RAVEN*]
Nevermore!

THE RAVEN.

President-elect Cleveland ought to love all Republicans. The Independent Republicans elected him, and now the Blaine Republicans are doing their very best to justify the action of the Independents. Even the most indifferent citizen must be convinced by this time that the Republican party will profit by retirement, if retirement leads to reorganization. Its leaders have devoted their leisure, since the election, to displaying before the world the extreme fatuity of their ideas and their methods. A party so hopelessly demoralized in defeat could surely not have been fit to govern.

When we say "demoralized," we use the word in its correct sense, and not as it is generally used, in the sense of "disorganized" or "broken up," The party is demoralized; the moral strength is gone out of it; it is spiritually unhealthy. The will of the people has put it out of power; the vote of the country having gone against it on an issue of its own making. Its duty is clear—to accept the situation with dignity and self-respect. But this appears to be the last thing considered in the counsels of its leaders. They are full of a contemptible and foolish resentment, and they are not ashamed to show it. They make no secret of their childish desire to "get even" with all those who in any way contributed to their defeat. Nothing is too mean to do that may annoy, embarrass or insult a Democrat or an Independent. Retaliation is the business of the hour.

The stupidity of all this is simply beautiful to contemplate. We have never looked upon the Democratic party as the incarnation of political wisdom; but when was the Democratic party so foolish as this? Suppose that after Hancock's defeat the managers on the losing side had solemnly gone to work to "read out of the party" every protectionist Democrat who was scared into voting for Garfield by General Hancock's ill-advised tariff letter. Suppose that they had announced their intention of putting outside the party lines every man who dared to hold an opinion of his own as to the fitness or unfitness of a candidate. Suppose they had been guilty of any similar idiocy. Would Cleveland have been elected in 1884?

He would not have been elected. And the Republican leaders are now taking a course certain to bring them to a second defeat in 1888. They are reducing their party to a faction. On the first of June, 1884, it was the Republican party. To-day it is, as far as they can make it so, the Blaine party. It has no principles, no convictions, no ambitions, no aspirations, no hopes, no aims, outside of what is expressed in this one article of faith, to which every true Republican is expected to subscribe: "When Steve Elkins and S. W. Dorsey and Powell Clayton and William Walter Phelps tell you to vote for James G. Blaine you must do it." A pretty platform for a party that a generation ago lived only to serve the country in the spirit of the loftiest, purest and most unselfish patriotism!

The quiet, respectable Republican must feel to-day much as did the Parisians in the latter days of the French Revolution, when everybody was trying to out-citizen everybody else. He may have thought, at one time, that his duty was done and his party standing assured when he cast his vote for the party candidate and paid the party assessment. But now he finds not only that he has got to be an out-and-out blainiac, but that if his neighbor be a little blainiacker than he, that neighbor will probably call him a traitor and a mugwump. And a quiet, respectable man must feel many temptations to take a mugwump's privileges when he sees his party leaders disgracing themselves in blainiac cabals in Washington and insulting the country as they have just insulted it with the silly, useless contention which came to an end last week in the United States Senate.

"THE SOUL OF BLAINE"—STILL ON THE RAMPAGE.

He organizes a little private St. Bartholomew's Eve of his own.

President Garfield, in spite of the squabbles of the doctors and the annoyance caused by Mr. Cyrus W. Field's patronizing subscription list, continues to improve. It is scarcely too much to hope that in a few more weeks he will have made sufficient progress towards complete recovery, to enable him to give some attention to his official duties. The country rejoices at the prospect; and good may come out of evil, for better government will be the result. Guiteau's brutal shot has killed many of the political opponents of President James A. Garfield. Sympathy for him has chastened their opposition and bitterness, and with the exception of men of the Arthur and Conkling stamp, who represent the worst of the objectionable features of American machine politics, everybody—whether he be Democrat or Republican—is ready to render a helping hand to facilitate the administration of the government. If the President completely recovers—that is to say, becomes as strong and robust, mentally and physically, as he was before the murderous performance of the crazy assassin Guiteau—he may thank his excellent constitution for it. He has lived so frugally, his habits have been so regular, he has done so much healthy work, without committing excess, that even with a cruel bullet in his body his chances of living to a good old age are probably greater than of many men who have never denied themselves any luxury. The President has almost as good a constitution as that of the United States.

Both have had a great deal to put up with. Everybody knows how the constitution of the President has been tried. But let us also consider how the no less healthy constitution of the United States has its strength tested. The monopolists are working all the time to ruin it. Their methods are as bold as they are vigorous. General Grant is the man who would have best answered their purposes, and they have not yet despaired of carrying out their purposes through somebody equally pliable. But we don't think now that they will do it with Mr. Garfield. We doubt if his views have the imperialistic character of those of the would-be-third-termer Grant. There is another disease which threatens our otherwise well-regulated constitution; it is the plague of office-seekers. It is a dangerous malady, and its cure cannot be a speedy one.

Ultimately, however, it will be thoroughly eradicated, and mere begging for patronage and office will become one of the traditions of the past. "To the victors belong the spoils" is a very pretty, but unwholesome doctrine, and will, we hope, be wiped out with the office-seeker scourge. Perhaps the mildest forms of disease which have made our constitution feel uncomfortable are cold water and the Roman Catholic Church. Neither of these things, in its way, is specially objectionable. Cold water, under some circumstances, is good both to drink and to wash in; but there are other fluids which at times are much more acceptable. Those who wish to confine themselves to water are welcome to do it; but they must not make fools of themselves publicly by cramming their weak-kneed doctrines down the throats of people who can drink liquor without necessarily making beasts of themselves. As for the Roman Catholic Church, it is just as good as any other, neither better nor worse—perhaps it is even better in its thorough consistency. It has only shown on few occasions a tendency to rub against our constitution, in claiming more privileges under it than it is justly entitled to; but it will in time learn to know better. In any case it hasn't hurt us much yet.

ENEMIES OF THE REPUBLIC.

Columbia to Garfield.—"They may annoy us; but they can't hurt us—we both have good constitutions!"

RIP VAN WINKLE'S RETURN.

Rip Van Winkle has come back again, after more than a score years' sleep, and we are extremely sorry to say that he has not met with the respectful reception to which his age, at the least, entitles him. A hoary head, we are told, is a crown of glory, if it be found in the way of righteousness; but there is reason to believe that this particular patriarch's snowy locks have occasionally been seen in paths which are not the paths of holiness, and that the ways of the ancient are not the ways of righteousness. Hence his return is not made an occasion for general rejoicing, nor for a popular ovation. This is sad, perhaps, but it seems eminently natural to those who know the political history of the country, and the figure he cut in it more than a century ago.

DEMOCRATIC HARMONY UNDER THE JEFFERSONIAN BANNER.

It is just the difference between generalizing and particularizing. So far, those who consider themselves the representatives of the Democratic party differ widely in their opinions. Indeed, there is scarcely a single point on which they have an opinion in common, unless it be that the Republican party ought to be turned out of office to make way for the Democrats. But then what about Mr. Pendleton's Civil Service Reform? How does it agree with Mr. John Kelly, his disgusting Board of New York rum-selling Aldermen and their "spoils" system? How can there be "harmony" between Mr. Randall's High Tariff and Mr. Hewitt's Free Trade?

On what principles are all these widely divergent politicians to organize or to arrive at any understanding? "On Jeffersonian principles," they answer. None of them seems to know what these are, not even Mr. Bayard, who would like to be the Democratic standard-bearer in 1884, although his chief occupation at the present time appears to be in dodging important questions. The Jeffersonian banner as things look now, runs a chance of getting pretty badly ripped.

President Garfield, by his withdrawal of all the New York nominations except that of Judge Robertson for Collector of the Port of New York, has rather astonished the country. Nobody, perhaps, feels more surprised than Senator Conkling. We doubt if he can yet believe it to be true. He has so long been accustomed to look upon himself as an autocrat—not only of the State of New York, but of the United States itself—that he cannot understand how even the President should attempt to call his authority into question. With our atrocious system of senatorial-territorial patronage it is, of course, utterly impossible to expect to get the right men in the right places—but the worst enemies of President Garfield will admit that, with one or two exceptions, his nominations have not been undesirable ones.

He has shown a sincere desire, we think, to please everybody, so far as was consistent with the duty of a President who owed his position to Republican votes. But Mr. Conkling was determined not to be satisfied. He cannot forgive Mr. Garfield for being elected, to the exclusion of General Grant, to whom Mr. Conkling hoped to be what Mr. Blaine is now to President Garfield—his right hand man. The deadlock in the Senate, by which the business of the country has been delayed, was caused in a great measure by Mr. Conkling who, after all, is nothing more than a mere tricky, bumptious politician, who has no more right to the title of statesman than an elephant has to be called a gazelle.

This wretched Riddleberger business, this truckling to Mahone, this perpetual talk about himself and his power have made Mr. Conkling, in the eyes of the country, something more than a nuisance. We rejoice that President Garfield has taken the first steps to curb this man's insolence. We are not aware that the country is beholden to Mr. Conkling for wise legislation of any kind. He is not that sort of man. All he cares for is to have a parcel of miserable place-hunters hanging to his skirts and to patronize them, when it suits him to do so. At first sight it might appear undignified that the President should have withdrawn names that were supposed to have been sent in after due consideration, but by the patronage system in the Senate there was no other course left to him.

The names that he withdrew were small-fry pets of Mr. Conkling; the name that he did not withdraw was that of Judge Robertson for Collector of the Port of New York—the President's own nomination. This was really the only way to force the question to an issue, to find out whether Mr. Conkling or Mr. Garfield was at the head of affairs. Mr. Conkling can no longer fritter away the time of the Senate in passing on his own nominations and shelving Judge Robertson, who naturally is distasteful to him, until next session. He has to decide whether or not he will have Judge Robertson, and thus show his attitude towards the administration. Mr. Conkling's authority, power and influence are at stake, and he is just vain enough and weak enough to declare war. We sincerely hope that he may be worsted in this unholy and unrepublican struggle. The atmosphere of the Senate-Chamber is foul with the contemptible huckstering and bartering of offices. The record of the Republican party is not so good that its so-called leaders can afford to fight among themselves for the spoils. The country relies on President Garfield's firmness at this crisis- firmness that will not only put a stop to the lofty pretensions of Senator Conkling, but also those of other Senators who may be inclined to follow in his footsteps.

A REVIVAL OF A BAD OLD PRACTICE.—FIGHTING WHILE THE FIRE BURNS.

(A pleasant prospect for the next four years.)

This is a great and glorious country. It is a country which for a hundred years has withstood the assaults of foes without and the shock of dissension within. It is a united country. Every citizen of it loves to support it and wishes to serve it for a salary or fees. This last statement is a lie. To read the newspapers, you wouldn't think it was a lie; you would think it was the solemn, sober truth. But it is a lie, just the same. There are still pure-minded, unselfish, devoted patriots in this country, and they are largely, very largely in the majority. But you don't hear very much about them at present. They went to the polls last November and expressed their views then on one side or another. Some got what they wanted, and others didn't. The first class is satisfied, and the other has to be.

The men who are now making so much noise in the newspapers belong to another class, which looks upon a change of the national administration as an opportunity for personal gain and aggrandizement, and which, by its persistent clamor and perseverance in the past, has managed very largely and too well to misrepresent the mass of the people. Will it do so again? We learn that the President-elect is harried and torn—by what? By his efforts to formulate a grand and beneficent policy to mark his administration? No—by his endeavors to satisfy the demands of place-hunters. In fact, our civil service as it is organized compels altogether too much attention from a chief magistrate with the best of desires and intentions. And the disgusting exhibition to which the country is at present being treated by the mob of office-seekers is the strongest sermon that could be preached in favor of reform.

OPENING OF THE NEW REPUBLIC CAFE'.

The people of Indiana seem to appreciate the efficacy of this mode of conducting a campaign, and everybody of the male sex who has a tongue in his head, both in and out of the State, appears to have taken the stump. Every dollar spent by either party in speechifying is worth five dollars invested in cape, helmet and torch equipments, and we would strongly advise both Republican and Democratic bar'l owners to put their money where it will do the most good. All eyes are turned on next month's election in Indiana, the Pivotal State, as it is called, although it is really no more pivotal than Rhode Island or Delaware. But we Americans can't live without excitement of some kind. If we can't have it legitimately, we make it or imagine it.

But Indiana, just now, does present a peculiar appearance. A number of would-be-orators and patriots—a few who are worth hearing and a great many who are not—have taken possession of every stump in the State, and are telling its inhabitants how they ought to vote. For, after all, it is a matter of some interest to a large proportion of the people of the United States as to the particular individual who is to have the privilege of drawing fifty thousand dollars a year and to live in the White House four years rent free. Whose turn will it be, in Uncle Sam's barber's shop, to sit in that comfortable high chair? If Mr. Garfield does not get there, Hancock will; and if Hancock fails, Garfield may have a chance. We are not thinking of the Greenback candidate.

Uncle Sam will have a great deal to do with one or the other of these persons during the next few years. His other customers are also waiting their turn—they eye the favored individuals wistfully; but they must wait, and very patiently, too. Some of them bewail their hard fate: they have waited so long—so very long. Perhaps customer Samuel Jones Tilden deserves the most commiseration—he *was* almost in the chair, but somehow or other he didn't get there; and now there are so many before him. But he is calm and hopeful, he does not get tired and go elsewhere—he lingers to see what the whirligig of time will bring round.

Who knows but that in years to come Kelly and Tammany may be friendly to him; and then, of course, his success is assured without the aid of Returning Boards or Electoral Commissions. We shall sincerely rejoice when the election is over and matters begin to assume their normal condition. No other subject appears to have any show at all. The newspapers are nothing more than mere campaign documents. If voters could but realize the value of the time they waste in reading all the political truck put daily before them they would be simply startled at their unconscious mental dissipation. The straight-forward, conscientious, honest, hardworking citizen is made the tool of the wily place-hunter or politician of both parties. More horrible things than ever are prognosticated should by any concatenation of circumstances General Hancock be elected.

The Republican horse has been duly entered for the Great Presidential Race. He is a noble animal, that horse, full of pluck and mettle, and with a fine record behind him for a twenty-five-year old. But in these matters it is all in the rider. A bad jockey will put a good horse out of the race, and a knowing chap in the saddle will get a wonderful amount of speed out of the poorest old back. So that is an unfortunate thing that the backers of the Republican entry have chosen a rider who is reputed tricky, and who is himself heavily handicapped. He carries weight, and a severe allowance. And on his back perches, like Black Care, the unshakable little Old Man of the N. Y. C. H

Still, there is good running to be expected there. The opposition entry must work hard for first place; and the prize is well worth the struggle. But the opposition entry is our old friend, the Go-as-You-Please Democratic Donkey. He is a noble creature, too, in his way. For twenty years he has been struggling for first place. Four times he has been hopelessly defeated; but he has always come up smiling, his ears erect and his tail swishing a graceful defiance to foes and flies. Last election he made a grand jog of it, and brought himself in first; but his jockey, being a bad old person, was barred out—which was very shabby treatment for the poor old donkey; and it is much to his credit that he again comes up to the scratch, stubborn and smiling.

But who will ride the Democratic Ass this year? The Bourbon Convention is assembled at Cincinnati, the various bar'ls are tapped, and the oratorical free-fight is declared open to all properly qualified comers. It is Chicago over again—a weak reproduction in Democratic style. At Chicago it was a question of Third-Term and Anti-Third-Term. Here, it is a question of Second-Term and Anti-Second-Term. The second term referred to is that of Mr. Samuel Jones Tilden. His first term was not a success; having been passed, for the most part, in the shady seclusion of Gramercy Park. Now he wants another. Mr. John Kelly thinks he has had enough. Others agree with Mr. John Kelly—including about three dozen candidates. Tilden is the Grant of Cincinnati. It remains to be seen whether his more modest aspirations will be crushed as Grant's were.

There is no lack of candidates for the Democrats to choose from. The party has never suffered from any trouble of the sort. It has always blossomed out into statesmen peculiarly adapted to presidential honors. Your average Republican wants to be an officeholder only, stowed away in some quiet, unobserved spot. But the Democrat is ambitious and lofty in his views; and flies high. The Candidates who seek the favor of the Cincinnati Convention are a small party in themselves. Among them are to be found some excellent men. There are many who, we can safely say, would make good presidents; and many of whom we can not positively assert that they would make bad ones.

Yet we think the chances are unpleasantly numerous that the Convention will distinguish itself by some royal blunder. Our only quarrel with the Democratic party is that it doesn't know enough to go in when it rains. It proposes to govern the country; and it has not yet shown that it can govern itself. Most parties are satisfied if their recalcitrant members "bolt" when a convention makes an undesirable nomination. But here is a party with a woful split in it before the convention is even called to order. We are not arguing about the principles of the Democratic party; we are only stating our dissatisfaction with its bad organization, and expressing a natural fear that a weak convention will bring forth a weak nomination, just at a time when, for various reasons, we should prefer to see a strong one.

Yes, we should like to see a really good name at the head of the Democratic ticket this year; and we don't see why the supporters of some one of the better class of candidates should not press bravely forward to victory, when we consider that he will probably have the prayers of the Reverend T. De Witt Talmage with him. For Beecher has declared for Garfield. He remarked, quite recently, at a political meeting, that he "could not forget the man who does and never speaks," which might also be said by other people. Then he went on to state: "I, first, second, last and all the time, am for General Grant; but, as I can't have my way, I shall be glad to take General Garfield. Since my favorite has been set aside shall I go to my tent and sulk? God forbid! I bow to the wisdom of that great Convention, and I am convinced that the man they have chosen is endowed with special capabilities for meeting the emergencies of our day."

THE POLITICAL HANDICAP—WHO WILL RIDE THE DEMOCRATIC ENTRY?

The Democratic Party has a Show, and Mr. Barnum is the showman—not old P. T. Barnum; but a smaller Democratic Barnum. He is showing General Hancock through the Old Curiosity Shop. It is quite a new experience for the General. He is a thorough Democrat, oh, yes; he has been a Democrat from birth; but he hasn't had very much to do with his party since it was his disagreeable duty to help defeat it at Gettysburg. In fact, he never did run very much with Democrats. He is a soldier, and a good one, and it has been his duty to defend the nation, and, naturally, this has brought him into the company of Republicans, who are rather more in that line. So, you see, he is quite a stranger in his own house. The Show contains many things that are new to him. This may account for his looking a little pale and startled.

"Just step right up, General," says Mr. Barnum, smiling blandly: "Guess you're astonished to find what an A 1, first-class Old Curiosity Shop we've got here. Didn't know your noble heritage as a born Democrat, did yer? Now here, by these highly interesting antiquities, you may see the rise of the Democratic Party. It's riz pretty high; but that ain't nathin' to the rise it's goin' to get. No, I don't mean it's goin' up. Never mind, cast your superb eye over this here. This is the Whipping-Post, the famous patriarchal institution of the South; and here are the Shackles and the Whips—the trimmings, so to speak—Lord, you can almost hear the howl of the Nigger—don't it seem lifelike? Ah, General, that there post was the Pillar of the Party.

Oh! them dear old days is gone, long gone; but mebbe we'll have 'em back again, if the South stays solid. You're a Northern man, General; do you remember how those chivalrous Southrons used to call us "Northern Mudsills," in their playful way? Sumner was a Northern Mudsill—there's the club that Prest Brooks laid him out with—chivalrous of Brooks, wa'n't it?

Now, here's where we get to the War—the unholy war that was waged agin the divine ordinance of slavery. You did some of the waging, General; but we won't think no harder of you, if you're solid with the South now. Here's the First Shot of Freedom—white freedom—strictly white, I mean to say. It was fired plumb into Sumter. Here's one of the Nigger Torpedoes—used to be set afloat in the bay, in blockade times. We ain't got many Yankee battle flags to show; but that's partly your fault, General. There—just see that—don't your heart beat faster at sight of that? It's the pistol that the Martyr Booth shot the Tyrant Lincoln with. Chivalrous of Booth, wa'n't it? We mighter had some of Lincoln's brains, that oozed out of the wound; but that kind of thing ain't much in our line. Since the war, our stock ain't so complete and rich in relics—we ain't had the chance. But you may like to glance at a few Repudiated State Bonds—we've got a neat collection of them—and here's our greatest triumph of late years—the Real Original Rag-Baby. There ain't no hard-money nonsense about you General, is there?

And here is, General Hancock, your new Mount. None of yer old Union War-Horses—this is the Genuine Old Democratic Charger—just wants your superb head to make it a complete animal." And then Mr. Barnum stops, and waits for the enthusiasm. General Hancock wipes his forehead, turns his fascinated eyes from the Whipping Post and the Shackles, and cries: "Great Scott, am I to be the Head of *that*?"

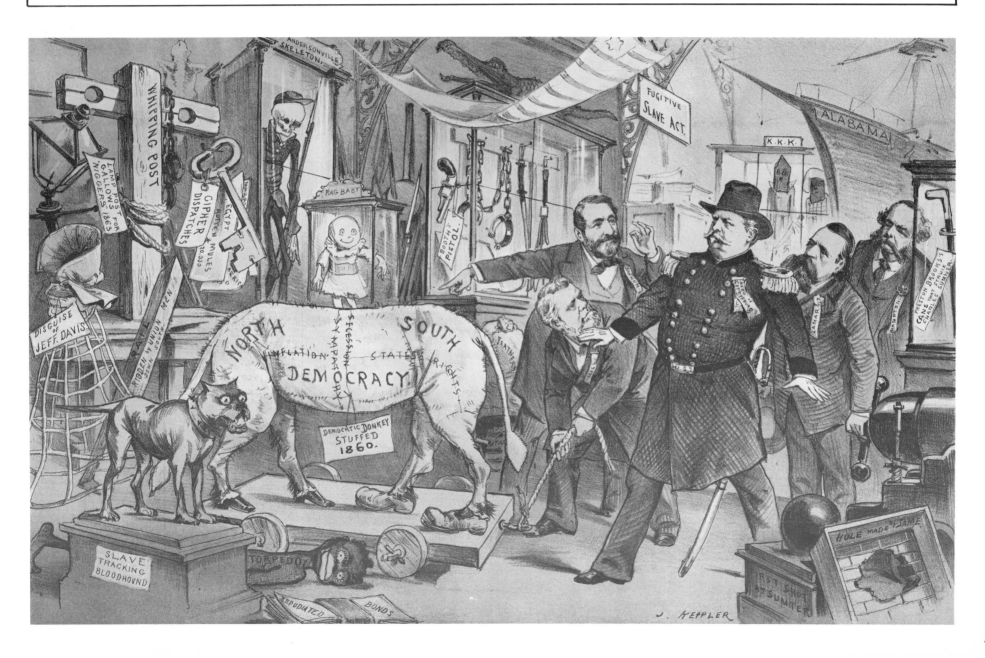

We are a nation.

This is shown in the way in which our government runs itself.

Practically, we have no government at all just at present; and, as a matter of fact, we really don't feel the loss. Indeed, it is a question whether we are not rather better off, as a people, when our President and his cabinet take it into their heads to wander forth to various parts of the country, far from the bustle and worry of Washington, yet not too far for remittances of salary to reach them.

Their absence at least limits the amount of mischief to be done at Washington. We know that in their wanderings they may, at most, make fools of themselves. Their opportunities of making the nation ridiculous are more limited than when they are in the active exercise of their official functions.

It is true that we pay them to serve us at the capital; but, it is only fair to say, it would be money in our pockets to pay them extra *not* to serve us, judging from the service we have so far received at their hands.

And when they show an agreeable willingness to neglect their duty and leave us in peace, it were manifestly ingratitude to a kindly providence to quarrel with so desirable a disposition on the part of our beloved rulers.

There have been found people injudicious and short-sighted enough to obstruct the irresponsible roamings of these in authority by loudly urging that in case of any sudden emergency—any unexpected complication with a foreign power—it would be desirable to have one or two officials at Washington to attend to the duties supposed to be confided to their charge.

Thoughtless objectors! Do you think that if some unlooked for unpleasantness gave the British lion occasion to roar at our own bald and bumptious eagle, said lion would be in any way influenced to cease his rumbling menace by the spectacle of good Mr. Hayes, seated, proud and asthmatic, in the presidential chair, supported at the post of duty by Mr. McCrary on the right, Mrs. Hayes on the left, and the New Centreville Sons of Temperance in the back-ground?

Do you think that the red man of the forest asks, before he draws his scalping knife, whether or no Mr. Carl Schurz be at work and Washington?

Do you think that the diplomatists of Europe and Halifax will tremble in their boots at the idea that Mr. W. E. Evarts is at home among his dictionaries at No. 11,549 H-and-an-eighth St., Washington, D. C.?

Do you think that the financial balance of the world is in the least disturbed by Mr. Sherman's drumming tours among the hard-money voters?

Do you think that the navies of the world will grow unduly audacious because Mr. Thompson is not at the helm of the solitary canal boat in commission that represents the fleet of the United States?

Do you think that the whole pack of picnickers are worth their salt, either as representatives of the people's dignity or as managers of the public affairs?

Nay, let us not disturb our rulers errant. Their dereliction does us no harm, and may do some good in various quarters of the country.

Many a Kelly voter has listened in delighted awe to words that he couldn't spell in a life-time, yet that dropped glibly as honey from the lip of Evarts; many an untutored Indian has worn his belt of scalps more proudly because of the taffied eloquence of Mr. C. Schurz; many a rural pumpkin has blushed a golden red at the honor of a sniff from the nose of Mr. Hayes. By all means, let our rulers junket.

A STRANGE CASE OF EPIZOOTY.

The attitude of the Democratic party of late has been very much that of the over-confident "sport." It has rested in a sweetly secure faith in the genial warmth of the Autumn weather—until the gale from Indiana and Ohio came along. The analogy ends here, however.

The Fall rains beat through the patched and ragged umbrella that shields the Bourbons' stock-in-trade; and the faithful old Democratic donkey is suffering from a bad attack of epizooty. Indeed, we hold the partisan howl of triumph to be as idiotic a bray as ever the influenza-stricken Democratic war-donkey set up.

But we are glad of the Republican successes because they put this Presidential contest on a squarer and fairer footing.

OVERTRAINING YOUNG HORSES.

It is rather early in the day to begin to discuss the chances of Presidential candidates for 1884. But we do not see very clearly how we can avoid doing so. It seems to be the fashion to assume that any man who is elected Governor of the State of New York need have very little difficulty in gratifying his ambition—if he has any-thing of the kind—in becoming President. Somehow or other we don't think that Mr. Cleveland will be our next President. Governor Benjamin Butler, who has been raised to a very high pinnacle of greatness, no doubt looks still higher; but we do not feel disposed to speculate on his aspirations. The training is a trifle premature.

DEMOCRACY'S DISASTROUS EGG-DANCE.

Well, no, as a rule it is not considered the proper scheme to smash the eggs in an egg-dance. Most performers try to combine graceful dancing with a maintenance of the integrity of the eggs. But, you see, that is where our performance is strictly original. That's her peculiarity. Yes, it is a rather startling system of dancing, and we are bound to confess that it hasn't taken the first prize yet; but if we were to alter our style—why, wherein should we differ from the other shows on the road? No sir, we want you to understand that this is the Great and Only Democratic Egg-Dance, and that we can smash more of our own eggs in one campaign than any other party in the world. Walk right in and we'll show you lots of fun.

PLATT'S POLITICAL PUPPET SHOW—HE PULLS THE STRINGS AND THE GREAT MEN DANCE TO HIS MUSIC.

It is beginning to be seen, by everybody except the old-school politicians, that the people can take a hand in politics when they like. The office-seekers of the old-time "practical sort" are slow to learn this lesson. Men like Evarts and Hiscock are still only too ready to dance to the piping of a manager like "Me Too" Platt; to do his bidding and help to elect his creatures; although they know that his ends are selfish, his means corrupt, and his influence and example in every way objectionable to the people. No doubt Messrs. Evarts and Hiscock—honest men, personally—deplore the necessity of serving such a man as Platt—of associating themselves with him—but they accept the necessity.

General Grant's friends are more than ever confident of his obtaining the nomination for the Presidency, and General Grant himself enters into the third-term campaign with much apparent gusto. But is he really sincere in his desire to be President once more, or is he simply a willing tool in the hands of the Republican Ring schemers? If the latter is the case—and we are constrained to believe it—General Grant is entitled to our sincere sympathy and commiseration. A man who has led such an active military life, and done so much for the country, ought to have been left to his own sweet will. Instead of which, his managers, finding that Grant was indispensable for their particular purposes, have been driving the poor man here, there, and everywhere, to be entertained by kings, princes and potentates, in order to furbish up the tarnished popularity that he enjoyed when he left the White House. After having trotted their man about like a prize bull until he is perfectly jaded, they then insist upon the poor fellow's going through the turmoil of a Presidential campaign. Miserable Grant, your story reminds us of that of the mythical Wandering Jew. Driven from post to pillar, with a war-record only as a staff, he sees before him a will-o'-the-wisp of a third term, which he fatuously follows, while the gravestones of strictly second term presidents loom up around him; but he cannot find rest for the soles of his feet.

This Presidential business will not down; it crops up on all sides in connection with everything, political or non-political. Few people realize that within a comparatively short time the Republican and Democratic nominations will be made at Chicago and Cincinnati. The excitement will be perfectly dreadful. It will be a godsend to the newspapers. The Republican journals will scarify the Democratic candidate; the Democratic papers will belittle the Republican candidate. The most terrible consequences will be predicted from the election of either. Should Grant be elected, he will serve a fourth term and then be Emperor. Then good-bye, the Declaration of Independence and everything else American! The consequences of the election of a Democratic President will be positively appalling. The Union will be immediately dismembered and split into half-a-dozen Confederacies, and Confederate brigadiers will find employment as the various Presidents. If the Candidate of the Okalona *States* be nominated, that dignified journal will come out with a short editorial something after this fashion:

"We have
Them now
On the hip,
We will
Never
Rest until they are
Skinned and eviscerated!"

Should the man of whom the *States* is in favor chance to receive the nomination, then shall we be told by the Lemars *Sentinel* that—

"The
Rattlesnakes
Have achieved a
Temporary victory.
But we
Will have
Revenge.
Blood
And
Gore.

This is the species of literature with which we shall be regaled for some time to come. What sensible people in Europe will think of our journalistic and political amenities will be hard to say, for the *State* and *Sentinel* are but mildly exaggerated types of our party organs.

THE MODERN WANDERING JEW.

TO THE CHICAGO CONVENTION.

The hours roll on, and bring us nearer to the holding of the convention which is to give us a Republican Presidential candidate. General Grant is urging along on his wild career towards Chicago, to receive his nomination. He is the locomotive that drags the train of his followers. Conkling is the engineer and Logan is the fireman. Don Cameron swings his signal lantern to signify that all is right ahead. Washburne is the switchman who switches the train on to the right track. In the car behind is a select company, consisting of Messrs. Shephard, Babcock, Belknap, Garfield, Williams and other gentlemen of the same profession.

THE HERO OF A THOUSAND FEEDS.

Grant: "I will eat my way to the White House, if it takes another four years!"

President Grant, for he is once more a President—of the Fair Commission—is still kept so much before the public that he runs a very good chance of degenerating into a nuisance. He has dined with so many people and at so many places, that the mere work of enumerating them would take a much longer time and more space than we would care to devote to it. The smallest village political organization—provided its creed is Republican—vies with the swellest social clubs in New York in doing him honor; and this honor invariably consists in sending him an invitation to dinner, which he as invariably accepts. His sword has not been beaten into a ploughshare, but into a carving-knife, and his spear has assumed the shape of a dinner-fork.

But, if General Grant really understood what a good dinner was—and we don't think that he has sufficient refinement in his composition ever to know—we should have nothing to say about these chronic free-lunches, provided they were simply for the purpose of giving the General something good to eat in his private capacity. But, as a matter of fact, they are nothing of the kind. General Grant practically invites himself to these feasts, and he does so for the purpose of keeping his name before the people as long as there is a chance of his being nominated for the Presidency. It is not pleasant for us to be constantly under the necessity of reading a lecture to General Grant. He has been a successful soldier, and we have had worse Presidents—but very few.

This perpetual junketing, undeserved and unnecessary, does little to raise General Grant in the eyes of sensible men, although the dazzle and glitter of the entertainments and the commonplace character of the speeches may have their effect on the vulgar. General Grant probably counts on such support for future honors, and herein he shows his shrewdness, for he knows perfectly well that on his simple merits as a statesman—he has been amply repaid for his soldiering—he is not in the slightest degree entitled to the fulsome adulation and notice he is attracting.

Senators who sought re-election, or of the legislators whose votes decide the momentous question. It was indeed a pitiable spectacle. The most talked-about, if not one of the ablest of the United States Senators going around with his hat in his hand and begging for support from men of whom, under ordinary circumstances, he would look down on with undisguised contempt! As things stand as we go to press, it can be only by some remarkable change in the political situation, or by extraordinary luck, that Mr. Conkling can once more take that seat in the Senate which he never really honored, and which he resigned in a fit of pique. But why is Mr. Conkling, with his Platt attachment, so anxious to recover that with which he parted so lightly?

Does he begin to realize that without his Senatorship he is like Sampson without his strength? Outside of Mr. Conkling's own feeling on the subject, we do not see why he should be re-elected. In fact, there are a host of cogent reasons why he should not. We are perfectly well aware that there can be no popular government without a certain amount of patronage. It may be small or it may be great. Under our "spoils" system, it is very great; but it exists, in one form or another, everywhere. But it was neither foreseen nor intended that government appointments should be reduced to the level of mere huckstering and bartering. And yet it is such work as this that the Senate, under the baneful influence of men like Conkling, chiefly passes its time in doing. Mr. Conkling does not wish to go back to the Senate to serve his country. He does not wish to make the Chamber ring with his eloquence in the advocacy of some wise measure with which his name may be hereafter enshrined in the memories of a grateful people.

He does not seek to reform bad laws. He does not seem to take an excess of interest in the Star Route disclosures. We don't hear of Mr. Conkling as exposing Navy Rings or Army Rings or Whiskey Rings; his tastes run in quite a different direction. What boots it so long as he can make some pet of his a Custom House officer or a United States Marshall? Suppose the country *is* robbed by swindling contractors, it is not of half as much consequence as that Bulldozer and Skilligalee, who have been "workers" shall be respectively window-opener and spittoon-cleaner to the Senate. It is very questionable if Senator Conkling ever aspires to anything beyond such things as these. If he does, his political record speaks falsely.

This explains why Mr. Conkling wishes to retrace his steps. This is why, after sawing off from the Republican tree the New York patronage limb and giving the Democratic donkeys a chance, he is so anxious to do his best to repair damages. This is why he writes undignified notes to ignorant Assemblymen, beseeching them to give him their vote. This is why—if it could be done with a shade of decency—he would even now go to President Garfield and ask him to let by-gones be by-gones, and promise never to oppose Garfield again in anything, and to confirm Judge Robertson every day of the week. But matters have gone too far. His resignation shows the fatal weakness of the character of the man. It shows that those who looked up to him as a leader were deceived. But Mr. Conkling may take the credit of having achieved one thing. He has widened the split—for split it is—in the Republican party. Nothing now remains for him but to get out of politics at once, and devote the remainder of his god-like existence to the cultivation of the ineffable curl on his forehead, and shot-gun tactics.

59

Cabinet-making is the order of the day. There is scarcely a paper in the country that has not had something to say with respect to the composition of President Arthur's cabinet. As a rule, however, the more it has had to say about it the less it has known; but it is easy for an obscure journal to acquire a reputation for acumen and knowledge by putting in all kinds of people in imaginary cabinets. Where all is uncertainty, the opinion or the information of the Cohosh *Clarion* may be just as valuable as that of the New York *Clamorer*. President Arthur has not taken us into his confidence, and we feel justified in making a remark or two on what his future policy will be, even if we cannot furnish to the public the names of the friends who are to help him carry on the Government.

There may, perhaps, be some undesirable men in the cabinet, but we venture to hope that they will not be men whom the people have good reason to believe ought not to be there. When the British King Henry the Fifth came to the throne he abandoned all his former dissolute companions, whose society he had enjoyed when Prince of Wales. He felt that now the responsibility of the supreme power rested on his shoulders, that the time had arrived by casting aside all youthful follies and doing his duty to the best of his ability. Is President Arthur going to be a Henry the Fifth? Is he going to say to his fishy political friends of his youth, "I can have nothing more to say to you because I am now King?" Must he intimate to the men for whom he has actually canvassed when he was Vice-President of the United States, that circumstances alter cases?

It will, we fear, be hard for him to do; but if President Arthur does not wish to make a failure of it, as have other Vice-Presidents who have filled the Presidential chair, there is no alternative. Our old friend Shakspere

gives us, as he always does, an admirable illustration of the situation. No two men could have been on warmer terms of intimacy than Falstaff, the fat and jolly but shiftless and unprincipled knight, and the Prince of Wales; but when the Prince came to the throne he was obliged to cut his acquaintance. All the drinking bouts, the bacchanalian festivities that they had enjoyed together counted for nothing. If President Arthur takes Mr. Conkling into his cabinet, there is certainly no good reason why Mr. Platt should not be offered a seat. Messrs. Conkling and Platt did not rise together, but they certainly fell together.

President Arthur has some other queer friends, too, and it will be as much as he can do to shake himself from their importunities. Some of them, as it is, are altogether too closely connected with him. To be sustained by Messrs. Gould and Vanderbilt is very good from a financial point of view, but we don't know that it has anything else to recommend it; certainly nothing in the shape of virtue or patriotism. There is General Grant, the would be third termer, who feels grateful to President Arthur for using his best endeavors to elect "his Senators," and who certainly will exhibit his gratitude by offering to assist the President in carrying out the arduous duties of the office. In some respects he will be found a more difficult man to deal with than ex-Senator Conkling, for he has great pertinacity of character, and has made some weak-minded people believe that he is a statesman as well as a soldier. General Grant may be a statesman, but the citizens of the United States don't want him even as an adviser to President Arthur. We wish we could make him understand this!

We cannot get away from politics this week. Do what we will, they are on all sides of us. When a man becomes President under the same melancholy circumstances as

Mr. Arthur, the political situation becomes more complicated than ever, and the public demands that the question be discussed in all its bearings. There have been queer rumors in the air concerning the President. Some say that he is a little better than a wooden man, and that his stolidity is such that it will be impossible to get him to understand what his duties are. On the other hand, we hear that he is the most vacillating person in existence; that he is swayed by every passing breeze, and does not know his own mind for five minutes together. Then there is a great deal of talk as to the degree of intimacy existing between him and certain prominent personages. He has been seen with his arms round the necks of Grant and Conkling; while others say that it is his practice to cut them when he meets them in the street.

The social arrangements in the White House, it is reported, will be of a most humorous and original character. The Executive Mansion will become a "beer garden." President Arthur will distribute his patronage from his imperial throne, and will give an office to everybody who asks for one, together with free lunch and unlimited lager and whiskey. But some of the rumors are more favorable, and on that account may, perhaps, have some foundation in fact. A brilliant aureole is said to surround the President's head; he will be the savior of the country, and he has already acquired the confidence of the American people. But there is one rumor which, as it interests us vitally, ought scarcely to be placed under that category: It is that President Arthur has an adviser—that adviser is, let us whisper, PUCK. If it be true—and there is no reason to doubt it—the country is certainly safe, and President Arthur's administration will indeed be the best since the Declaration of Independence.

A GRAND SHAKESPERIAN REVIVAL.

(Which we have but little hope of seeing on the stage of the national capital.)

THE "WALKING DELEGATE."

Senator Gorman's infamous bill making it a misdemeanor to exact from an employee a pledge that he will not join a labor organization is not likely to become a law; and if it did become a law it could not be upheld under the constitution. But it should not be forgotten that the man who is guilty of this shameless piece of demagogy is the representative of the element in the Democratic party which is opposed to the principles and policy of Mr. Cleveland. It gives us an opportunity to see the real character and value of that element—and to judge fairly of what it aims at.

OUR NATIONAL DOG-SHOW.

The year has rolled round again to the dog-show season, and, not to be behind the times, we present our canine cartoon, which is really worthy of study. The animals are familiar to everybody, and need no comment, either on their beauties or their peculiarities.

A PRESIDENTIAL CONJUROR.

It was our boyish idea that the whole duty of the President of the United States was to "eat molasses candy, and swing upon the gates." President Arthur could tell us better. We doubt if any man before him found the presidential chair thicker stuffed with nettles. An unpopular man, he succeeds a President whose memory is peculiarly dear to the hearts of the people. He goes about his business with the unpleasant feeling that a sharp-eyed nation is watching him to see if he will do anything out-of-the-way. Hanging to his coat-tails is the wreck of a party thoroughly hated and distrusted by the people—a party? a section of a party, rather.

PERSUASIVE NYMPHS TRYING TO LURE THE COY INTO THE PRESIDENTIAL WATERS.

Is Mr. Tilden to be a candidate for the Presidency? We read the *Sun* carefully every day, and try to learn from its editorials what Mr. Tilden's course is to be, but without obtaining any enlightenment. One editorial may perhaps raise our hopes—we see our way perfectly clear, and look forward to November twelvemonth, when we shall have the happiness of recording our vote for him. A few days after, these hopes are shattered by the announcement that Mr. Tilden would not in any circumstances be President, although there is no doubt that, if nominated, he would be elected.

Another week may elapse during which time the *Sun* "booms" two or three likely men, but it always returns to its first and only love, Uncle Samuel. Other Presidents may have done very well in their way, but there was never a President—nor will there ever be a President—who could, would or should equal Samuel J. Tilden. Please, Mr. Dana, tell us what is the use of talking about Mr. Tilden if he is not a candidate? And is he a candidate? If not, are you going to make him one against his will, with the help of Mr. Watterson and Mr. Hendricks and Mr. Hewitt? You will pardon our saying so, Mr. Dana, but Mr. Tilden is becoming a nuisance, and we shall be glad when we hear he is finally out of politics, if he is ever going to get out.

WONDERFUL SAGACITY OF THE REPUBLICAN ELEPHANT IN WALKING AMONG EGGS WITHOUT TOUCHING THEM.

The party became a party without principles. Elected to office by the acceptance of an illogical proposition, it logically assumed that logic was of no account in practical politics; and, on *that* assumption it proceeded. "I saved your house from burning down—give me the management of your business"—this was the position it took. Finding that so absurd a claim was allowed, why should it trouble itself to be reasonable in dealing with the people to whom it addressed itself? "See," it said: "they think so little of their public business that they will give its conduct to us for such an inapplicable reason. Let us profit by such folly." And so, for fifteen years certainly, politics has meant, to the leaders of the Republican Party, not opposition to the extension of slavery, not the freeing of the slaves, not the assertion of the principle of national unity; but, simply and solely, the traffic in public offices for private gain. We are perfectly willing to say that to most Democratic politicians it means exactly the same thing. But we do say that to the one candidate of the Democratic Party—the one man the party can nominate and elect—politics means only an endeavor towards good government; and that he is a man strong enough to make his party follow him.

GARFIELD'S TALLYHO! SELECTING THE PASSENGERS.

The Administration Coach is drawn up ready to start on its four-years trip. A nice new showy coach it is, too. How it will look after it has traveled the hard public road for the long presidential term it is hard to say. Perhaps some of its spick-and-span beauty will have worn off a little. A good deal will depend upon its passengers, and how they are disposed to bear their share of the burden of the traveling. If they are an ill-behaved or quarrelsome lot, they will have to be ejected, one by one, and their places supplied by more desirable passengers. These little stoppages will not improve the appearance of the coach. They may happen to coincide with the mud-puddles along the route.

This coming term will end the first hundred years of the American Presidency. Shall the century begun with Washington at the head of our government end in disgrace with James G. Blaine in that sacred chair? Is not this the great question we have to face? Look at it clearly, and see its magnitude. See how small all considerations of policy, of convenience, of party fealty must appear beside it. Consider what that question involves. The election of Blaine does not mean only that we shall have a bad man in the Presidential seat. We have had bad men there before, and the country has survived it. There might be far worse things for the nation than the election of a bad man in support of a good principle. Such painful political necessities may—must, perhaps—come to every country. They must be accepted, not thoughtlessly or lightly, but in deep seriousness and sober regret.

But we stand in no such case to-day. If we elect Mr. Blaine we elect a bad man as the representative of a bad principle. Knowingly, we have never done this before. Even the defenders of slavery were put in power by the votes of men who honestly believed that slavery was at least a desirable institution. But nobody can honestly think political corruption a desirable, or even a defensible thing. And nobody who will read the testimony that is abundantly offered by the best men of the two great parties can doubt that James G. Blaine is the living exemplar of the idea of deliberate, systematized political corruption. It is not merely that he has done dishonest and dishonorable things. It is that he, and the men who defend him, and with whom he allies himself, defend, excuse, palliate this dishonesty and dishonor, and that they are known to practise what they preach.

So that is more than the question of having a good President or a bad one. We have to ask ourselves whether we shall formally approve Right or Wrong. Is there any doubt that this is the issue put before us? If you vote for James G. Blaine you vote for a man who has been openly proclaimed, by reputable citizens and responsible newspapers, a liar and a corrupt official, and who has neither disproved the charges brought against him nor punished as slanderers those who brought them. If you vote for James G. Blaine you vote for a man who is willing to assume the holy trust of office with the burden of this odium on his shoulders. Is not this enough for honest men—or must the candidate stand at the cross-roads and cry "I am unclean!" before they will acknowledge his uncleanness?

And if you vote for Grover Cleveland you do not vote for the South, nor for the Democratic party, nor for slavery, nor for State sovereignty, nor for free trade; but for a man who has been chosen as a candidate by the wisest Democrats and the most patriotic Republicans, just because he best represents the principle of honesty in public affairs, and because he is able to give us that pure and clean government in which he believes.

THE HONOR OF THE COUNTRY IN DANGER—10-29-84.

It is rather difficult to picture to one's self the intellectual life of an inveterate reader of the New York *Tribune*. How does he manage to exist among men of the nineteenth century? How does he exchange ideas with his fellows? Let us try to fancy in what a world of extravagant unrealities he lived. Of the actual condition of his country, of the opinions of other citizens, of the character of the men who compose the national government—of all these things he knows absolutely nothing. For instance, three years ago he believed for weeks that a certain man was the President-elect, when a certain very different man enjoyed that honor, beyond all question. And when his chosen journal at last told him that it had deceived him, why, it made no difference to the inveterate reader. He went right on believing what it said, and living in the gloom of its profuse and variegated mendacity.

Just think of what that poor devil believes as to public matters. He thinks that the President of the United States is of a character so vile and vicious that history scarcely furnishes a parallel for it. He believes that this monster lives only to revive the Southern Confederacy and to betray the Union into the hands of the "copperheads" of 1861. He believes that these copperheads are still living, in the vigorous prime of life. He has had to believe—perhaps believes still—that the President is in a deep and dark conspiracy to place Southern men in power, and to inflict every possible wrong and indignity upon all loyal citizens of the North—especially upon the veterans of the Civil War. Yes, he really believes all this, although he must know—he can not be wholly shut out from other sources of information—that this same President has been all his life, until he went to Albany to act as Governor of the State of New York, an esteemed citizen of Buffalo, N, Y.; that he does not even know what the South looks like, and that by birth, breeding, education and every association of life he is Northern.

A man must be a fool to believe such things, you say? Well, it looks a good deal that way. But a man may be quite sensible and fair and honest in all other affairs of life, and yet be an irrational, disingenuous fanatic in politics or in religion. The *Tribune* reader believes all this nonsense—or makes believe to believe it—because he wishes to. He has been disappointed in the game of politics; a man has been elected who was not his choice, and he is trying to make himself think that his duty lies in opposing the will of a majority of his fellow-citizens. He does not care to take the trouble to find out whether they were not right and he wrong. He only seeks an angry man's revenge, and he will do anything, say anything, believe anything to ease his irritated mind and keep alive in it the idea that he was right and his opponents were wholly wrong. It would be a curious experiment to isolate a *Tribune* reader for a few months—long enough to let his brain recover, in some measure, its normal functions—and then to lay before him the unimpeachable statistics which would show him that the President elected in November 1884, had proved an excellent, faithful, sensible, honest, patriotic public officer. He is not, like the defeated candidate, a great and perfect genius, a hero, an unequalled statesman and a plumed knight; but he is a good President. The worst that can be brought against his administration is that he has made some unfortunate appointments to minor offices; of these the most have been made at the instance of one shrewd, specious, plausible politician of the unscrupulous sort—Arthur P. Gorman. That President Cleveland should listen to this man is much to be regretted. That his having been deceived by Gorman gives anyone a right to question his honesty of purpose not even a *Tribune* reader would assert, if he made even the slightest investigation with a view of finding out the truth.

A VETERAN RECRUIT.

The winnowing has begun, and the winnowing will go on for many a day to come, and the souls of men shall be sifted, and the fame of men shall be purged as with fire. For the day of judgment has come for the American politician, and he is judged by his deeds, and by them shall he stand or fall. Truly, as the days go on, it will be a purgatory for the men who want to be President. They will be examined and criticised for the benefit of every voter in the land. They will be on trial before a court that knows no rules of evidence, and where every question is admissible.

We predict weeping and wailing and gnashing of teeth before the summer is half over. Nobody dreams yet what an imbecile scoundrel his favorite candidate is. But all the world will know in a few weeks. His "record" will be carefully raked over, and the smallest fault in his past will loom up in lurid horror. These will be sore days for many a good, easy man. The sensitive spirit of Mr. James G. Blaine, of Maine, will be mightily vexed. The soul of Mr. John A. Logan will be harrowed, and his long established character as a grammarian will be utterly destroyed. General Grant will learn that a republican people can never forgive a display of imperialistic tendencies. Mr. S. Jones Tilden will find out how old and feeble he is, and will make the acquaintance of several of his own ailments of whose existence he had no previous suspicion. And the state of moral health of various other prominent men will be pleasantly diagnosed. It will be death on the politicians; but fun for the people.

There are, actually, only two prominent candidates for the office of President who have political principles, and believe in them. We put aside, of course, the small fry—the Prohibitionists who are in the field only to secure the enactment of such sumptuary laws as the Constitution forbids; the Socialists and the Land-Confiscators, who do not know what they really want, in this free country; the Friends of Labor, who do know what they want, and who want it in cold cash. Setting these aside, there are two men—Grover Cleveland and James G. Blaine. Mr. Blaine has a political creed. He believes in turning politics into a business for his own profit—in taking public office in order to make himself useful to capitalists and corporations in those various channels in which a legislator or an executive officer can be serviceable to men who wish to control legislation and the appointment of public functionaries. He believes in distributing the offices within his control among the people who will best help him in his speculations. He believes that all who disapprove of such a scheme of public service are dudes and Pharisees. Here is a creed simple, clear and comprehensible. Mr. Blaine certainly stands for a principle.

Mr. Cleveland believes in turning politics into a business—for the benefit of the people. He believes in carrying on the government as any honest business should be carried on—as well and as economically as possible, with the aim of securing the best results for all interested.

This is also a creed, and one that you would think would be generally acceptable, on the face of it. And yet, Mr. Cleveland, in putting this plain and sound theory into action, is having harder work than any President of the United States has known, with the one exception of President Lincoln. The practical politicians of his own party howl at him because he really believes and tries to put in practice what he has solemnly professed before the people. The theoretical politicians scold him because he has not been able, in three years time, to utterly eradicate a political system opposed to his own in every detail, that has been established for the better part of half of a century. It is an easy thing to have a stock-jobbing creed and to live up to it, or to have no creed at all, and to live up to any thing that is asked of you. But to make up your mind to do the right thing, regardless of consequences, is very often a much more difficult matter. And when a man makes up his mind to this, and goes honestly to work, undeterred by the fact that in four years neither he nor any other human being can undo what has been done in fifty years—why, this paper, for one, proposes to hold up that man's hands. We are convinced that Mr. Cleveland is trying to give the people an honest, non-partisan government, on good business principles. If ever we find that we are mistaken, we shall let our readers know it. So far, we have only been strengthened in the conviction upon which we acted in 1884.

It is very hard that when a lot of men want to clean out the Augean stables, they can't be permitted to do the job in peace. The stables are very dirty, there is no question about that. And the trifling objection that the cleansing party is a little dirtier than the stables only raises a side issue. Here they are, several hundred thousand industrious Democrats, just crazy for work, hankering after work, and work is refused them. This is hard. It is unjust. It is, moreover, humiliating. Here is the venerable Mr. Dana standing outside of the fence and shouting: "Turn the rascals out!" And not a rascal will turn out. "The Republican party must go," plaintively observes the friend of Hancock and Tilden. And yet the Republican party settles itself down as if it felt pretty fairly at home, and rudely and unfeelingly declines to go.

Yet perhaps it is not well to trust too much to arrogance and that possession which is nine points of the law. It takes only one little legal quibble to upset a strong case; and only a trifle is needed to turn the scale hopelessly against the Republican party a year from next November. For a long time we had to take it on trust that the Government stables were in a really unclean condition; but now there is remarkably little doubt of the fact. The uncleanness is conceded: the point is only—who shall do the cleaning? The Republican party, having carefully fouled its own nest during its twenty odd years of occupancy, is now as confident as ever that the country may trust it to restore the nest to a condition of virgin purity. It is a little doubtful whether the country will agree with the Republican party in this matter. And if, by any chance, the country does give the job to the Democrats, what an upturning of heaped and stale corruption there will be!

STILL WAITING.

When the Chicago Convention, convinced of the hopelessness of conducting a canvass with James G. Blaine at the head of the ticket, nominated Benjamin Harrison for President of the United States, there was a general expression of satisfaction throughout the country that we were about to enter upon a campaign of principles, not of personalities,—that the battle would turn less on the characters of the nominees than on the platforms upon which they stood. In fact, we were promised a fair fight, and the party which had nominated Grover Cleveland at St. Louis, confident of the irrefutable logic of its claims, welcomed such a contest. Has it been such a contest? The personal element has largely disappeared, it is true; but the honest advocate of tariff-reform and the other great principles of government which Grover Cleveland represents finds himself confronted at every turn with appeals based upon statements whose only foundation is in the fertile imaginations of their promulgators, by conclusions boldly stated to be drawn from facts which really offer no foundation for them, and even by arguments which can not logically be derived from the lies upon which they are supposed to depend. It may not have been a campaign of personalities, but it has been a campaign of misrepresentations.

There is one thing certain. If Grover Cleveland is nominated for the Presidency, the Democrats will have the nicest set of men at the polls, next November, that they have seen in a good twenty-five years. And the fine old Bourbon Democracy may well afford to smile superior, in that hour, to blainiac jeers. Their new colleagues may be "dudes" and "Pharisees"; but even one who is a dude, and moreover a Pharisee, hath he not a vote, like unto other men? Verily, there is no ridicule, no jeer, no scoff, no fling, no merry jest that availeth aught against the solid argument of the vote that is cast. Dudes and Pharisees though they be, their votes have a solid Bourbon value. Other considerations apart, we should like to see Cleveland nominated, if only to note the manners of the Democrats on receiving into their family party the protesting pick of the Republicans. It would be a pure joy to watch the sturdy Jeffersonians making a hospitable attempt to put on a few unwonted elegances and graces, to make their allies "feel at home." But there is a strong chance that we shall have to deny ourselves this pleasure.

Hunger sharpens all wits but Democratic wits. After twenty-five years of tantalizing deprivation of the good things of office, they have now the chance to establish themselves in the comfortable place of the Republicans under circumstances that will make it very difficult to oust them. If they elect their President in November, they will elect him because a great number of Republicans have risen in open revolt against the corruption and tyranny of their own party as it is now governed.

These Republicans—would it were possible to beat the idea into Democratic brains!—do not belong to the class which, within the ranks of Jefferson, mainly causes trouble by its independence. Their secession is not at all the same thing as the act of secession when performed by Mr. John Kelly and his merry men. A Tammany Hall secession means simply the preservation of the Tammany Hall equilibrium by the shifting of a certain body of men to balance the transfer of a certain amount of money.

But the Democrat is respectfully invited to note a delicate distinction between the respective cases of Tammany and the Independent Republicans. It is indeed so fine a distinction that many Democrats will refuse to consider it at all. Yet we assure them that we are not hair-splitting, nor yet straining the simple truth when we point out to them that they can not use men who come into their ranks as temporary allies, moved by principle alone, as they can use those who come to them on the simple basis of barter and sale. If Tammany's block of voters is once properly secured, it matters very little to Tammany what candidate its purchaser may put up. Tammany, certain that its price will be paid, is perfectly willing that the people should amuse themselves by thinking they are electing the unobjectionable man who is nominated by the party, and who will be delivered over to Mr. Kelly as soon as he begins his term of office. Or you may put up a bad candidate. It is all the same to Tammany. It takes a great deal to turn the Tammany stomach; and it takes very little whiskey to fire the

Tammany soul; and when "the boys" are ordered to hurrah, much it is they care whose name soars from their strident throats. They know well that they are hurrahing *for* Mr. John Kelly and their own pockets. Consequently, the deal once made, the price once agreed to and payment guaranteed, there is little need of consulting Tammany's private feelings. But, O dearly-beloved brethren in the Democratic ranks, don't go away with the idea that you can treat in similar cavalier fashion the dissatisfied, insulted Republicans who look to you for salvation from the disgrace which the election of Blaine would bring upon them!

It was not money nor the hope of money that set them where they are now. It was not a miserable sectional jealousy. It was not prejudice. It was not self-seeking of any sort. They left the Republican Party because they could not honorably lend it aid. They will give you help if they can honorably do it. But they will not step one inch toward you if you ask them to fight a man who is as objectionable to them as the man whom the unthinking majority of their party has forced upon them. These are not an organized horde, to be sold and handed over in a lump; even if their leaders were purchasable, they themselves would act individually as they are now acting in a body. In fact, their case is only analogous to that of Tammany in so far as Tammany's is analogous to that of the mule. They can kick. And, dear Democrats, they will kick against the nomination of a bad Democrat—as readily as though he were a bad Republican.

The Grand Old Party still appeals to the country as the divinely commissioned and only genuine instrument of salvation in matters political. It still insists upon its dogma of infallibility, and will not submit its claims to the test of reason. Because it was right in some things in 1861, it assumes that it must be right in all things in 1886 and at all times hereafter. This style of argument, however, hardly goes well with its very elastic and variegated creed. According to the greatest and most authoritative expounders of the blainiac gospel. Civil-Service Reform is all right, if it is Republican Civil-Service Reform—but, of course, all wrong if it is Democratic Civil-Service Reform. Tariff Reform is all right, if a Republican introduces the bill—all wrong, naturally, if it comes in the form of a measure from the Democratic side of the House.

This sort of talk does not take as well, though, as it did a few years ago. People are beginning to see that the country can bear a Democratic administration without going hopelessly to the dogs. The sun rises and sets, the crops are grown and gathered, men go about their business, and our paper currency is still good for the purchase of bread and butter and winter clothing. The people are beginning to think that after all, it doesn't make much difference whether wise and honest government calls itself Republican or Democratic.

Mr. S. J. Tilden is evidently going to make a struggle—and a pretty severe struggle, too—to be President of the United States during the next four years. All his preparations have been made with judgement, and he is going to fight on the particular line he has marked out for himself if it takes all summer. There are very many worthy people in the Democratic party who do not like Mr. Tilden, and would be rejoiced if he would withdraw from the contest. But they can't help themselves, for Mr. Tilden is a Democratic hard fact—and there is too much burning jealousy among the aforementioned worthy Democrats to permit them boldly to repudiate Mr. Tilden and put up a better and a stronger man. What with his bar'l, and his fraud grievances, Mr. Tilden is literally the skeleton in the closet—which almost has the effect of making him a candidate in spite of himself.

This is not the case with General Grant. His third term candidacy is entirely in his own hands, he could withdraw, if he chose, at a moment's notice. General Grant was not a good President. He was a bad president. His partisans point with pride to the *strong* government that he inaugurated, especially down South. It was a strong government bolstered with carpet bags and supported by bayonets, and Grant, if he had his own way, would like to be at it again on the same principle. The mild milk and watery wish-washy rustic Mr. Rutherford B. Hayes is usually credited with administering a weak government in the sweet South. It may be weak, but it is certainly a much more wholesome style of thing than anything that Grant could give in the event of his being unhappily hoisted into the White House for a third term.

THE "STRONG" GOVERNMENT 1869-1877. THE "WEAK" GOVERNMENT 1877-1881.

Certain of General Garfield's supporters have put forward a plea in extenuation of those unhappy lapses from strict political virtue on the part of their candidate over which we have mourned from time to time. They frankly admit that the statesman of their choice has been guilty of certain dishonorable actions; but they ask that his fault may be condoned on the ground that the profit of his wrong-doing was painfully small. He sold his honor, they say, for $329. It was a very trivial affair—really not worth talking about. If it had been $329,000—well, one might say something; but who would be so mean-minded as to condemn a man for a little retail immorality of that sort? This is, however, only the old plea of the indiscreet young woman in Marryatt's story; and it is much less deserving of consideration in his than in her case. The amount of the theft is not an index to the moral character of the thief; and the only difference between a big steal and a little steal is that the small sinner has thrown himself away, as the late Mr. Field put it, "without sufficient cause."

But the duty of enlarging on this high moral truth may well be left to those Bourbon organs which, for the first time in twenty years, have an opportunity of howling in the interests of virtue. The agony which Mr. Garfield's crookedness has caused those noble sheets is something to be comprehended only by people to whom it is at once a luxury and a novelty to have to uphold beautiful principles in the way of business. For our own part, we can't say we fully understand it. It sometimes seems to us as if the Democratic Party had its hands full in taking care of its own candidate. Not that *his* moral character has hitherto needed looking after; but he has now a hard road to travel, and still harder associates to travel it with; and it will be no easy job to keep his skirts clean, while he is in his present company. For General Hancock is a heavily handicapped man. His shoulders are broad; but they have a mighty load to carry. The country looks upon his party with a firmly-grounded suspicion. It is all very well to say now that all Democrat, are not traitors; that the Southern "claims" will not be paid; that everything is lovely in the old slave-states, and that the political goose hangs high. Nobody ever said that every Democrat is a traitor. But a good many traitors have been Democrats, which is unpleasant. The Southern "claims" won't be paid; but is not that because the country at large wouldn't stand it? Everything *may* be perfectly peaceful down South; but there has certainly been enough turmoil to give an excuse-for-being to the much-denounced "demon of radical misrule." The Democrats want all the morality they have for home use.

FORBIDDING THE BANNS.

The bride (Garfield):—"But it was such a little one!"

It seems incredible that at this stage of the campaign there are still weak-minded, feeble-souled wretches who have not made up their minds which side to take in the fight. We can understand the out-and-out blainiac— the man who calls his candidate a plumed knight and a spotless hero and a brilliant statesman. There is nothing strange or puzzling about that man. Either he is lying or else he is a fool. And we can understand the loyal and conscientious Republican, who thinks, or thinks he thinks that by electing a Democratic President we shall give the country over to Democratic damnation. He is honest, prejudiced and misled. But the conscienceless creature who sits on the fence and waits to see which is to be the winning crowd, that he may join it—he is a marvel of contemptible weakness.

And it is curious to note the process by which he has been evolved. This is the same man who last June was shrieking wildly that the voice of the country would vindicate Blaine—that he would be elected by an unprecedented majority. He had no proofs of Blaine's honesty; he had no arguments in favor of trusting a political trickster with the highest office in the land. But he could, and did shout that Blaine would be elected. That was to end the Independent revolt, and the whole question of the political immorality of the Republican candidate. Blaine was to sweep the country like wildfire, and his stained record was to be cleansed by a great vote of vindication.

Very noisy he was, this wild blainiac, in the early Summer months. Loud was his denunciation of the Democratic party. He rejoiced in calling Governor Cleveland a hangman, and in predicting his assured defeat. He was happy, chipper and contented under his disgrace. It was nothing to him that his party was soiled by the nomination of a corrupt leader; the party was going to win, and that was enough for him. He was not be left out in the cold. All that he valued in the party was its success, and that, he felt, was certain.

Would you believe that it is the same man who is now silent, watchful, uncertain; dodging political discussion, furtively hunting for "straws" to tell him which way the wind of popular favor is blowing? And what a very hard time he is having of it just now! The promised wildfire has not swept the country. The "aggressive campaign" that was laid out so bravely has turned out a pitiful, sneaking, defensive campaign. Day by day has revealed the weakness of the cause to which he allied himself solely because he thought that it was strong. And now the last great prop of his enthusiasm has failed him. Ohio—Ohio was to show the tremendous undercurrent of popular feeling in favor of Blaine. Ohio was to kindle the fire that should destroy Independents and Democrats in one common holocaust.

HELPING THE RASCALS IN

A BURGLARIOUS SCHEME THAT MAY BE SUDDENLY SPOILED.

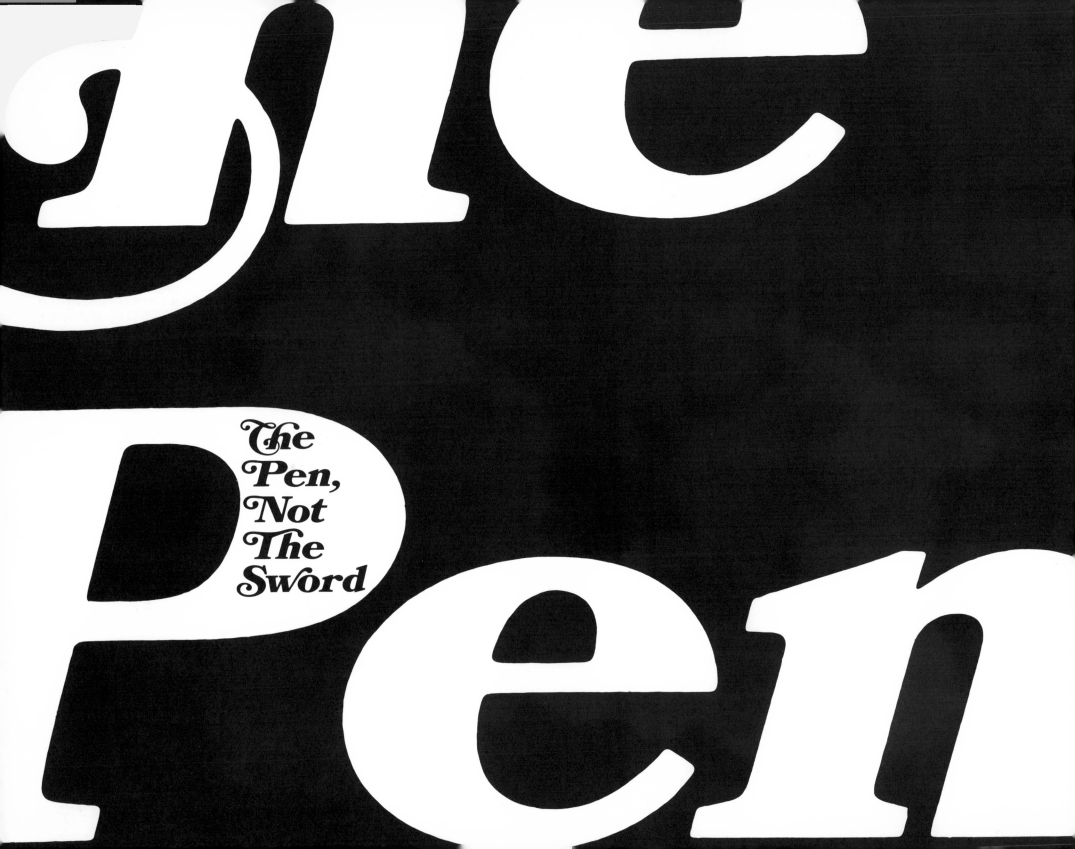

The Pen,
Not
The
Sword

IMMIGRATION SOCIAL MEDICINE

Immigration was largely responsible for the great increase in population in the United States between 1880 and 1900, for about nine million immigrants arrived in that twenty-year-span—nearly as many as in the preceding sixty years during which records were kept. Allowing for mortality and the return of immigrants to their native country, the total addition of foreign-born in the country was less than half, roughly about four million. Economic conditions or political disturbances in their native lands at first sent hundreds of thousands of Irish, German and Scandinavians to the United States. After 1890, the character of immigration changed, and these were followed by a rush of Italians, Poles and Russians. Amounting to one-third of the total number of immigrants, they were less akin racially, socially and religiously than most of the earlier comers.

The most available opportunities for labor or business were the industrial centers and cities of the East. These areas became overcrowded with new Americans, eager to share in America's bounty but needing Americanization. Of the Irish immigrants, 45 percent settled in the big cities; of the German, 38 percent; while other nationalities had lesser quotas. In 1885 only 31 percent of the inhabitants of Boston, Massachusetts, had been born in the United States; the rest were of foreign parentage.

The immigrant usually sought the section of the country where he could find employment in his particular trade. The miners from Wales and England naturally went to the coal mines of Pennsylvania; the Scandinavians founded their own colonies in Minnesota and Wisconsin; the Germans stayed to some extent in the large cities but scattered into Illinois, Pennsylvania and Missouri, where a large colony was founded in St. Louis, and to the farms of Ohio, Michigan, Wisconsin and Iowa. Another influence on where they settled was the presence of friends or countrymen upon whom the new immigrant could depend for help or advice. Since many had come at the solicitation of friends or relatives, or with the aid of money sent by them, they naturally sought out these relatives when they arrived on these shores.

There were certain forces which tended to counteract this clannishness among the immigrants and which gradually fused the different characteristics into one American nationality. Economic prosperity caused the new citizen to want many of the things he saw about him, and led him to seek a high standard of living. This separated him from many habits and traditions of his native country and gave him a feeling of superiority when he revisited the old home or came into contact with later arrivals. It differentiated him from the recent immigrant and gave him a feeling of belonging to the country in which he prospered. This affection increased with his children and grandchildren until they became completely identified with American customs, manners and thought.

In application to politics many immigrants were ignorant of their rights and this made them important to political leaders. Suffrage generally gave them much more esteem than they were accustomed to at home, and this attached them more firmly to their adopted country. No doubt our politics suffered from this additional vote, but it had a nationalizing effect upon the immigrant. However attached the Irishman was to the cause of home rule or how proud the German was of the military might of the empire, his feelings were gradually directed toward the country where he found economic prosperity and political recognition.

The English language was another blending force. In most cases the immigrant found it necessary or desirable to learn our language, and if he did not, his children did. Thus he became further identified as an American. In some cases the thickly populated communities managed to maintain the foreign speech and the old religion for several generations, but the moment the immigrant ventured into higher education, commercial work or politics, he was forced to learn English. It was impossible to completely isolate the little communities.

In the course of time, the foreigners became more amalgamated through intermarriage, except for the black race where there was the insurmountable color barrier. In the case of the immigrant this did not exist, and even the impediments of difference in language, customs and religion were gradually removed. Where one nationality was highly concentrated, most men chose wives of their own race, but where nationality was sparse, the men married women from other nationalities. The immigrants of British birth showed the greatest inclination to marry American women, obviously because there was no language obstacle.

It is evident that the enormous influx of immigrants had a great effect on the political life of this country. Whatever the character of the immigrants, it was not likely they had the same political philosophy as the original settlers. Through the establishment of suffrage and the short naturalization period, their strength at the polls was soon felt, and as soon as this vote was worth controlling, it was utilized by the unscrupulous politician and party manager.

The requirements for citizenship were: 1) Preliminary declaration three years before admission (modified in some cases); 2) Proof of five years' residence in the state; 3) Proof of good conduct, attachment to the principles of the Constitution, etc.; 4) Renunciation of any title of nobility; 5) Declaration, on oath or affirmation, that the person desiring admission will support the Constitution of the United States and that he renounces his former allegiance. The evident intention of this act was to admit all persons of good character, who came to this country with the intention of staying here, to all the rights and privileges of American citizens.

The immigrant was granted the privilege of citizenship, including the right to vote, without any test of fitness for it. The courts made it merely a matter of form, for any alien who had been here the required length of time and complied with the requirements as to the previous declaration of intent, and who could bring one or two persons who would vouch for his good character, was at once admitted to citizenship. With the enormous number of applicants every year it was impossible for the court to test the character of each very thoroughly, but it was the custom not to conduct any such examination at all—in fact a clerk conducted the brief examination while the court was busy with other matters. Furthermore any court, either state of federal, could naturalize aliens, so the states had authority over this matter which was of national importance. Often the applicant could neither read nor write—what could

he know about the Constitution of the United States?

The result of this admission of foreigners to political power before they were prepared to be incorporated into our political system was an attempt on the part of politicians to win with the immigrant vote, particularly the Irish and German. Some of these naturalized citizens retained certain prejudices in respect to their old homeland, or had ideas not in keeping with those of other Americans about them. For example, the Irish wanted our foreign policy to be conducted in accordance to relations between England and Ireland, and they felt that we should protect naturalized citizens in acts hostile to a power with which we were on friendly terms. Politicians yielded to these prejudices, and politics became corrupt by attempts to win these votes. The German vote in many localities controlled the action of political leaders on the liquor question, at times against the desires of the community. The admission of foreigners to political power had tangible effects on the laws of our cities and states.

The bad influence of the immigrant vote degraded local administrations all over America. The foreign-born were easily controlled by leaders of their own nationality who used their voting power to gain possession of the city government and administer it for their personal gain. Positions in the local administration were filled with political workers from the immigrant rank, and contracts were jobbed out to their political supporters. Bribery rapidly developed into direct buying of votes at the polls, a practice which spread to state and national elections. Many high government officials owed their positions to some corrupt ward leader.

Socialism and anarchism also affected our political life. These movements were led and carried on by persons of foreign birth, and were importations of foreign agitators who came to America for the sole purpose of making converts to their doctrines. These agitators abused the rights of liberty which they enjoyed in America and interpreted the freedom of speech and agitation which were allowed them as evidences of the weakness of our government. These alien agitators were men who used freedom for the purpose of conspiring to bring about social revolution by violence. Unrestricted immigration was beginning to affect our political life.

It is true that the immigrants did not take to agriculture as readily as they did to mining and mechanical industries, possibly because of the capital required to purchase and stock a farm, but they were found in large numbers engaged as agricultural laborers and related occupations. The census as early as 1880 showed nearly

800,000 immigrants in agriculture over the ten percent of the whole population so engaged. At the same time one-half of all men employed in mining were of foreign birth. It was this unskilled but hardy labor that enabled the country to establish its vast railroad system.

It is interesting to note that the process of immigration was expanded by various means. Paupers and the poor were admitted through arrangements of their own country to emigrate, the British government having been the most active in this "assisted emigrant" movement. It had done so for the purpose of relieving the pressures of population, especially in the poorer areas of Ireland and Scotland. It was assisted by poor-law authorities; by charitable societies and persons; by remittances and prepaid tickets from relatives and friends in this country; and by steamship agents and brokers who made it a business to induce people to emigrate and had advanced money to them or paid their passages and collected the money after their arrival.

Transportation for the immigrants was a profitable business, and the competition among steamship lines was intense, each company having its own agents throughout this country. One steamship line had no less than thirty-four hundred such agencies, and this demonstrates that the immigration movement was being promoted by persons in America rather than those from foreign countries. The price of the passage was regulated by competition of the steamship companies in America, and was high or low according to agreement or for traffic, and was not fixed according to the competition of the emigrants on foreign soil nor to the cost of service. The prevailing rate was from twenty-three to twenty-six dollars, of which three dollars was the agent's commission.

The rivalry of the steamship lines led not only to employment of more agents but also to the payment of commissions to any person who would sell tickets. Books of tickets were placed in the hands of so-called bankers (exchangers), boardinghouse keepers and even saloon keepers. For every ticket sold the agent received a commission, and it was natural for these agents to use their influence to persuade immigrants to send for their relatives and friends, promising to secure work for them when they arrived. In many cases they sacrificed a part of their own commission in order to sell the ticket, and in other cases they even advanced the money under an agreement of repayment out of the first earnings of a new arrival.

This brought even further schemes to induce emigrants from the other side, by using agents in the foreign countries to sell tickets to intending emigrants. The Italian agents went a step further in order to make the business more profitable: they would occasionally find a "tramp" steamer that would transport the emigrant at less than the regular rate in order to make a cargo. They chose to issue their own tickets which entitled the purchaser to a passage to America, but at a time designated by the agent. If they could find a "tramp" steamer, the emigrant would be brought to the embarkation port and put on board. If no passage could be obtained, these tickets were exchanged for fares on one of the regular steamship lines.

On foreign shores we had a group of agents whose object was to persuade men to emigrate with the promise that profitable employment would be found for them when they reached America. The peasant was persuaded to sell or mortgage his little farm or vineyard, in many cases to leave his family, with the belief that work was plentiful and well-paying in America, and that he could soon send for his family or support them better until he returned. If the emigrant had no property, his passage was paid by the agent, with promises that he would repay a larger sum out of his earnings. In America, the agents had their men receive the immigrants whom they contracted to be responsible for all sums. These men often exploited the immigrants in various ways: they found board and room for them at exorbitant rates; loaned them money at usury; sold them bills of exchange and prepaid passage for their families; received bonuses for their employment; and furnished laborers for railroad companies with board and lodging included in the contracts. Although there were thousands of unemployed men at that time, the immigrants were continually brought over. The whole business of immigration was being abused, and it was harmful to America as well as to the immigrant.

Switzerland was the first country to pass a comprehensive law to prevent the abuses of indiscriminate emigration, and their example was soon followed by other countries of Europe. This legislation marked a new attitude on the part of European countries toward unrestricted emigration.

In 1885 immigration to the United States was further restricted by passing a law prohibiting the importation of laborers under contract, but the provisions of the act were poorly enforced, owing to the difficulty of procuring evidence as to the actual contract or agreement. Had the contract labor law been strictly enforced, few of the millions who have come to America since its enactment could have landed.

SENATOR EDMUNDS, in introducing his bill prohibiting the manufacture and exportation of dynamite for illegal purposes, has done a good deed, and one that will entitle him to the respect and gratitude not only of foreign nations, but of Americans as well. The world seems to be full of dyed-in-the-grain, cowardly blackguards just now, who have no higher ambition than murder and destruction, and, unfortunately, the nitro explosive offers them a cheap and easy means of gratifying their savage instincts. It is not enough that the decent portion of humanity should regard the dynamiters and their kin with loathing and detestation. Such wretches must be coerced by the laws, and if the laws as they exist cannot reach them, others must be framed to meet their cases.

In the large accession to our population, which we annually receive from Europe, we are compelled to take the good with the bad, and many are welcomed to these shores whom we could well consent to do without. The sewers of Europe are constantly pouring out their noxious contents upon us. We feel the effects in such incendiary meetings as that which recently took place in Chicago; in such overt acts of malignant and cowardly vengeance as instigated the dynamite explosion at Norwalk. It is already our interest as well as our duty to co-operate with the authorities abroad to suppress these crimes. Free speech need not be interfered with, and yet we should check the preaching of incendiary doctrines. The liberty of the Press may remain unimpeached, and yet we can consistently suppress such publications as the *Dynamite Monthly* and O'Donovan's organ. THE JUDGE wishes that Mr. Edmund's bill could have been made sweeping enough to embrace these prints and speeches; but, as it stands, it is a step in the right direction and the rest will follow. The United States is already tired of being regarded by the scum of European nations as vantage ground whither they can retire when hard pressed by the laws they have broken, and whence they can launch their murderous schemes at our friends across the water, as soon as those schemes ripen to fruition under our protecting flag. The United States still has a warm welcome for emigrants; but they must be emigrants in good faith, not flying assassins, who merely claim our hospitality that they may escape the consequences of their past atrocities and have leisure to scheme fresh ones.

The great American public has no sympathy for dynamiters.

COLUMBIA'S UNWELCOMED GUESTS.

M. Pasteur has offered to go to Egypt and study the origin of the cholera epidemic, as well as the means of suppressing it, or, at least, of keeping it within bounds. If he is successful in his daring errand, and is able to telegraph to this country an accurate description of the personal appearance of the only original Jacobs of cholera germs, wouldn't it be a good idea to have some of the members of our ornamental Board of Health stationed outside the harbor, on board of the pilot-boats, to watch for the coming of the "dread infection," and, so to speak, strangle it in the bud? It is not likely that much more practical measures will be taken to prevent the importation of this most deadly of diseases. A city that tolerates such a Board of Alderman as ours, that lets its noble harbor be filled up gradually by the criminal carelessness of its own scavengers, that revels in unclean streets and filthy and pest-producing suburbs, is not exactly the city to be awakened to a sense of its danger so long as the danger is not at its very doors. And yet cholera may at any moment sail calmly into this port, an "assisted emigrant" that we cannot ship back to Europe.

Motel Schapirstain, Benzien Maradecki, Israel Belo-certowshi, Jechel Kartakowski, Oscher Abramowitsh, Sacharja Macowiski, Golde Kaschmivski. These are not Nihilists, but are simply the names of some Muscovite Jews, who have fled from tyranny and persecution in Russia to enjoy freedom and protection under the broad banner of the Stars and Stripes. In spite of a few professional American Jew baiters, such as Mr. Hilton and Mr. Corbin, the people of this country are very glad to welcome this addition to the population. They will make much better citizens than noisy and impracticable Irishmen, who are forever abusing the British Government, and never doing anything to remedy their so-called wrongs, except committing a number of cowardly murders at home and hurling silly newspaper threats from abroad.

Persecution, indeed! If Irishmen wish to know what race in the world has suffered from persecution, we would point to the Jews. Yet they have endured it calmly, peaceably and patiently, and have always triumphed in the end without shooting landlords from behind hedges or blowing up public buildings with dynamite. We do not mean to say that the Jews are the greatest race that ever existed, but they have many remarkable and admirable qualities. They are a practical and sensible people, and it is more astonishing that they should be so when the superstitious belief of a large majority of even the modern Jews is considered. To believe that they have been specially marked out by the Deity for favors and rewards, and that a savior is coming at some future period to lead them to a certain Asiatic district, may be very consoling; but it does not appeal strongly to common sense.

Not that the belief of other denominations is founded on a stronger basis than that of the Jews; but then the Jew must not complain if the Buddhist, the Mohometan, the Roman Catholic, the Greek Catholic, the Protestant or the Mormon claims for his particular belief all that the Jew asserts belongs to him alone. Who is there competent to decide the question? Uncle Sam, as the modern Moses, will decide it in his own peculiar fashion, and without getting into a polemical discussion, either. All he says to the persecuted races of Europe, whether Jew or Christian, believer or unbeliever, is: "You are welcome to America."

"Practise any religion you please; they are all the same to me; but don't quarrel about your belief or unbelief. If you wish, cover the land with churches and synagogues; but avoid sectarianism in your schools, your hospitals, and your charitable institutions, and in every shape. Sectarianism is the parent of bigotry, ignorance and intolerance, and I dont want these things about me. I don't invite you Jews to come here because you are Jews, but because I want a lot of intelligent and ill-used people to become citizens of my glorious Republic. As my ancient predecessor, Moses, did with the Red Sea, I do with the Atlantic Ocean. The waters are divided, and you can safely pass through them to the land of liberty, and leave oppression, persecution and brutality behind you."

THE MODERN MOSES.

THE CHINESE INVASION.

"The Chinese must go," so says riotous Dennis Kearney. Yes, they must go to New York, to Boston, or even to Philadelphia, the inhabitants of which cities will be very glad to see them. They will be formidable rivals to Bridget in kitchen and house work, generally, and it *is* about time Bridget was threatened with a rival. If on their arrival in New York they help us to get rid of some other crying nuisances, we shall thank the glorious climate and constitution of California. We talk about rats leaving the sinking ship. This, then, is the effect thereof.

PROHIBITION AND OBSTRUCTION.

Everybody knows that the theory of no rum unavoidably means free rum and free poison. That is the record of every so-called prohibition state, from that of Niel Dow to those of St. John and Benedict Arnold. You can no more get rid of alcohol than you can of mud. To abolish it would be to impoverish a hundred legitimate industries. You must regulate it, as you regulate all mercantile commodities that, used improperly, bring suffering and regret. This truth, however, is mere whistling against the wind. You can no more talk to a prohibition crank than you can to that aged theological reformer who declared that rather than to submit to redemption for a certain personal enemy he would sink the universe to the deepest depth of the bottomless pit.

IMMIGRATION SOCIAL MEDICINE

During the last quarter of the nineteenth century, a unique phenomenon occurred in the United States: wealth multiplied more rapidly than population. In no other country were there so many material possessions. The nation had prospered, yet its wealth was unevenly distributed. One of the most pronounced signs of the times was the extreme concentration of wealth among the few. Rapid economic expansion was made possible by centralization of private enterprise in the hands of a few Eastern industrialists and the federal government policy. Without huge investments of Eastern capital, the natural resources of the West would have been undeveloped for years. Previously, the Western economy had depended on only a few products: lumber, grain and minerals. When the Industrial Revolution spread into the West, a higher degree of managerial organization became necessary to facilitate profitable expansion.

Some noteworthy philanthropic endeavors occurred during the latter years of the nineteenth century. Not all millionaires misused their fortunes. Much of Rockefeller's millions went to higher education. Carnegie built libraries and established pension funds for college professors; his gifts totaled over $300,000,000 before his death. Other wealthy men gave huge sums to many benevolent causes, but the fact remained that only a few could amass such wealth, while the great majority could barely maintain a subsistence level.

In the 1880s and 1890s, radicals such as Henry George spoke out against plutocracy, pointing to the dangers of concentrated wealth. Other radicals spread discontent among the working classes by preaching equality of economic opportunity. This struggle for human rights and economic reform had such names as populism, progressivism, bolshevism and socialism. Plans were proposed for preventing the future accumulation of fortunes and for distributing existing fortunes. Federal and state income taxes were imposed so that the captains of industry would bear a greater share of public financial burdens. Some men in high positions advocated inheritance taxes to reduce great fortunes.

Programs for social reform were many and varied. For example, some reformers echoed the sentiments of their colonial ancestors by advocating prohibition. The movement made little progress; many men who were teetotalers objected to prohibition on the grounds that such legislation infringed on personal liberty. Immigrants, most of them accustomed to drink since their youth, aided the adversaries of prohibition. In fact, distillation of liquors became an immense and highly profitable business which employed thousands of people. Despite a boom in the spirits business, the prohibition movement became a nationwide issue. Party leaders made efforts to keep the issue out of politics. The exception was the National Prohibition party, which had entered every presidential contest since its foundation in 1872. This party never carried a single state; its highest vote was 270,710 during the 1892 campaign. Other organizations in the same field were the Women's Christian Temperance Union (W.C.T.U.) and the Anti-Saloon League, both of which pledged to do battle against "Rum Power." Before the turn of the century legislation for restriction of the sale of intoxicants was put into effect in all states, usually as local option laws. Two states were completely dry—Kansas and Maine.

The liquor industry fought tooth and nail against the prohibition movement and spent enormous sums in influencing legislators and elections. In the cities, they used all conceivable measures to prevent the enforcement of blue laws and other regulatory acts. They wanted to keep the liquor flowing as freely as possible. Saloons were usually operated jointly with gambling-houses, white-slave traffic and other vices. Saloons and liquor occasionally had a corrupting influence on politics. Gradually the liquor trade antagonized the public. Many believed that the business had a debilitating effect on society and ruined the lives of thousands—not only of drinkers but of their families. Many businessmen realized that drinkers were less dependable, less efficient and more troublesome than nondrinkers, and many business establishments turned toward a policy of hiring only teetotalers. Prohibition gained a foothold in the

South where drunkenness was responsible for many crimes perpetrated on the Negro population.

Between 1880 and 1900, the population increased by twenty-six million. Nearly a fourth of this number settled in only four states: New York, Massachusetts, Pennsylvania and New Jersey. The remainder spread over other areas. Many located on the rapidly diminishing government domain that had been available to homesteaders. Between 1890 and 1900, public land shrank to half of what it had been in 1880. In 1880, there were five territories in the West which had less than fifty thousand inhabitants each. After the discovery of gold, silver and copper, these territories rapidly became populated. By 1900, only Wyoming and Nevada had not exceeded the hundred thousand mark. Westward expansion resulted in a decline of the farm population in Iowa and Illinois. The mineral strikes served to offset the 1884 depression—a factor which contributed to the rapid expansion Westward.

The American Indian was the victim of population expansion. His frontier and hunting land disappeared; substantial portions of reservations were appropriated by railroads. The ranchers looked with envy at the vast plains given to the Indians for hunting grounds. The Indian territory that was once remote was not vulnerable to pioneer encroachment. The government had relocated the Indians for the last time: land for another relocation was no longer available. The only solution was accommodation between the two civilizations. White men would not tolerate the uneconomic use of Indian lands. Paltry government economic assistance failed to upgrade the Indians' economic status. A new solution was proposed. Individual ownership was to replace tribal ownership on the reservation. In 1887 the Dawes Act was passed, providing for the allotment of lands to individuals. A quarter-section was granted to the head of each family; smaller acreage went to others. To protect the Indian against land-sharks and speculators, the Dawes Act stipulated that the property could not be sold for a period of twenty-five years. Under the same act the Indian also received citizenship. It was hoped that ownership of land would relieve the government of rationing, annuities and other tribal subsidies.

In order to enlarge the public domain for white settlers, the government made efforts to buy portions of the Indian reservations. In 1885, Indian reservations amounted to 225,000 square miles. One-eighth of this total was still enough to give 320 acres to each of the 250,000 Indians west of the Mississippi. The government was to invest money from sale of tribal land in a tribal fund, rather than paying each tribe directly. The government also spent more money for Indian education. In 1888, fifteen thousand Indian children were enrolled in schools. A compulsory education act was passed by Congress in 1891 and all Indian children of eligible age fell under the program. For some, day schools were established, but many were taken from their homes and placed in reservation boarding schools or schools off the reservation, such as the Haskell Institute at Lawrence, Kansas, or the Carlisle Institute in Pennsylvania.

The Indian problem was far from settled. Treaty rights were violated by careless or overaggressive settlers. Cattlemen made unjustifiable attacks on the Indians in Colorado in 1887. Earlier, the Apaches in New Mexico threw the Southwest into a panic when they murdered a hundred people during one uprising. Government mismanagement of Indian agencies and violation of treaty obligations resulted in open warfare on the Sioux reservation in the Dakotas in 1890. In the Battle of Wounded Knee, General Miles' troops killed five hundred Indians, and thirty Army soldiers died.

As people reacted to social ills, reform measures gained support. Before the nineteenth century came to a close, social reform ideas were widely discussed throughout the country. Regulation of labor practices was an area of grave concern. Labor needed governmental agencies to represent them. The first state to establish a bureau of labor was Massachusetts. By 1885 similar bureaus were set up in several other states. These bureaus studied the moral, physical, economical and sanitary conditions under which employees worked. Labor leaders complained to the bureau on issues of low wages, working hours, industrial accidents, unemployment and similar matters. Reformers contended that special legislation would diminish or eliminate the unhealthy conditions to which the worker was subjected.

Reformers launched attacks against poverty and slum misery. Thousands of industrial workers, including immigrants, lived in tenements. They paid millions of dollars annually in rents to slum landlords. Much of the misery in the slums was due to inefficient municipal government and to inadequate regulation of business conduct. The independent spirit of Americans was hard to guide and restrain, and in politics as in business nearly everyone looked out for his own personal gain first. The tenets of Social Darwinism provided rationalization of such behavior. Authorities were slow to legislate and enforce building and health laws. Unsafe and unsanitary tenements caused many fire disasters and filled the tuberculous wards in the hospitals. The crime rate of the cities became extremely high, but the fault was not entirely with the law. The best intentioned officers found it difficult to cope with cheap theaters and unprincipled and unscrupulous swindlers of every kind who preyed upon the poor and unfortunate.

The settlement house was the effort of the philanthropic minded, educated, and well-to-do people to assist the poor. It was not intended to be a charity center. The people who founded these social settlements did not force religion upon anyone. They invited the poor to classes and clubs and they visited families in their homes. These citizen reform movements occasionally pushed corrupt government officials out of office, but the old order usually returned under cover. Law and order leagues and societies for good citizenship served as meeting places for civic-minded people. They felt that the surest method to reach their goal was the education of young people. The first of these civic clubs was the City Club of New York, founded in 1892. This club served as the springboard for a wave of reform.

Reform spread from government to business. American business expansion had created keen competition which often made man selfish and ruthless. The ethics of earlier times did not meet the requirements of the new business complex; sordid business practices often prevailed. Profiteering reached new heights and national legislation had no marked effect on the business community. On the other hand, credit expansion by business illustrated the reliability of businessmen.

One of the most trying problems was that of industry. Industrial ethics permitted the employer to prescribe the working conditions. As a result, workers were underpaid and could barely afford life's necessities. There were other questions involved in the labor struggle: freedom, justice, and social betterment. The problem developed into a power struggle, the employee demanding increased privileges and a wider recognition of labor union legitimacy. Hostility bred hatred and suspicion. As the worker gained more privileges by means of united effort, he also developed a determination to profit at the expense of his employer, despite the reform measures adopted by business.

The church took small part in all these social movements, even though reformers were often church leaders. Laborers attended churches in large numbers, even though they felt the church was too much in agreement with the capitalist. Ministers in the pulpit were outspoken in their demands for social reform, but most people believed that religion did not include social affairs, also that the church should be as separate from business and industry as from the state.

Sociological courses were incorporated into the curriculum of the colleges. Students of reform Darwinism left school with a glowing desire to engage in many forms of social service. In earlier times, these young reformers would have trained for the ministry.

Social problems were complicated by the influx of a large foreign element into the population. Immigration threatened the social structure because the immigrant was not readily assimilated. Another social problem that was almost purely American was the rural community. The exodus of youth to the city left some farm areas with a labor shortage. In rural areas, isolation kept people individualistic, often ignorant, and sometimes antisocial in conduct. Moral conditions were usually better than in the cities, but culture was on a low plane. There was emptiness rather than unpleasantness in rural life. Given these conditions, young people could not be condemned if they yielded to the city, with its glitter and magnificence, its economic opportunity, and its many recreational activities. If they were ambitious, the city offered a chance to succeed. If they wanted only pleasure, the city could offer all forms of amusements. Their brawn and intellect was the making of the city but contributed to the impoverishment of the country which they left. It was feared that if the exodus weren't stopped, the strength of the nation would be in jeopardy and the agricultural resources would dwindle. The situation was so alarming that action was taken to make rural life more attractive.

The overhead electric trolley transportation system was first tried in Richmond, Virginia, in 1888. Successful on a small scale, it was quickly built in Boston, where previous plans had been made to use a cable system. Other cities followed in substituting the trolley for the horse-drawn car. In 1890 the ratio of horsecar to electric power on street transit lines in all cities of the United States was about four to one; by 1900, the situation was reversed.

This made it possible for a larger population to live in the suburbs of cities, thus extending the social and economic impact of city life. More than one-half of the increase of population of Manhattan, New York, between 1890 and 1900 was north of Eighty-Sixth Street, seven miles from the southern tip. Suburbs were made possible in sections that were inaccessible by steam trains. New York, with its boroughs, grew from less than 2,000,000 in 1880 to 3,437,000 in 1900. Within a radius of twenty-five miles from New York City Hall, there was a population of nearly 5,000,000. Better transportation facilities led to concentration of business in large department stores and high office buildings.

Arc-lighting was introduced in 1880 and this was followed by the use of the incandescent lamp. The application of electricity to industry was pursued with renewed vigor. In 1900 the average annual per capita expenditure for electricity was about seven dollars, which represented about $1.25 for electric equipment and supplies, $3.00 for electric transportation, $1.50 for telephone uses, $.75 for telegraphic service and $.50 for miscellaneous use.

The telephone became a part of business communication in 1880. At first it was regarded as a luxury; but by 1890, it was considered a necessity in the commercial world. With the expiration of many patents, the costs of service were reduced. Telephone convenience to home and office led to the establishment of exchanges in suburban areas of cities and also in small towns. Even outlying farms were brought into communication. In 1900 there were over forty-two hundred exchanges with nearly two million subscribers, a ratio of one to forty of the population.

The bicycle craze in the nineties created a great social revolution. The new type bicycle with equal-sized wheels and pneumatic rubber tires could be mastered and ridden by people of all ages. It put thousands of people in a new environment. The fad died out before the decade was over but it had added fun and gaiety to American life as nothing had before.

Bicycling led to a change in women's styles. Skirts became shorter and the bloomer and tam became familiar wearing apparel for the lady cyclist. Boys wore knee pants until their teens; older boys and men in long pants used a trouser clamp to keep the leg of the pants from getting caught in the pedal sprocket. The baggy knickerbocker and bulky sweater became standard attire for men. Many men wore these clothes to work, which marked a great change from the stiff and conventional style of the past.

HOW TO GET OVER THE PROHIBITION LAW.

The great electoral sweep has shown one thing in a very distinct manner, that the majority of the people are not going to be deprived of their beer and whiskey, because a few canting cranks think it wicked to drink liquor of any kind. Drunkenness is of course a terrible evil, but can't be eradicated by any such nonsense as prohibitory laws. A man ought to be allowed to eat and drink what he pleases, and, if he is fool enough to get drunk, he must take the consequence of his acts. What with the closing of liquor saloons, and the efforts made to introduce a prohibition clause in the constitution of the different states, the only place left for a man to imbibe in comfort will be in a balloon.

BARTENDERS' STATUE OF LICENSE LIGHTENING NEW YORK.

Is it possible to secure passably-decent men to administer city governments in this country? Why do the enormities and deformities of human depravity always come on top in the Metropolis?

Why is it possible to find only blackmailers to suppress gambling and prostitution, beer-guzzlers to execute the license-laws, wolves to guard the sheep?

For a variety and a surprise, why cannot we have one department of law administered by others than law breakers?

Does THE JUDGE rant? All the world has read the investigation of police conspiracy with gambling houses, dance houses, prostitution houses for the protection of the one and the profit of the other. A police-inspector's son was a living witness to what ought to have been the damnation of the service and to have caused a popular upheaval of reform. Did anything come of it?

Policeman Conroy commits a most brutal murder, and gets simple imprisonment to be ended with speedy pardon by some Democratic governor at the behest of Democratic pals, probably.

A police sergant poses before the public in the brilliant role of ravisher of young girls.

These savage beasts are not placed over a helpless people by a conquering tyrant. They are the full blossom of the attempt at self-government! Of all the unspeakable crimes to be charged up by History against the Democratic party, the record of its government of the Metropolis is the foulest category.

This is "how we live now."

What are the Intelligence, Culture, Wealth, Feminine-Refinement, Christianity of New York going to do about it?

"There have been times and incidents when the strike was the only court of appeals for the workingmen, and the evil lay in the abuse of strikes, and not in the use of them. The method used to bring about a successful termination of strikes, the abuse of property and even of persons, has brought the very name into disrepute, while sympathy for the laboring men is dying out. More and more clearly defined is the line becoming which divides the honest man, satisfied with a just remuneration which he has truly earned, until by his own effort he can rise to a higher position in life, and the loud-voiced 'bomb thrower,' who, scarcely able to speak the English language, seeks to win his own comfortable living from those who have worked for it, presuming upon the imagination and arousing false hopes in the hearts of those who are still more ignorant than himself. Among sensible men the day for all this is past."

These are the words of Mr. Arthur, the head of the Brotherhood of Locomotive Engineers, which is the most powerful and successful labor union in the country, the only one that has no internal dissensions, and that enjoys the respect of the country. They are the words of a man who has been a manual laborer, and who has given up his work only to go into the nobler business of preventing strikes and maintaining harmony between employers and their employees. His work is not the work of the Powderlys and Ironses and McGlackins. His purpose is to help laboring-men, to keep them at their work, to show them the only true way to prosperity, and to protect them from bad counselors and false leaders. This has for years been his task, honestly and ably performed, and the men who call him chief are themselves honest and able enough to value his help and listen to his counsels.

"Among sensible men, the day for all this is past." For all what? Why, for all the vile work which Powderly and Irons and McGlackin have been doing for three years. For all this so-called "labor agitation" based on the utterly untenable idea that the laborer is worthy of more than his hire. For all this riot and bloodshed and miscellaneous violence and disorder by which "Labor" has sought to assert its "dignity." For the unmanly cruelty of the Boycott, and for the degrading slavery of the Knights of Labor. Mr. Arthur is right: the time is past, among sensible men, and it will soon be past among all men. The action of the Typothetae in New York is but an earnest of the action that must be taken by decent men of business throughout the country. Organization for the infraction of the laws and the ruin of trade must be met by organization for the upholding of constitutional rights and the preservation of prosperity. It is very hard to make the workingman understand this—that if he would exact justice from his employer, he must himself be just—that if he breaks the laws, he must not expect that the law will protect him in his assault upon the law-abiding. And this has been the teaching of the Knights of Labor, of the District Assemblies, of the Socialists and the Anarchists—that if a workman be dissatisfied with his work or with his wages, he is superior to all laws, civil, national or moral. The disturbance which is the outcome of such doctrines put into practical application, can have but one end. The people have been patient and forbearing. They have been willing to believe that the working-folk were, as a rule, unfairly treated. They believe this no longer; and before long they must believe that the workingman is the enemy of peace, order and industry. When they do believe this, and begin a war of reprisal, there will be even more distress and misery than we have yet seen. And this is what must surely come of the folly of men who have yielded up their independence, their self-respect, their very manhood, to the tyranny of "organizers" who make their rich living out of over-worked women and half-starved children.

BETWEEN SLAVERY AND STARVATION.

Two "systems" are the curse of our American schools, public and private. One is the text-book system, and the other is the marking system. They go hand-in-hand and do their work together. Their work is the over-straining of young bodies, and the dulling of young brains. The idea of these two wretched schemes is to save the teachers a little labor and a great deal of brain-work. They make it possible, in fact, to be a teacher and yet know nothing; thus enabling a large class of worthy but ignorant people to get a living with reasonable ease and certainty. Many a man who would otherwise be seeking vainly a position as assistant entry-clerk or light-porter is to-day getting a respectable salary as an instructor of the young—a position to which he could never aspire were it not for the text-book system.

The "system" has simplicity to recommend it, at least. A publisher's hack writes a text-book—an English grammar, or a so-called history of the United States or the World, or a first book in natural History. Whatever he may call it, it is nothing better than a spiritless transcript of dull generalities and dry technical or statistical facts, culled, often with little attempt at accuracy, from such standard authorities as may be accessible to him. Then another hack, who calls himself a teacher, hands this book to the children given into his care, and tells them to learn so many lines or so many pages a day. He does not teach them; he merely tells them to learn. When the time for recitation comes, each child repeats all or a part of what he has committed to memory, while the hack compares the recitation with the printed page. If the recital and the text book agree, the child gets a credit of such and such a figure in a record-book. If there are discrepancies, the child gets a smaller figure. If the two do not agree at all, the child is marked nought or zero. At the end of the week the hack adds up the child's figures, divides the total by the number of the recitations, and gives the result—say 778.33—as John's or Eliza's

average of scholarship. This is written in a printed form, and sent to the child's parents, to be signed and returned. It will be seen that there is no undue strain upon the teacher's brain. It would be more difficult to measure tape and make change in a dry-goods shop.

But what a senseless, soulless "system" it is for the poor helpless children. The industrious child toils and strives and learns by rote a vast mass of dry, cold fact, of the significance and value of which he knows nothing, and which it is beyond the power of his young and untrained memory to retain for any length of time, or to properly assimilate in any way. The idle child contents himself with imperfect recitations, takes home his record of "low average scholarship," and accepts the consequent punishment, whatsoever it may be. And we are inclined to think that often-times he goes out of his school-slavery, better off than the child who has strained his mental capacity in the acquisition of useless knowledge or knowledge that he can not use—which is the sort of knowledge that most text-books give.

This assertion is sweeping; but it is essentially correct. The text-book-taught boy can "bound" the states of the Union, can repeat the names of the presidents in proper order, and can tell you when each monarch of England came to the throne. But what does he really *know* of the history, character and resources of his own country? What does he understand of the lesson of England's growth and the grandeur of her past? And how has he been taught to find out for himself? He knows of two books of reference—the Encyclopaedia and the Dictionary. Take these away from him and he is all at sea. The learning of the ages is at his disposal, in countless public and private libraries; but he has no knowledge of what study really means; he has no power to distinguish the useful from the useless—he has not *learned to learn*. History is for him a matter of dates; geography a matter of statistics. He can not understand that a man

may know all that is worth knowing of Louis the Fourteenth, of France, and yet have to go to his book-shelves and take down a work of reference to find the dates of Louis's birth and death.

If this were the worst of the text-book system it would be bad enough; but it is not the worst. A base venality has made it doubly a curse. The multiplication of text-books has been carried so far that even the most ignorant and thoughtless of "parents and guardians" must suspect the existence of a disgraceful alliance between the publishers of school-books and a certain class of school-teachers and school-superintendents. The books used in many of our schools are changed with a frequency that can not but excite suspicion. The book that was the standard last year is supplanted by a new one this season; the boy who has an edition of 1885 is ordered to get one of 1886. Parents may protest; but the books must be bought and paid for, or the responsibility for the boy's lagging behind in his studies does not rest with the school-teacher. Of course, the influences which are brought to bear upon the teachers and commissioners do not often take the form of gross bribery. In most cases the school authority obliges the publishers only because they oblige him in various ways—by giving him discounts on books and stationery for his own use, we may suggest, by way of instance. But, unfortunately, it is impossible not to believe that in many instances the influence goes a great deal further than this. On no other ground can be explained the feverish anxiety shown in many schools to pile study upon study; to load down weak, half-grown children with books upon books; to enact tasks—always under this text-book system—which wear out young bodies and young brains, and bring our children to a premature, one-sided development of the mental faculties, at the expense of strained and enfeebled frames.

THE FORCING PROCESS IN OUR SCHOOLS—
ONE OF THE RESULTS OF AN UNHOLY ALLIANCE.

Times have not greatly changed, after all, since the trial of the famous case of Bardell *vs.* Pickwick, (Dickens's Reports, 1,288.) Justice Stareleigh is not so familiar a figure upon the American bench; but we have our Dodsons and our Foggs, and Master Bardell is still led in to make his mother weep bitter tears, for the edification of the jury. It is a curious thing that we have hardly a judge in our courts who is not hopelessly trammeled by legal tradition and fear of the letter of the law that he dares to check the antics of the Tombs shyster who acts as though he owned the entire courthouse. This creature, whose services are to be had by every thief and ruffian in the community, defeats the ends of justice daily, by all manner of illegal means; and it is only once in a long while that he gets some small part of the rebuke which is his due. The judge on the bench is in deadly fear of the awful exception, which may bring about a reversal of the verdict, on the ground that the court has erred. So he lets the iniquity go on, and witnesses are bullied, insulted, confused and misrepresented, the sympathies of the jury are appealed to in ways never contemplated by any code of legal procedure, and the verdict comes in dead against the law and the evidence.

The "family tableau act" is at present one of the most popular means of influencing juries in favor of murderers or worse men. The wife of the defendant comes into court, dressed in sober black, and tearfully embraces the social lion who is on trial. She leads by their little hands her weeping children, carefully washed for the occasion. If only the family cat could be brought along to purr softly at the prisoner's feet, the picture of a happy home circle would be so sweetly complete that no jury would so far consider the binding nature of an oath as to part the misled husband from his loved ones. Perhaps, as things are going now, we shall not have very long to wait before the cat becomes a possibility. We may even see the cook-stove—or a neat working-model of it—burning cheerily in the court room, to suggest the charms of the domestic hearth still more forcibly to the mind of the tender-hearted juror. A kind friend who has asked for our opinion upon this practice reminds us of a recent case where a disgusted District-Attorney was obliged to off-set the family tableau by bringing the mangled remains of the domestic criminal's victim into the halls of justice, and, so to speak, slumping them down in full view of the jury, as he asked that members of the tribunal should consider, to some extent, the feelings of the widow to whom those members belonged.

This sort of thing has been mostly in use in capital cases; but it seems to have a wider usefulness. We have just had an example of its application in this city, and no doubt it was, in the case to which we refer, largely instrumental in causing a miscarriage of justice. Of course, it is a wretched trick which can not be thoroughly checked—it is an abuse of wholesome privilege, indeed. But some check may be put upon it, if a judge has the courage to act. Where, however, we are to find the judge whose knees do not grow weak at the thought of the deadly exception, we know not. He certainly is not likely to be found in the ranks of the elective judiciary.

Bring out the old red cutter, light, almost, as a trotting-sulky. Hitch up the little bay, the bay that you knew as a colt that you yourself broke in. He has Morgan blood in him, and his sire had a record of 2:39½ when it was something of a distinction to beat two-forty. His dam was the first horse your father bought for your mother's use, when he had paid off the mortgage on the old place after years of honest, wholesome work. Hitch up, for a holiday ride. Your hard week is done, and She is expecting you, down there in the brown house under the hill. Ah, at the gate she is, the good girl, not ashamed to show that she is looking for you. And now you help her in, and tuck the buffalo-robe around the little feet on the hot brick, and jump in by her side, and gather up the lines, and get his head right for the road, and go *clk!*—and off you fly.

And now you are skimming down the road, and Her cheeks are flushed with the snapping air and the excitement of the ride; for the little bay is getting down to his work and slipping past everything on runners. Good reason why he should, too. He has never been chromolithographed, with a margin-full of pedigree; but it took a great deal of sound human stock to produce him. He is the product of generations of wise, temperate and useful labor. He, and his sires before him—they were all well-fed, well-trained, well-exercised by men who worked for their living as men ought to work—conscientiously, thoughtfully, and for good and reasonable ends. It is not strange that their horses should be like them,

for the horses were not only a part of the economy of their lives, but sharers of their love and consideration. And so that little bay, got by Wisdom out of Labor, goes proudly trotting down the road, well ahead of all his fellows—when *zip!* there is a jingle of strange bells, the b-r-r of steel on hard snow, and past you flashes a gorgeous sleigh, shiny and black, oddly shaped and oddly decked, and the sealskin-coated driver turns back on you a fat, over-fed, insolent face, and smiles at the poor devil who thought that his home-bred little bay could beat the great forty-thousand-dollar trotter about which all the newspapers are talking.

The forty-thousand-dollar horse, good friend, bought with money accumulated at that mean kind of gambling which uses stocks and shares instead of cards and chips. Gambling none the less it is, and dishonest gambling at that. This man's father gambled himself rich, and his son is going on, gambling up riches upon earth, to be corrupted and to spread corruption, to tempt thieves to break through and steal, to spread right and left the curse of overgrown and illegitimate wealth. Go back, good friend, with your old-fashioned red cutter, with your little home-bred bay horse, go back with the simple girl who is to be your wife and your helpmate; go back with your outworn ideas of industry and honesty and honor—what place have you in this day of gambling monopolists—what place have you on this road that is leading us all to the confines of a tyranny worse than the tyranny of imperial despotism?

FEARFUL CONSEQUENCES OF A GENERAL STRIKE.

The public has of late been pretty extensively regaled with accounts of strikes in a large number of trades. In a cartoon we have endeavored to show the probable result of strikes in certain trades. It would be awkward if no horse-shoers were available to fit our steeds with their iron congress-gaiters and slippers. We should have to encase the animals' legs in our own private top-boots and Oxford-ties, in which we are accustomed to promenade the Avenue. Again, suppose the car-drivers struck: the glorious spectacle of the directors hauling along their own cars—which would do them good—would be exhibited. A general strike among the cabinet-makers might utilize the family cooking-range in a way never contemplated by art or nature.

ANOTHER BIG THING—
THE MARRIED MENS' LODGE—
NIGHT HOOK-AND-LADDER CAB COMPANY
NO MORE LATCH KEYS NEEDED.

Almost every married man has a lodge-night, and every man, be he married or single, has a night-key. The troubles of the night-key are so well known that they occupy no mean link in the chain of jokes that constitute American Stock Humor. If a man has his night-key in his other trousers, he can not remain out late; for if he does, he will be obliged to ring the bell, and then his wife will know the exact time of his arrival. Therefore, he carries a night-key always, and guards it as he does his gold watch. When he gets on the stoop, he can't find the key-hole until he has called a policeman, and then the key is full of lint out of his pocket, which he has to pry out with a pin. After he gets in, he is as apt to go down in the cellar and go to bed in the refrigerator as to go up-stairs and retire to his regular couch.

Therefore, our artist has struck upon a novel idea which should prove the abolition of the night-key. All night-key carriers should get together and form a stock company, and call it "The Married Men's Lodge-Night Hook-and-Ladder Cab Co." It would be a great satisfaction to the man who is out celebrating the election to know that a cab is standing outside to take him home just as soon as he can not stand alone. The man could fall asleep on the mattress inside, and, on arriving home, could be shot right through his window into bed. The hooks on the end at the window-sill are intended for a pair of boot-jacks. These Johns, or jacks, as they are usually called, take off the boots of the victim as he goes along, and this keeps his footprints from becoming imprinted on the snowy surface of the counterpane. It is very probable that "The Married Men's Lodge-Night Hook-and-Ladder Cab Co." will become so popular that there will be imitation cabs that you can't tell from the originals to save your life.

IMMIGRATION SOCIAL MEDICINE

The story of the rise of scientific medicine to some was magic, while to others it was mystery, but having overcome ignorance and quackery, it now is the most beneficial of the sciences known to man. A long and difficult struggle has at last produced tangible achievements in the prevention and cure of disease and prolongation of life.

The last few hundred years encompass such discoveries as the bacterial cause of infection, one of the greatest triumphs in man's struggle against his environment. Primitive man still believed disease was one of his misfortunes, brought about by spirits and supernatural forces: to cure or prevent disease the spirits must be forced or bribed to leave. The function of the earliest physicians was to heal their friends, but to cause sickness upon their enemies. We would call these physicians medicine men and they practiced both white magic healing and black magic destruction. Medicine was a mixture of superstition and religion, but it also had some very practical measures, and some of these primitive practices were used as late as the eighteenth century.

It was among the Greeks that scientific approaches to medicine were first formulated, in that they were the first to divorce religion from medicine, and make its practice not magic or superstition. To know is science, but merely to believe one knows is ignorance.

Bad health had been looked upon as an act of the Gods, or a personal matter between the patient and his doctor. Soon it was discovered that some of man's diseases were hereditary, others were social in origin, or were occupational diseases, caused from the use of certain chemicals such as in making matches or pottery. Slowly it dawned on the public mind that disease due to heredity or to personal faults constituted a costly burden for industry and perpetuated society with reduced efficiency.

Near the middle of the eighteenth century there were accelerated epidemics of smallpox and cholera. This aroused great interest in public health, and city councils and state legislators were forced to act in the interest of public health, to achieve victory over ignorant and often virulent opposition, as well as the disease itself.

Dr. Josephine Baker symbolized those labors as "Fighting for Life." The highest type of men have the intelligence, the independence, the integrity and the courage to admit their errors and seek after the truth without bias. Cholera infections have definitely been related to invasion of the human body by specific germs or virus. Cholera is seldom if ever seen in the United States. Infected water is the most common cause of cholera. There are foolish people who talk about the germ theory. Germs are not a theory, no more than other things that live and reproduce. Anyone with a reasoning mind should be willing to grant that the germ actually causes the diseases. The best way to avoid disease, is to keep away from people who have them.

Men who have given us modern medicine are men such as the French surgeon Ambroise Paré who discarded the practice of cauterization which tended to increase infection. Roger of Palermo prescribed burnt sponge for goiter, mercury salves for skin diseases, and Joseph Lister made his announcement of the antiseptic principle.

William Harvey discovered circulation, but the actual discovery of blood flow is less important than the method by which he arrived at his conclusions. He applied mathematical measurements to vital physical phenomena and was the first man to do so. About this time there was an instrument coming into use destined to be one of the most valuable of all medical discoveries, the microscope. This instrument was first used by a Jesuit priest, named Athanasius Kircher, and later there was Robert Hooke, whose book on micrographics so fascinated others beginning study in that field. It was Hooke who first recorded the cellular structure of plants.

Jan Swammerdam first understood and described the

119

red corpuscles. Italian Marcello Malpighi was the great microscopist who founded histology as a science, and it was he who brought out the final step in Harvey's demonstration of circulation: he saw the capillaries, and demonstrated the essential vascular structure of the lungs, about which Harvey had only speculated. It was an English chemist, John Mayow, who demonstrated that change of color was due to exposure to air. This is but a little of the rugged work, such as that represented in the discoveries of Harvey, Malpighi, and Leeuwenhoek.

Edward Jenner's work has an importance aside from its practical usefulness, for he made a pure application of the control experiment, as well as using prophylactic methods to prevent smallpox, and it is Edward Jenner to whom we owe the vaccination against the disease.

Philippe Pinél was a pioneer in the care of the mentally ill. Against the advice of authorities, he cut the chains from the mad, and treated these poor men and women as if they were ill, opening the way for modern care of the insane.

Psychiatry was a new approach in the nineteenth century. The old Vienna school founded in this century had its greatest importance because it was the site of the work of Ignatz Semmelweis, who made the first practical step toward the control of puerperal infection. Semmelweis demonstrated the conception of blood poisoning from infection, but was laughed at and persecuted. In disgust he left Vienna and went to Budapest a broken man, to die within a few years.

The rise of Edinburgh to medical eminence was a result of the prominent physicians John Morgan, William Shippen, Jr., and Benjamin Rush, who in turn served as surgeons-general. Although they left no major contributions to medical progress, they stressed the importance of research and hygienic practices.

The better physicians often occupied high social positions, and this was the era of famous quacks. At the same time social change was affecting medicine, for it was in these years that the "anatomy laws" providing subjects for dissection were formulated. This move did much to compound the intense popular opposition to medical study then existing. This country's feeling against medical research culminated in the "doctor's mob" of New York City, when it was necessary to call out the militia to quell the rising against the hospital and physicians.

The professional level was raised by state control of licensure and appointed boards of examination. The Carnegie Foundation exposed abuses in medical educa-

tion and proposed reforms through grants for medical centers, some of which went to Vanderbilt, George Washington, Duke, and the Universities of Chicago, Rochester and Iowa. Although these measures brought about a rise in quality of physicians, it was nevertheless a time when art and personality and show, rather than science, ruled medical practice. Many of the most successful physicians had no medical education, for a few schools were turning out thousands of doctors—there were twenty-one medical schools and over fifteen thousand practitioners. Some were known as the "physicians' factories," and although this factory procedure was illegal in many states, by 1890 there were 112 medical schools with faulty instruction. Medicine had become a social necessity.

Due to the inventive improvements of this century, the stage coach, the sailboat, the candle, the filthy city without sewers gave way in turn to the railroad and the automobile, the steam boat the paraffin lamp and then electricity; and then a clean city with sewers, pure water, clean streets and clean homes. The important changes that made the modern city possible were entirely due to the advances of medical discoveries. Dorothea Lynde Dix of Boston was one who literally forced upon a reluctant public the duty of providing for the mentally ill. She was responsible for more than thirty of our state mental institutions. Likewise, Florence Nightingale organized nursing, the very keynote of the medical progress of the nineteenth century. Such physicians as Morton, Long, Wells, Pasteur, Koch, Lister and Reed are men who have altered our ways of living and thinking more profoundly than the warriors and traders and even the philosophers.

The beneficial "anatomy laws" were formulated soon after the disreputable "Burk and Hair" affair of Scotland, also called the "anatomy murders," for these men undertook to procure subjects for the anatomy rooms of medical schools by the murders of inconspicuous citizens.

The list of medical advance continues: René Théophile Laënnec was the originator of the stethoscope, and Horace Green published his treatise on diseases of the air passages, known as Laryngology. Ernest Krackourizer expanded the field with the Laryngoscope, while Samuel D. Gross wrote significantly on intestinal lesions, respiratory organs and surgery. This was the first comprehensive work in English.

Karl Basedow described exophthalmic goiter; William Stokes recorded his account of the heart block; Thomas Addison wrote on pernicious anemia; Rudolf Virchow

commenced his studies that were to be consummated in his great thesis of cellular pathology. Decade by decade came the great discoveries which have shaped modern medicine.

It is in this period that Claude Bernard founded experimental medicine, when he commenced his study of the glycogenic function of the liver. Ten years before he had come to Paris an aspirant to be a dramatic poet, but two men influenced his career and led him on his way towards his great physiological contributions. Medicine owes an everlasting debt to these men: Saint-Marc Girardin, the critic, who advised him to give up poetry, and his teacher, the great Magendie.

The Weber brothers, Ernst and Eduard, were in Leipzig showing that impulses in the vagus nerve affect the action of the heart, one of the fundamental discoveries of physiology. Next to Jenner's vaccination, anesthesis was the most useful and the most humane treatment for disease. It was discovered by three different men in three different places: Crawford Long in Georgia, Horace Wells in Hartford, Connecticut, and William Morton in Charlestown, Massachusetts. The English Quaker surgeon, Joseph Lister, was founder of the antiseptic principle, but the final events connected with the introduction of ether occurred in America. Shortly before the ether anesthesia was discovered, there was a great deal of discussion of the use of hypnotic trance during operations, but nothing produced the complete absence of pain, other than anesthesia. The first demonstration of surgical anesthesia was made at General Hospital in Massachusetts.

Diseases were now given classical names and lengthy descriptions: Brown Sequard described ascending paralysis; Thomas Addison published his descriptions of the disturbances of the adrenal gland; Grolfe the details of retinal embolism; Perkin aniline dyes; and Karl Credé of Leipzig made his important observations on obstetrics.

Hermann von Helmholtz developed the opthalmoscope and the opthalmometer with which he was able to elucidate the mechanism of accommodation. Important as are these practical contributions of the great Helmholtz, his most fundamental work was in the field of mathematical physics.

In the years following there were great pioneers of modern surgical technique, such as Theodor Billroth, Ernst von Bergmann and William Halsted. Modern surgery of the abdomen, the brain, the chest, and the joints dates back to Lister's time.

Carl Wunderlick was teaching at Leipzig when Max von Pellinkofer of Bavaria, who later headed the first institute of hygiene, obtained with Carl von Niot the basic knowledge of energy metabolism. It was in this decade that Carl Wunderlick wrote his classical treatise on bodily temperature and disease, and the practical use of the clinical thermometer dates from his time.

Two more outstanding events of medical importance occurred at this time, but both found their usefulness in later years. Gregor Mendel, an Augustine monk of Brünn, reported his results from experiments in hybridizing peas, but it was not until the beginning of the twentieth century that it came into prominence as the basis for Mendelian law of inheritance. Likewise, Henri Dunant was the man who conceived the idea of a people united to help the sufferers in war and disaster, and in his honor the Swiss Flag was adopted to form the symbol of the organization of the International Red Cross.

Lister's discovery of the previous decade and the work of Pasteur and Koch overshadows all other medical events of the time. Louis Pasteur was not actually a physician, but came into the medical field with his knowledge of chemistry. To prevent bacterial growth he developed the process of heating fluid, which came to be called Pasteurization, in his honor. Robert Koch, a country doctor in Prussia, had as a hobby the close inspection of all manner of things under his microscope. He had studied the anthrax bacillus and worked out in his crude laboratory the complete life history of this organism. He was the founder of modern bacteriology, and later made the momentous discovery of the cause of tuberculosis. That year he isolated the tubercle bacillus and showed that the disease could develop only after infection with the organism, opening the way for eradication of a disease, which at that time was called the "Captain of the men of Death."

This inspired the search for all disease bacteria, with the result that the majority of the more important pathogenic organisms were identified, as the bacilli of cholera, typhoid, diphtheria, tetanus and meningitis, to name only a few. It was also about that time that Pasteur announced his discovery of a method preventing rabies, the Pasteur prophylactic treatment.

Major Walter Reed on this continent headed the "yellow fever" commission, which demonstrated the role of the mosquito in the transmission of yellow fever, while Karl Credé advanced his method of preventing ophthalmia in the newborn. It was twenty years later that a similar prophylactic procedure was to be developed by Elie Metchnikoff for the treatment of syphilis.

Before this time there was no conception that human disease might arise from similar animal parasites, until Alphonse Laveran of Paris discovered the mosquito carrying malaria. This brought on a rash of similar discoveries: Sir Patrick Manson showed the mosquito carried the filaris bancroftic; Theobald Smith demonstrated that ticks were the intermediary host in Texas fever of cattle; Charles Nicollo showed the mosquito as the carrier of malaria and yellow fever, the tsetse fly bearing fatal sleeping sickness; the flea that transmits bubonic plague, and the louse that carries typhus.

Perhaps nowhere is there a greater commentary on simple practicality of modern medicine than in this field of diseases borne by insects, for it demonstrates the practical aspects of the discoveries of modern medicine. In building the Panama Canal, yellow fever and malaria had made this district "the white man's grave"; yet today, the Canal Zone boasts of being one of the healthiest districts in the world.

Late in the nineteenth century, medical science was led forward by achievements in chemistry and physics; Emil Fischer, a Berlin professor, had succeeded in synthesizing caffeine; two other practical contributions to medicine were those of Marie and Pierre Curie in discovering radium, and Wilhelm Konrad Roentgen of Wurzburg discovering the X-ray. Roentgen's discovery was known throughout the world in a week and was used in medicine within a month. James Lind held the clue to vitamin deficiency, and he showed the efficiency of lime juice in preventing scurvy.

Fritz Schaudinn of Germany discovered the cause of syphilis, while Von Wasserman developed the diagnostic serum test for syphilis in the same year in which Metchnikoff described a specific prophylactic measure. Paul Ehrlich, founder of chemotherapy, announced the first cure of syphilis, one of the rare finds in therapy. The future may hold a leading role in medicine for this field of chemical therapy.

The greatest practical result of organotherapy has been the isolation of insulin by Banting and Best, bringing about a new era for the diabetic patient. The discoveries in the field of the vitamins are well known although they are still so new that we cannot even speculate upon their eventual outcome.

Medicine, we have seen, has risen from mystery and magic to science. The science of the laboratory is a science of modern medicine. It is not to the research worker that we turn in pain, but to the physician. Man is now protected against disease, is relieved of pain and cured by discoveries. These were the landmarks of the nineteenth century.

"When it is not one thing it is something else" that agitates the mind and threatens the health of the New Yorker. His favorite health resort, Central Park, is now pronounced infected. Its drainage doesn't drain; its waters are covered with scum so thick that the little tailless tadpoles take their cues and go gamboling on the green; the statues and the obelisks are shaky, the lawns are forlorn, and the Lady of the Lake paddles about with a gondola in the shape of a coffin. All this in the minds of nervous citizens.

If "the Lungs of New York" are diseased, through what shall it breathe? Where shall the sole find rest from malaria? Indeed, between malaria out of doors and tumbling dwellings when in-doors, there seems to be only one safe resort, only one secure style of habitation for the urban. He might as well emigrate to Greenwood or Cypress Hill at once.

But there is another suggestion: Suppose all these sanitary scares are the result of a collusion between the fecund reporter and the versatile Coney Island speculator! It is a noticeable coincidence that the malaria and the summer resort seasons open together. There's matter in this, and one could find it out.

To the poor and crowded population the condition of our parks is no trifling matter, and next to insuring safe and wholesome housing, the city authorities should guard from infection the only outing places of half a million of our people. But they wont, probably. City officials can be safely depended on to do only one thing—draw their salaries regularly.

If "de mortuis nil nisi bonum" is to be written over all men's graves, and a sort of general essence of perfect goodness is to exhale from the memories of those who have gone before, there is no reason why we should make a sort of cross between a May Festival and a picnic in bestowing earth on earth.

It is common to sneer at our fellow-citizens of Irish descent for the very exuberant way in which they go a-merry-making when one of their "cousins" dies; but in those classes in which there is greater wealth, and to which we look for greater intelligence and all those social proprieties which go to make life beautiful, we can find the funeral folly quite as absurd as it is with Pat in his tenement house.

When Death steps into the home-circle and places his cold hand upon one of the number, the shock that almost stills the hearts of the survivors is not to be assuaged by the set words of sympathy from strangers; still less by much kissing, easily-shed tears which make the house as damp as on a washing-day; or a deluge of pillars, crosses and anchors in all sorts of flowers from the florist's.

The very loneliness which makes the death-scene of Colonel Newcome, when he answered "Adsum!" one of the most touching scenes in fiction, is the feeling which stirs the deeper and truer parts of our nature, and urges us to close the world out from knowledge of, or sympathy with, our grief, and makes us cry: "Leave us *alone* with our dead."

Yet, such slaves are we to the fashions of the times we live in, that we sacrifice all the finer feelings of our natures and go in with the mob. The house where Death reigns closes its blinds, to be sure, but the ostentatious crepe which dangles from the door is a notice to all the world that the pompes funèbres are in full fig within. The street is lined with carriages from which alight hundreds of the acquaintances of the dead, bearing flowers; and the florist's assistants stagger up the steps under loads of flowers arranged in every shape that bad taste can suggest. The coffin is a casket; it's a wonderful piece of handicraft from the cabinet-maker and the upholsterer. The basements and dining-rooms are thronged with searchers for the funeral baked meats—and wines; and when the day of sepulchre comes, the car-

riages, the dresses, the floral display, sometimes the bbrass-bands, and the church ceremonies form a pageant; they are pabulum for the pen of the reporter with a descriptive turn, but—they are not grief for the dead.

It may, perhaps, be said that if people have money for all these things, they have the right to please their fancy, that it is only a matter of taste, and that we have no recognized authority to declare, ex cathedrâ, what is good and what is bad taste.

All this is true; but the example this funeral pomp sets to people of limited means is absurd to the dead and cruel to the living. The desire to give the dead a fine funeral—much as we give an opera singer or a Talmage a good send-off when they voyage across the Atlantic—is strong in the hearts of the poor; and great are the shifts they put themselves to, many the sacrifices, and heavy the mortgages they lay upon their time and labor to make the "send-off" as showy as possible. It is a fact that in this city a dead man's clothes have been pawned to obtain a more showy coffin for his remains than could otherwise have been purchased; and many a poor widow, after lunching a houseful of hungry "mourners" has gone to bed at night, after burying her dead, with her larder and her pocket-book both empty.

Some Catholic bishops have set the seal of their displeasure against the long carriage parade at funerals; and some sensible people are beginning to add in their newspaper notices of a death: "It is particularly requested that no flowers be sent." These are moves in the right direction, but it would be better to reform it altogether.

When a man, illustrious for the great things he has done for mankind, shall lie down in death, a people who love his memory and who mourn his death, can rise up in the sincerity of their grief and do him what lavish honors are left them to pay him. But this continual display of mock grief, this pageantry of woe which is constantly paraded through our streets, blocking commerce and rendering it almost impossible for a man to cross the ferries of our East River without a corpse or two on the boat with him, should be done away with. It benefits the undertakers, the "dealers in mourning," the florists; but it is in bad taste, it shows a shoddy state of civilization, and it tends to still more impoverish our poor.

The PUCK BUILDING stands on Houston Street, only a stone's throw from Broadway. As you approach it from that great thoroughfare, you find Houston Street much like all its neighbors, crowded thick with shops, warehouses and places of refreshment for the hungry and thirsty. It is like any one of Broadway's arteries about the midriff of the town—just between the down and the up of the huge city. But if you come toward it from the east, you see the tall red structure towering above blocks of two and three story houses, for you must pass through the realm of poverty and squalor if you would reach that northward-running strip of New York which is given over to prosperous, pushing Business. Broadway is full of tall stores, with plate-glass windows and ample doors. But on each side of Broadway, only a few blocks to east and west, stretches in a dismal parallel a poor quarter of the town. There are poor quarters higher up; but for airless, ill-lit misery, these down-town regions stand pre-eminently poor. They are the oldest; the most crowded, the least cared-for, though they shoulder the palaces of our "merchant princes."

There are thousands of business-men who walk home from their offices six days in the week. Of these there are few who turn out of Broadway before they reach Fourteenth Street and the region of the well-to-do. Yet anyone who chose to set his face to the east and follow any street between Canal and Bond might find much to interest him. He would see something interesting in the way of babies, for instance. There are babies everywhere in these streets. They are in the windows, on the stoops, on the sidewalks, in the middle of the street. Some of them are in their mothers' arms; some are carried by elder sisters or brothers; most of them are toddling about at an age when no child should attempt to toddle, and bowing out their rickety little legs in so doing. They are nearly all of them dirty, which is not an unnatural nor necessarily an unwholesome condition

for babies. But what you notice first in all of them is that their skins are dull and colorless. They raise pallid, putty-like faces toward you as they scramble out of your way; and you see the same unwholesome shade on the features of their mothers, standing just within the doors, trying to get a little fresh air.

And there is no fresh air there. It is all spoiled and thickened in dirty streets and badly ventilated, foul-smelling tenements. If a breeze comes up from the East River, the life is taken out of it before it gets half way to the Bowery; and it is poor stuff to fill the lungs of babes who draw their sustenance from mothers but half nourished on unfit food. Of all the thousand things that are needed in these close streets, the one that is needed most, or most immediately, is fresh air, for both babes and mothers.

Do not misunderstand what is said here. The responsibility for all this misery does not lie at the door of Society; the blame for it all, for this sad spectacle of limp mothers and pale children must be given to the ignorant and self-willed men who insist upon pushing into an over-crowded city, and adding to the supply of labor beyond any possible demand. That dull-eyed baby in the arms of the neatly dressed woman on the stoop yonder is the fifth child of a street-car driver. The father makes twelve or thirteen dollars a week, of which he pays three for the rent of two miserable rooms. For twelve dollars a month he could hire a well-built comfortable little house in New Jersey, and find all the work he could do lying ready to his hand, to be paid for at the rate of $1.50 day. Of course, it would be such work as the community needed; but it would be only such work as any man of ordinary strength and sense could do. And for doing it he might have for himself and his wife and his children the blessings of pure air, wholesome food and good surroundings of every sort. But the work does not happen to be horse-car driving , and

the place does not happen to be New York, and so his baby must breathe its little life out in this dull and deadly air, and his wife must grow old before her time, and he must sell himself, body and soul, either to the railway company which pays him his wages, or to the labor union which takes them from him.

But, all the same, these women and babies suffer in the hot air of a New York summer; and it is not their fault if their husbands and fathers force them into this misery. If we can do anything for them, let us do it. And one thing we can do—give them, from time to time at least, fresh air and a glimpse of more beautiful and cheering things than the shabby streets have to show. On Thursday of this week twelve hundred mothers and children will sail down the bay and spend the day on Staten Island, getting breathable air into their lungs, and learning that there is a world outside of New York. PUCK will send them, and the St. John's Guild will take them, for it is a part of the work of that grand organization to manage such excursions whenever the money is supplied for the purpose. A PUCK excursion is a good "starter" for this year: are there not some among PUCK's readers who will see that the great white Floating Hospital of the St. John's Guild does not lie idle at her dock through the rest of the summer? In one way or another, almost everyone may help the city-bound poor in the hot months. If you can not send out an excursion, you can send a child for a fortnight's "fresh air" outing. That luxury will cost you about three dollars. And if you have not three dollars, but have the country fields about you, remember that a box full of wild-flowers—common to you, but uncommon enough in tenement houses—will be taken by the express companies free of charge and delivered to the Flower Mission, at 20th Street and 4th Avenue, and thence distributed among those who need the ministration of flowers.

126

The Season of "Commencements" will set in early this year. The College Commencement is an institution peculiar to the country. It is the fancy frilling to the annual examination, like the slashed and puffed paper around the neck of a boiled ham. It is the efflorescence of the sophomoric idea—the cheap luxury of under-graduate ambition. The dozen or so athletic chickens whom every one of the innumerable colleges of our beloved land yearly labels with a meaningless A. B. or A. M., and sends forth to confound the world with strange new varieties of ultra-modern wisdom, club together with the younger fledglings of their collegiate coop; hire a hall, and electrify their immediate relatives with the brilliancy of their fancy, the depth of their thought, and the Demosthenian draught of their lungs.

But there are two or three colleges and universities that do not greatly hanker after the publicity of the "Commencement." These institutions of learning are situated in Philadelphia, Pennsylvania. They are colleges with a "specialty:" namely, the production of physicians on the cheap and rapid plan. They are very good colleges in their way—very good indeed. They will take your butcher or your baker, or your candlestick-maker, and turn him out a complete, ready-made doctor in less than no time, and on the most moderate terms. Nothing is necessary—no study, no love for the profession, no intellect—nothing but a face and a pocket full of brass. Yearly these fertile institutions send their huge quota to the ranks of what Carlyle called "the true ministry"; and the grip which these graduates of patent labor-saving universities have on their "business" is enough to startle the plodding old practitioners to whom the *profession* was a holy mission, to which they gave the labor, the reverence, the devotion of their lives. But where is the old-fashioned practitioner by the side of the Philadelphia

physician? The "Eclectic" College man can kill ten patients while the old fogy is curing one: he can spread disease like a pestilence incarnate; he can maim more men, if his taste happens to run to surgery, than a first-class civil war. Why, at the end of a long and busy life, the Philadelphia physician, sitting at the door of his noble mansion, and looking proudly over the well-filled aisles of his own private graveyard, can say to himself, with sweet complacency: "It's just as well that I never took the trouble to study—always got along just the same."

The Philadelphia Doctor-Mill certainly does its best to cast discredit upon two noble professions; and no doubt does to some extent besmirch the skirts of all the honest teachers and healers in the country. In England, no doubt, such practices would, in the end, prejudice the entire peasantry and yeomanry against schools and physicians in general. Fortunately, the American public is intelligent enough to discriminate between the false and the true in both professions. In any case, the Doctor can take care of himself. He is a staple—a necessity. The teacher is worse off; but we firmly believe that he is sufficiently respected to be safe from any injury from this source. We hope, indeed, that the American citizen has a steadfast and abiding appreciation of the value of Education in every form. He talks about it—talks a great deal. If he really has at heart the welfare of the institutions he is so proud of saying that his forefathers founded to keep the nation out of the darkness of ignorance—if he really understands the value of "popular education" and all that is meant by his buncome phrases—if he really does, he will look at the exhibit on page 96 of this issue; and see if it does not suggest to him the propriety of waking up and taking a little interest in the matter.

THE PHILADELPHIA PHYSICIAN-FACTORY.

There are as many fashions in schools of medicine and curatives as there are in Parisian styles of women's dresses. No matter how wild the theory or system may be—no matter how much opposed to common sense—some noodles will be found who will be prepared to swear by the new system, and to follow it to the death—and death it very often is. The brutal attack on the President has given a number of the professors of the newest doctrines an opportunity of advocating certain treatment. Some of the recommendations were positively grotesque in their absurdity; and yet we do not doubt that there are many people who believe that every other method but the new one proposed was wrong. It says very little for the progress of the science of medicine that there should be so much uncertainty about it. Were two doctors ever known to agree absolutely on any point?

For ourselves, we have not a profound belief in homeopathy. And yet Hahnemann, its founder, cannot with justice be called an imposter; and thousands of intelligent people enjoy themselves in taking frequent doses of pellets and globules, and look down with undisguised contempt on the "regular" practitioner, and on those who allow themselves to be treated by him. There are, likewise, many worthy persons who have profound faith in patent medicines. The consumption of these nostrums is not, as is generally supposed, confined to the poorer and ignorant classes. Rational men and women—rational on every subject but this—scan with eagle eye the advertising columns of the newspapers, and buy and use the latest thing in medicines—the bigger the advertisement, the more they buy of it. Advertising must pay the manufacturers of these compounds, or how could such enormous fortunes be accumulated out of them?

The consumer expends two or three dollars for something, the actual value of which is not as many cents. We have no desire to keep up the conventional joke about all doctors being licensed murderers; but it is very certain that there is more quackery in this country than in any other. We have too many doctors and too many quacks, and Americans are proverbially too busy to take the trouble to find out if the medical men they employ are worthy of confidence. America suffers from a multiplicity of medical colleges, three-fourths of which ought to be abolished. At many of these Western institutions it is as easy to get a diploma—and not a bogus one, either—as it is to get your boots blacked. Half-a-dozen frame shanties form a city, and one of the shanties is called a medical college, with a full staff of professors.

A staff of professors professing every branch of medical science, heard and unheard of. These gentlemen, and the graduates they train, are frequently very ignorant men, and they do much to lessen the respect for the profession. It is far too easy a matter to become a doctor. Theoretically it is a noble calling, and the path to it ought to be beset with difficulties. There should be a few well-equipped colleges in different parts of the country, and all the "Blanche, Tray, and Sweetheart" ones ought to be ruthlessly wiped out of existence. Students should not be admitted without a rigid examination to prove the possession of culture, and sufficient training to enable them to benefit to the fullest extent by the instruction they seek. At present, M. D.s, in every State of the Union, are as plentiful as blackberries, and many of the men who bear the title are about as worthy of it as some of Superintendent Coleman's street-sweepers. No wonder quacks flourish when there is often so little difference between them, and those who are not technically quacks.

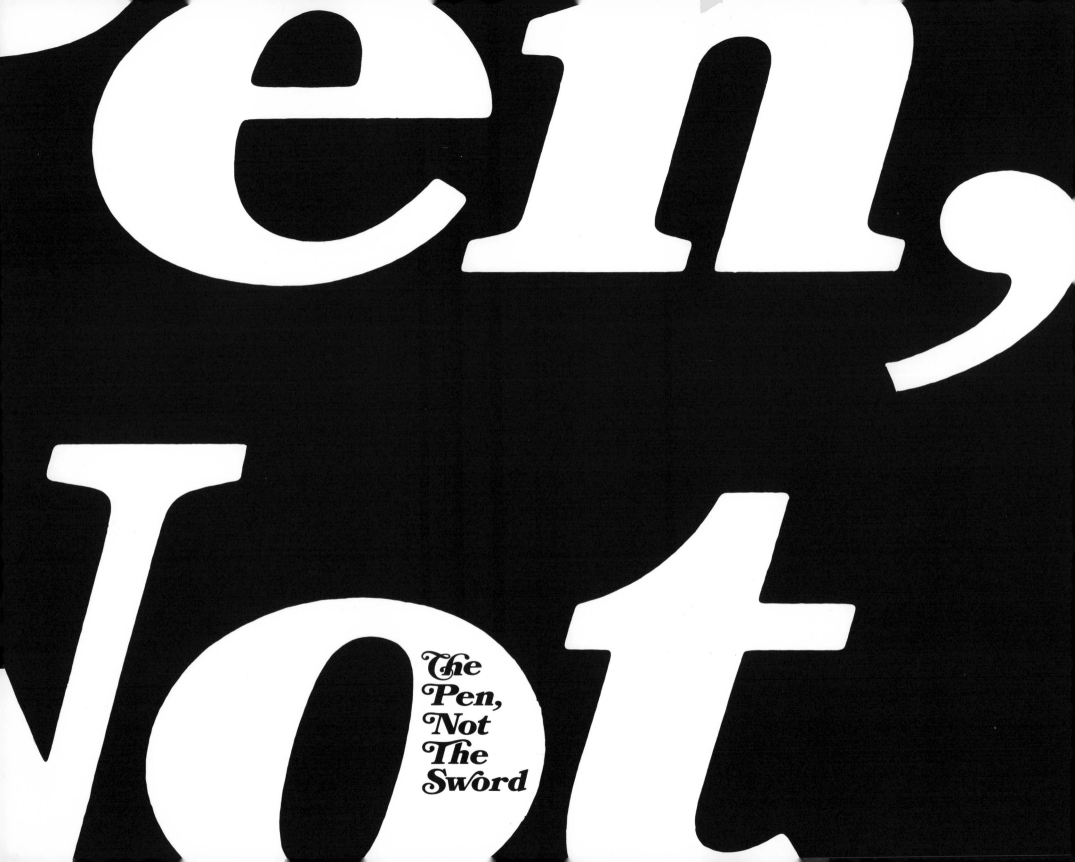

The
Pen,
Not
The
Sword

RELIGION

In order to get a comprehensive idea of the numerous religious bodies, it is necessary to classify them. They fall naturally into three divisions, the Christian, Jewish and miscellaneous. The Christian division, the largest numerically, is divided into such classes as Catholic, Protestant and Evangelical or non-Evangelical, and quite independently of these broad classifications are the denominational groups, or families. Under the heading "miscellaneous" are included Taoist, Hindu, Confucianist, Buddhist, Theosophist, and Culturist. This division is numerically small and relatively insignificant. The Jewish division embraces simply the Orthodox and Reformed Jews.

Catholic

The Catholic church provided the ambitious immigrant with effective means for its own advancement. The Catholic school has been particularly effective in this respect, especially at the college level, for it has helped to preserve and perpetuate the faith.

Somewhat later in the controversy over Americanism, this issue emerged. In an Apostolic letter which Pope Leo XIII directed to Cardinal Gibbons, he warned against certain tendencies which a number of European theologians claimed to discover in the American Church, among them overemphasis on the active virtues, at the expense of humility, charity and obedience; putting natural virtues above the supernatural; and employing untried methods of attracting non-Catholics to the faith. Although Cardinal Gibbons immediately replied that no one in American prelates, priest or laity, held these views, and a few years later the Pope told Archbishop Ireland to forget the whole matter, there can be little doubt that what Pope Leo XIII was warned against was not altogether unrelated to practices in the American church. No such institution can remain part of American life without revision of Catholic thinking on problems of the church and state; it is part of the Americanness of American Catholicism.

Cardinal Gibbons, however, had already established friendly relations with Terence V. Powderly, the Catholic head of the Knights of Labor. When he went to Rome in 1887 to receive his Cardinal's hat, he was able to convince Pope Leo XIII that an expression of his fears would be both unjust and disastrous. Since that time, the Catholic church has remained prolabor and has shown a deep concern for retaining the allegiance of its working people; in the years after the turn of the century, it has been estimated, about two-thirds of the membership and a substantial part of the leadership of organized labor was Catholic.

The decisive point in fixing the church policy toward labor was in 1880, when the Canadian hierarchy obtained a Papal condemnation of the Knights of Labor on the grounds that it was a secret society infected with socialism and given to violence. In 1891 the encyclical of Pope Leo XIII gave way to social reformers. The Catholic hierarchy gradually began to swing to the leadership of the liberal Cardinal Gibbons.

Catholic agitation had occurred in the early 1850s, particularly in connection with the arrival of Bishop Bedini as apostolic visitor. In 1854 rioters in St. Louis killed ten men, and, a year later on "Bloody Monday," nearly a hundred Catholics were slain and homes were burned in Kentucky. By this time anti-Catholics had become the leading principals of the so-called "Know Nothing Party."

At present, the Catholic church in America operates a vast network of institutions of every type and variety: colleges, hospitals and orphanages. The Catholic youth organization has six million members. This system constitutes a self-contained Catholic world, with its own complex interior economy and American Catholicism's resources of participation in the large American community.

The Church in Nineteenth-Century America

Catholics, Protestants, Latter Day Saints, all bodies not Jewish or Pagan, are a denominational family. All Methodist bodies are branches with a common stem, a common name, a common type of doctrine and certain common features and usages. Various Lutheran bodies are a denominational family, as are the numerous Baptist bodies. A denominational family is a number of branches closely affiliated in history and in common characteristics.

The word *Protestant* in the title of the Methodist Protestant church does not, at least historically, mean evangelical or anti-Catholic, but actually anti-Episcopal. Much confusion often arises from such similarity.

The Negro of the United States had no religion but the Christian religion. He is not a heathen, like our native Indian, but worships the Christian God, although he nevertheless is more or less superstitious, symptomatic of the tenacity with which we cling to belief in signs and times and lucky and unlucky. The secularism that pervades the American consciousness is essentially of this kind; it is thinking and living in terms of a framework of reality and value remote from the religious beliefs simultaneously professed.

Developments in the physical and biological sciences in the late nineteenth century affected religion in America, for new scientific concepts increasingly tended to cast doubt on the validity of the established religious beliefs. Sizable numbers of church members, determined to keep the old faith pure, split off from the parent church during these spiritually trying times.

In fashionable churches, ministers leaned toward what they called "applied Christianity," later named social gospel. One reaction against the established churches took the form of an evangelical revival, which swept the middle and lower classes. This wave of emotionalism in religion began to wane after the turn of the century, but the general shift of emphasis from theology to society that characterized religious thought had a lasting effect on American church life.

The unsettled times, revolutions in agriculture and industry and rapidly changing social patterns all contributed to spiritual unrest. People were searching for some emotional and spiritual stability, and the number of churches increased at a faster rate than the growth of population.

A trend toward "localized Christianity" was the Y.M.C.A., imported from England, and its counterpart, the Y.W.C.A., which had expanded to two thousand chapters by 1900. Likewise, the Salvation Army had begun work in 1879 among the urban poor, and settlement houses appeared in many cities.

The spiritual needs of the times reactivated many faltering denominations, although the moral vigor of the American churches was so radically changed that many churches today are in reality social institutions with programs, vocations classes, nursery schools, and concerts.

Mormons And Latter-Day Saints

The Latter-Day Saints, like the Mormons of Utah, trace their origin back to the movements begun by Joseph Smith, claiming to represent his movement and to be true to the principles proclaimed by him. Sometimes called nonpolygamous Mormons, they deny that the revelation concerning polygamy which was communicated to the church in Salt Lake City by Brigham Young was genuine.

This recognized church accepts three books as being of Divine origin: the Bible; the Book of Mormon; and the Book of Covenants. In doctrine they adhere to the

134

Trinity, to the atonement of Jesus Christ, to the resurrection of the dead, to the second coming of Christ and to the eternal judgment, believing that each individual will receive reward or punishment in strict measure according to the good or evil deeds done in life. They hold that men are to be saved by faith in God and Christ, by forsaking sin, by immersion, for the remission of sin, and by laying on of hands. They believe that revelations of God are still given by the Holy Spirit.

As for marriage, they believe that it is ordained of God and that there should be but one companion for man or woman in wedlock until the contract is broken by death or transgression, and they characterize the doctrine of polygamy or plural wives as an abomination.

Jewish

The first company of Jews came from Brazil and they established the first synagogue on Mill Street, New York City. It was called the Shearith Israel (Renant of Israel) and the society is still active in existence, occupying a building on West Nineteenth Street. According to custom, ten males above the age of thirteen can form a Jewish congregation, so it is quite probable that there was Jewish worship before the first synagogue was opened.

Jewish congregations were soon organized in Savannah, Georgia, and in Philadelphia. Some used the ritual of the Portuguese Jews, others, that of the German Jews. The Jews of America had no religious head, and each congregation was autonomous and responsible only to its members. It is said that an effort in New York to bring the Orthodox Congregation under the care of a chief Rabbi was not wholly satisfactory. There are two branches of schools of thought in the Jewish religion, the orthodox and the reformed. The Orthodox Jews accept the Schulchan Aruch as authoritative in all its requirements. It is a codification made by Rabbi Joseph Kars in the middle of the sixteenth century, of the laws and ceremonies expounded by the rabbis of the Talmud and handed down from generation to generation by tradition, providing for the minutest details of Jewish life. Those who accept it consider it as binding as the law of Moses.

For Reformed Jews the departure from orthodoxy may be slight, such as worshiping with the hat off, the mingling of the sexes in the synagogue and the introduction of the organ and female choir.

Protestant

For Protestants, each denominational family or branch goes back to the same source historically and has the same name, the same confession of faith, with two or three exceptions, and the same system of government. Various bodies as the Lutheran are a denominational family, as are numerous Baptist bodies and so on. A denominational family, therefore, is a number of branches closely affiliated in history and common characteristics.

Nowhere have denominational families developed as in the United States. In no quarter of the globe have the Lutherans or the Methodists, the Presbyterians or Baptists, the Friends or the Mennonites, separated into as many branches as here in this land of perfect civil and religious liberty.

No denomination has thus far proved to be too small for division. It is not easy to define clearly and to apply discriminatingly the term evangelical, for example. It comes, of course, from the Greek word "evangel," for which our Anglo-Saxon "gospel" or good news, is the close equivalent. It is supposed when we say certain denominations are evangelical that they hold earnestly to the doctrine of Christ as found in the New Testament. *Evangelical* and *non-evangelical* are terms used generally to designate classes of churches in the Protestant division, the evangelical churches being those which hold to the authority of the scriptures, the Trinity, the deity of Christ, justification by faith alone and the work of the Holy Ghost in the conversion and sanctification of the sinner.

As a further example of the subdivisions of American Protestantism, among the Presbyterians there are four bodies of the reformed variety. One is called the Reformed Presbyterian Church in the United States of America; another the Reformed Presbyterian Church in North America; one has a synod and the other a general synod. But it is not always easy to remember which has which.

There are distinctions in their monthly organs; one of these has a blue cover, the other a pink cover. The blue covered organ represents the general synod and the general synod represents the Reformed Presbyterian Church in North America. The pink covered organ represents the synod, and the synod represents the Reformed Presbyterian Church in the United States of America.

BOYCOTTING THE POPE.

His Holiness the Pope is in a bad way. His most faithful Irish subjects have gone back on him. They have told Leo in very plain terms that they will take all the theology he can give them, and more, too; but they decline to have it adulterated with politics. His Irish flock prefer to make their politics for themselves, and no one can deny that they have succeeded in making a first-class article. The homage that the Pope has lost has been transferred to Mr. Parnell, and His Holiness may be said to be boycotted. It is pretty hard lines for a well-regulated establishment like the Church of Rome—which has done pretty much as it liked for many hundred years—to suddenly have allegiance to it renounced. But it isn't the want of allegiance that is bothering it so much: it is the Peter's Pence that goes with the allegiance.

OUR SPIRITUAL GUARDIAN

It is not a pleasant picture for the conscientious Christian who believes in going to church regularly and listening to the word of God as expounded by the clerical gentlemen who may happen to have the floor.

These men—these pastors, to whom practically the care of our families is confided, are disgracing themselves.

It is not a question of the misfortune of any one denomination, disgraced by these unworthy guardians. Protestant, Catholic, Atheist and Jew are alike interested in the exposure and punishment of the public teacher who betrays his trust and misuses his privileges.

TWO OF A KIND.

Our beloved old friend, the Pope of Rome, is once more troubled in his aged mind. It is the Free Masons this time. He has fulminated against them, and we trust that he feels relieved. He says that they are base believers in reason—a charge which has the distinguished merit of originality. He likewise says that they are opening the way to natural science, which, he further remarks, is a bad thing for virtue. He says that the Free Masons are paving the way for communism; and, generally, he thinks that they are in a parlous state. And having delivered himself, he relapses into dignified silence and leaves the daily journals of this misguided world to cut his communication down to a stick and a half, and to make irreverent comments on it at that.

That mighty, free and independent power, the Labor Vote, seems to be always in the possession of people entirely unconnected with Labor. Up to Tuesday of last week, when the Chicago elections were held, the Anarchists owned it. Now the Roman Catholic church is making large and enthusiastic bids for it. The bids are, perhaps, too large and too enthusiastic. Archbishop Gibbons, in his famous letter, based his approval of the Knights of Labor upon the general principles—principles as general as he could make them. But Cardinal Manning, not having the knowledge of "practical politics" enjoyed by his American coadjutor, has frankly stated, in *his* missive, that he wants the Knights of Labor to help him in spreading the power of the Romish church in America. The Cardinal is quite plain and unaffected in his language; he makes no bones of it; he says his say, and we have no reason to complain that we can not understand him. If the Knights will work with the church officials, he thinks that the temporal power of the Pope may be increased in the United States. Americans will please take notice.

We can not see that there is any reason for crediting with good sense and sincere principle a body of men who will ally themselves to-day with the sworn foes of law and order and to-morrow with the agents of papal despotism. If the so-called Labor Party is merely an organized band of political Hessians, ready to work with any other party, good, bad or indifferent, that will divide the spoils of office with the walking-delegates, why, let the Labor Party put its advertisement in the newspapers, and honestly announce how many votes it has for sale, and how many offices it wants for them. That would be a straightforward and manly way of doing business. But to flaunt the red flag in Chicago and to elevate the papal crown and keys in Baltimore, and still pretend to the possession of a cause, an ideal, a vital principle, is both shifty and silly. If there is a vital principle underlying this political movement, it can not be in harmony with both of two conflicting ideas. It can not hunt with Anarchy and hide with Papacy.

We have asked in vain, over and over again, for one clear, plain, common-sense statement of the nature of the "grievance" on which the Labor Party is founded. We get no answer that is to the point. We hear hysterical denunciations of monopolistic capitalists, of oppressors of the poor, of mysterious people who are wronging the workingmen. But of plain solid English fact we get nothing. The nearest approach to a direct answer that can be got out of millions of spoken and written words is Mr. Chauncey M. Depew's inspired utterance to the effect that it is a grievance which can not be defined. It must be admitted that this is not a satisfactory framework for a political platform. Any collection of men might go office-hunting on this basis. When a man starts out to alter existing conditions of society, and explains that he does so because he has a grievance against society, though he does not know what the grievance is, nor where it hurts him, his explanation may fairly be called inadequate and illogical. Yet this is all the organizers of the Labor Party have to offer by way of explaining their presence in the political field.

Since this appearance can not be accounted for upon the hypothesis of a definite and explicable grievance, we must look elsewhere for the cause of it. And we have not far to look. With no positive assertions of political principle, with no clearly-defined system of reform, with no policy that any human being can understand, the Labor Party can not possibly benefit its adherents in any way, no matter how much power it may acquire. What, then, is the object of its existence? In our opinion, to benefit itself. For the Labor Party is, after all, only another name for the horde of organizers who live off the workingmen, and have their headquarters in a palace in Philadelphia. These organizers—master workmen, walking delegates, or whatever they may call themselves, are pretty well paid by the workingmen for whom they have invented a grievance, but they want something more than large salaries. They know that there is money in the office-holding business, and that money they propose to get. And so Labor must go into politics.

A BUSINESS ALLIANCE.

Leo XIII.—Bless you, my children!—I think we can work together nobly in America.

This is PUCK's second visit to the camp-meetings, and it is almost as sad a visit as the first. *Then* he saw the positive immorality of these huge gatherings, which brought all manner of people, of both sexes, together under circumstances, in parliamentary phrase, "not conducive" to health and decency. Now he sees the negative unrighteousness of their inception—something scarcely less sad to look upon.

The camp-meeting of the day is *not* a religious festival—emphatically not. It is much more like a business speculation. This statement may seem shocking to the good people who have been brought up to look upon these institutions of the Church as essentially sacred and beyond the reach of profane criticism. But this is not an age when people may look askance upon an utterance because it is startling and painful. The vital question must be: Is it true? In this case, the reader has the proof before his eyes. Let him go to the camp meeting with an honest determination not to lull his conscience to sleep with canting phrases about "worship on the bosom of nature" and "holiness among the trees;" but to assure himself squarely and fairly that he is taking his amusement in a wise and proper way. His amusement? Yes—that is what he goes there for, if he tells the truth to his own conscience. Let him go on this frank basis, and what will he find out for himself? Something like this:

Camp-meetings are usually held on grounds owned by a corporation, which corporation sometimes gets a bill through the local legislature exempting its property from taxation—a dishonest and unpatriotic trick. The managers of the grounds arrange with the railroad or steamboat lines to carry passengers to the camp-meeting at reduced rates. This is an inducement to the public,

and the public carriers profit by it. Indeed, they may be called, in a sense, partners of the camp-meeting organizers. This union of forces having been made, the real camp-meeting business is begun. The "privileges" are sold. Beer and tobacco are not sold within the grounds, being carnal and unholy; but there are ginger-beer, peanuts, candies, religious literature of all kinds, "tenting" equipments, oil-stones, cough and colic medicines, fruits, newspapers and a few other small trifles, the dealers in all of which must pay roundly for the privilege of selling their wares within the sacred ground, just as they would have to in a pedestrian tournament. Then, if the camp-meeting is of the "advanced" class, there are croquet and lawn-tennis and bathing-house privileges to be let to the highest bidder. And when the camp-meeting actually opens, the money pours in from the rental of tents, from collections taken up, and from a dozen other sources. Does it all go to the heathen, do you suppose?

It does not, and it is about time that the humbug was exposed. The average camp-meeting is got up as a scheme of profit by speculators as worldly-minded as the men who run picnic "parks" up on the East River. It is simply a form of popular amusement, and the aureole of religion is thrown round it as an advertisement. It is in no wise a "means of grace." It is often a most unhealthy dissipation. What shall be said of the conduct of these spiritual teachers who are willing to lend their influence to money-making schemes frequently much less fair, much less profitable to the public than an ordinary old-fashioned carnal circus? Are they faithful stewards in the Biblical meaning?

We say frankly that we can not believe that any attempt will be made in our lifetime—that it is unlikely that any attempt will be made in our childrens' lifetime—to place our federal state under the control of the Roman Catholic church, directly or indirectly—vast as might be the advantage to that church, clear as her intentions may seem to many excellent citizens who are in the habit of looking upon her and speaking of her as the "Scarlet Woman." That it would be a very pleasant and comfortable thing for the Roman Catholic church if it could establish ecclesiastical and temporal power in the United States, we have no manner of doubt. That the church can safely undertake any such job in the United States we have all manner of doubt, for the best reason in the world—just simply because the United States is the United States, and the United States is no place for any such undertaking.

So far, so good. You wholly agree with us, don't you, you good Americans who read this page? But do you consider that if you ever gave a good chance to the Roman Catholics who would like to see the temporal powers of the Pope established in this country as it was once established in European countries, you are giving it now? If you allow the President, whom you elect, to use his high office solely for the purpose of building up a Republican party organization, designed to control the government and, in case of necessity, to counteract the power of the people at the polls; if you allow him to turn men out of office and to substitute others, not because the men turned out were not good and efficient public servants, but because the men turned in will help him to re-election: if you allow him to disregard the needs of the whole country, and to devote the whole power that you have placed in his hands to making his party your permanent rulers, you are doing for him just what you might do for a Roman Catholic President who was determined to establish the temporal power of the Pope in the United States.

But, you say, a Roman Catholic, with this purpose never could be elected President of the United States. True. But why should you know, before his election, that he had that purpose? Why should you know, even, that he was a Roman Catholic? The man whom you elected last November was well-nigh unknown to you.

Before his election he pledged his word that fitness should be the sole test in his appointments to office, and that the men he would select to manage your public business should be selected to serve you well and faithfully. You elected him, and he has thrown his pledges to the wind. It is notorious that he has kept neither the letter nor the spirit of his promises. It is obvious that the party leaders who put him in power never expected that he would. They put him where he is that he might help the Republican party to get a lasting grip on the United States government. Yet, before election, he declared to the people that he had no such intention. Why should not a Roman Catholic do for his church what this Republican has done for his party? We would not suffer it? Perhaps not. But why do we suffer this? And why do we allow in a Republican the same tyrannous disregard of public rights that we would resent in a Roman Catholic? And, as a matter of practical business, if one can grab the whole government, what excuse will you find for stopping the other if he tries to do the same thing?

The suggestion, made by some ingenious and mysterious European notable, that the next Pope of Rome may possibly be an American, has stimulated the imagination of many active-minded journalists, and has probably had a mildly exciting effect on the spirits of those faithful sons of the Church who still believe in a possible restoration of the temporal power of the Supreme Pontiff. That an American Pope, enthroned in Rome, would be what the theatrical people call an "attraction" can not be denied. Whatever the masses of Protestant America may think of the Pope—or of the necessity of having any Pope at all—he is certainly, considered as the chief inhabitant of the Vatican, a very imposing, interesting and aristocratic figure. He has, so to speak, a style about him such as pertains to no European monarch. Even the haughty Czar of Russia has to travel about on special railroad trains, like any common American millionaire, kissing his brother potentates on both cheeks whenever they appear at the junction stations. This last can not be altogether a pleasant job, and it certainly awakens the jeers of the populace and moves to contempt the members of races who believe that a kiss where two sexes are not united is an unnecessary and offensive performance—like buttering butter, for instance, or offering two contiguous slices of bread for a sandwich.

But the Pope takes no railroad journeys and kisses no casual sovereigns. He sits at home in his palace, and the toe of his embroidered slipper is kissed by the thronging faithful. He is attired in robes of unspeakable richness, and when he has anything to say he says it in Latin. In all possible ways he presents such a spectacle of dignified grandeur that the other great ones of the earth look quite shabby and commonplace beside him. If America could really produce such a lace-robed and tiara-crowned autocrat, it would be strange indeed if the select four hundreds of our large cities did not instantly dethrone poor Albert Edward and set up the new idol in his place. What chance would a stout, elderly gentleman in a frock coat stand against pontifical magnificence? What need would there be to look for our ideal of lofty humanity to the heir apparent of the British throne, if we had an American magnate who would, so to speak, sweep the Prince of Wales into oblivion with the tail of his robe?

And if the various select four hundreds were thus affected, what would be the stimulus applied to the hundreds of thousands of Hibernian descent who have made America their home and kept up their worship of an Italian Pope? They have the happy faculty of being Irishmen and Americans at one and the same time—with the Irishman noticeably preponderating. Now, the Irishman in them is a Roman Catholic, and if you ally the American in them with the papacy, you have a combination which is about 90 per cent. Roman to 10 per cent. of combined Irish and American. With this combination, it is not to be wondered at if they should dream of a Roman Catholic America—which would be, to all intents and purposes, an Irish Catholic America.

Is it a dream that is beyond all possibility? We think so. We can not imagine any combination of circumstances, as things stand at present, which would make possible the union of any church with our American state—least of all can we imagine any combination of circumstances which would make possible the union of the Roman Catholic Church with our state. The sentiment of the people is too strong, too nearly unanimous, to bring such a union within the bounds of possibility. It may be attempted. Our children may live to see the attempt made. But, if it ever is made, they will certainly see more good Catholics opposing it than supporting it. The American idea is a great educator.

THE POPE'S DREAM—A ROMAN CATHOLIC AMERICA.

With a table globe, we can consult our "Cook's Tourists' Guide," or the railway and steamship advertisements in the daily papers, to find a sure, speedy and direct route; purchasing the necessary ticket therefor, we find ourselves, in due time, at the haven we seek.

But if we desire to soar beyond this habitable sphere, and flit away above, (or below,) the routes and the guides are so many, so contradictory, and so confusing, that the poor man, who would fain be *en route* to Heaven, gets himself completely mixed and finds himself at a standstill. In point of fact it is so very hard to decide how to get to Heaven that large numbers of people, it is said, make no effort at all to get there; and, as Heaven is acknowledged to be a "Land of Supreme Delight," it seems to us that these lying "Guides" with their contradictory routes, who prevent mankind from rushing there directly, should be incontinently squelched.

We say *lying* guides advisedly; and are they not? As they all disagree, they cannot *all* be right; and if any one of the crowd is right, are not all the rest lying guides?

Suppose a man goes over to Brooklyn, or wherever else the meandering Doctor Fulton happens to have a church or a hall, and gets himself well soused, head over heels, in that worthy divine's baptismal tub, so that he is assured he is going swimmingly to heaven, wouldn't he feel just mad when St. Peter barred the Gates against him and told him he ought to have come by the Episcopal Ritual Route, *via* Rev. Cream Cheese! Or, if a worthy soul, for years, pours all her big and little sins into the ears, and nearly all her dollars into the lap of a snuffy old prelate, that she may secure passage to the Bright Beyond, wouldn't it be rough on her to find herself switched off to the Infernal Sing Sing and held there on a charge of "mummery and worshipping of false gods?" And there is our good brother Talmage. Think how it would be if all the devout people of England, Ireland, and Brooklyn who hope they are dancing on to Heaven with him, should be brought up with a round turn in—well, say in Hades—and be made to dance on hot plates with the peculiarly uncomfortable application to their persons of a hot poker. And if the happy-go-lucky guidance of Mr. Beecher be taken, isn't one as apt to step down and out into outer darkness as to meet with disaster on any other route?

It may be said these are extreme cases; but is it not the fact that all these Guides set themselves up as showing the only true route? Does not the mitred Bishop tell you that the Protestants will go to Hell, and that Salvation is only to be found (if paid for) in the True Church? And do not the stiff and starched presenters of the Protestant idea assure you that all Roman Catholics, and all the other divisions and sub-divisions of their own creed, are on the "wrong road?"

It is all very much like the scenes enacted on our piers last summer when the rival steamboat runners assured passengers that only *their* boats landed at the proper place, and that all opposition boats would either burst their boilers or get stuck in the mud. All of which was con-foosing to the timid pater-families with many young ones and weighty lunch baskets.

But it is too uncertain and mixed-up at present. A man isn't even sure how he can go to Hell, if he wishes; certain creeds and teachers asserting there is no Hell. We hope this confusion worst confounded will soon be straightened out, for at present all we can do towards realizing our hopes is to obey the laws, be a good citizen, be kind to our neighbors, mind our own business, and do no man wrong.

145

A personal Devil is an encouraging, cheerful institution. Men rather need to flatter their depravity by imagining that there is a monster who is responsible for most of their sins—a diabolical slugger, so to speak—who has superinhuman knocking-out powers.

But the human heart is above all things fearfully and desperately lazy, as well as wicked—and so men hire some one to do devil-fighting for them. Though they profess to believe "resist the Devil he will flee from you," they would a little rather someone else should do the resisting and take the dust of the "wicked flee whom no man pursueth."

Of course, while the champions of righteousness are off for an outing, men have no defenders, and Satan has his way, because they have not been taught to resist him for themselves. The system breeds moral cowards and sneaks; makes churches spiritual hospitals and infirmaries, and ministers moral dry-nurses to their parishioners. And if one of these keepers of the fold goes wrong, his whole system collapses. But in the present undeveloped state of man's religious nature this babe-and-suckling system seems necessary.

Therefore, it is with a sense of relief on behalf of the poor victims of Satan, that we see the clergy returning, invigorated, to the fray. Of course, we know that they can't whip; that about the time they get Satan "in chancery" the Almighty will come to his deliverance and set him on his divinely-appointed roving mission again. But, just the same, we admire pluck—in others—and clap for the clerical party. May they punch more of him than he does of them!

But there are plenty of people who do not fear his Satanic Majesty, if they believe in his existence. One of the most unterrifiable of this class are those who make a profession of religion "for revenue only."

The metamorphosis of the camp meeting from a genuine, if crude, religious service to a speculation, is evidence that this class of offensive sectarians has greatly increased.

Take such a sanctified real-estate speculation as Ocean Grove, or Asbury Park, and compare it with the simple, unselfish camp-meeting of the past generation, if you want to realize the necessity of some one to again make a scourge of small cords and go through the temples of worship to drive out "those who sell doves and the changers of money sitting."

"TIME!"

The Preachers' Vacation Ended.—The Old Fight Renewed.

FRANK BEARD.

From more or less authentic sources we learn that Cardinal Gibbons thinks that the Catholic Church ought to approve of the doings of the Knights of Labor, by way of "taking the part of the weaker against the stronger." Thus is the papal benediction demanded for the thousands of Knights who, in knightly way, hurl their brick barts at the head of the helpless and solitary scab who takes the job that the proud Knight rejects.

This is all very well for Cardinal Gibbons. He may hold what opinions he pleases, and may express them as he pleases, so long as he keeps within the law of the land. But there are a few other people interested in this matter, and it is time that they were heard from. We want to hear something about the rights of the Plain People—the people who do not call themselves laborers, or Knights, or Amalgamated Brothers or anything whatever; but, who do their work and mind their own business, just the same. We want to find out what "rights" belong to the plain, common public. For two years we, the ordinary honest citizens of this republic, have suffered every form of annoyance at the hands of a small minority of the population—a minority mainly of foreign birth. Our business has been interfered with, our railways and street-car lines have been put out of running order; our streets have been filled with rioting cowards; the laws which we obey have been openly violated, and rapine and murder have been preached in public places. And this is all—solely and entirely—because a man named Terence Powderly, an Irishman out of a job, desires to experiment with certain theories of his own, for the benefit of some people who have discovered that they have a grievance, although they do not know what it is.

At last one public man has shown that he has the courage to speak his mind upon this business, even though it may put him in the way of losing votes. Mayor Hewitt has talked common, honest, American sense about what is called the labor question; and there is some faint hope that other public officers else may be brave enough to follow his example. One thing is sure—the long-suffering people need a spokesman to assert their rights. Since the relations between our various classes of citizens seem to be undetermined, perhaps it may as well be understood now that there are certain things which the majority of the people in this country will insist on, sooner or later, as fundamental necessities in the make-up of society. Here are some of them:

This country is going to be governed by its own laws, and by the common law on which they were founded.

A man has the right to work at any honest trade for any price or compensation that he chooses to take; and he has a right to sell goods for whatever he thinks fit.

A man has a right to conduct his business as he pleases, to employ whom he pleases, to discharge whom he pleases, and to do what he pleases, so long as he offends no law of the State.

A man has the right to own land or buy other property that he acquires according to the existing laws.

No man has a right to commit acts of illegal violence or to attempt the overthrow of the constitutional government.

There are other things that the citizens of the United States will insist upon, when it comes to the test; but these few will do to begin with; and the sooner the fact of their positive permanence is generally accepted, the better for every one concerned. This is a country with laws and a constitution, and its system of government is not to be overthrown by any body or class of men, whether they have a grievance or no. If they can not legally right their grievance under the most liberal system of laws that has ever existed on the face of the globe, they must let it go unrighted. The fault is in themselves; not in the laws.

These plain facts deserve the careful study of the Powderlys. Quinns and Henry Georges in general. By the indulgence of the great body of citizens, these men have been playing their mad antics for the last two years. They have driven hundreds of men to beggary and starvation; they have paralyzed business, jeoparded the savings invested in railroad and manufacturing stocks for the benefit of widows and orphans, and have caused more riot, bloodshed and murder than can be accurately computed. Soon or late, the time must come when the law-abiding public will no longer stand this impudent defiance of decency, and will rise up in its might and deal with its disorderly malcontents forcibly and decisively. And when the day of reckoning comes, it will be uncommonly hard for the Powderlys and Quinns and Georges. They have drawn under their control a vast number of men whom they can not now fully control. Should a revulsion of feeling occur among these thousands of uneducated, excitable, mis-directed men, making their leaders unpopular, nothing but superior physical force will save the objects of their anger. Mr. Powderly has "organized" his laboring-classes, and has promised to better their condition. When his "organized" followers find out—as they must, in the end—that instead of bettering their condition he has made it worse—well, they are just as likely as not to haul Mr. Powderly out of his gorgeous Philadelphia palace, and handle him like a common "scab."

THE NEW ALLY OF THE KNIGHTS OF LABOR.—DOES THE CATHOLIC CHURCH SANCTION MOB LAW?

Since the departure of Mr. Brigham Young to the happy hunting ground his successors and his widows have been singularly quiet; indeed so much so that many people had well nigh forgotten the existence of such an eccentric people as Mormons.

But of late there have been premonitory symptoms of a greater interest being taken in their proceedings.

Mr. Cannon, the energetic and conscientious delegate from Utah Territory, has recently had a few words to say on the subject of the people among whom he is a shining light. The Mormons will not allow themselves to be wiped out with impunity, in spite of Mr. Evarts, the whole Cabinet, and Mr. Hayes to boot. They are going to stick to their round dozen of wives apiece—whether anybody likes it or not. Of what use is it to live in a free country if there is to be the slightest interference with one's volition? Surely the authors and expounders of the Book of Mormon ought to know more about what is right and wrong than Congress, and all the other inhabitants of the United States put together. If they don't they must learn to know, and the Mormon, his sisters and his cousins and his aunts, will take a hand in giving the lesson.

Uncle Sam naturally trembles in his boots at the polygamous threats, and is doing his utmost to resist the Mormon onslaught, and, at the same time, to get in a little offensive work on his own account.

In such a campaign it is obvious that the Mormon forces would have the advantage. If Uncle Sam's troops are armed with Sharpe's or Remington's rifles, of what effect would be such weapons against a well-drilled corps of reserve wives, who would keep up a heavy, raking fire of pillows from their bedstead stronghold on the vanguard of the enemy, who might have the temerity to make an attack?

An old guard of superannuated female spouses would now be ordered up on the right, and their martial appearance in coal-scuttle helmets, and armed with broomsticks, would be calculated to scare Mr. Leonidas's treble century at Thermopylae.

And when the extra reserve, in the shape of harridans with a breastwork of kitchen-utensils and artillery of wash-tubs loomed up in the distance, there would be nothing else for even the bravest U.S. troops in the Union to do but to cut and run. Mr. Elder John Taylor, as the chief rooster of the territory, could then crow vigorously, and shake defiantly his luxuriant tail-feathers.

This is the humorous side of the picture, and we don't object to having our joke about it; but we really think if the demoralizing and disgusting system of Mormonism were abolished to-morrow, the effect would be a wholesome one on the country generally.

It is not a question of mere narrow church doctrine. It is not a question of Monotheism, or Polytheism, or Deism, or Materialism. It is simply a question of common decency and common sense—a question the settlement of which must show civilized man's superiority to the brute.

No, Mormonism ought to have no place or recognition in this country.

The Pen, Not The Sword

TARIFF
CIVIL SERVICE
LABOR
SILVER COINAGE
MONOPOLIES

The tariff question, on the whole, received less consideration than other matters in the mid-nineteenth century. While there had been some improvement in the tariff structure in the early 1870s, the duties in force were exceedingly high, the same ones levied during the Civil War for the purpose of revenue rather than protection, and some complaint had arisen over the function of these tariffs. Although they had been criticized by some theoretical political economists, the tariff had not yet become a political issue of significance. The chief reason some favored revision was that revenues from the high duties were overflowing the treasury, withdrawing money from circulation and increasing the temptation for government expenditure. The surplus in 1881 amounted to $101,000,000 and in 1882 increased to $145,000,000.

In May of 1882, Congress created a commission to study the situation, and after an extended investigation, the commission recommended tariff reductions of at least 20 percent. Republican supporters of protection joined with like-minded Democrats, notably ex-Speaker Randall of Pennsylvania, who represented large manufacturing interests in his state. After much debate on the subject, Congress passed a new tariff act in 1883, which provided such slight reductions they were scarcely noticeable, while in some cases actually raised rates.

During the fiscal years 1882 to 1885, the excess in revenue over expenditures amounted to $446,000,000 and the public debt was reduced from $1,820,000,000 in 1882 to $1,375,000,000 in 1885. Only a small part of this amount could be withdrawn at a request of the treasury (about $195,000,000 in 1885) and no decrease beyond that was possible except through the choice of bondholders to sell or buy the redemption of greenbacks. An excess of revenue was expected as long as the existing schedules of tax rates were preserved, as long as no large appropriations were legislated. The consumption of tobacco and beer kept step with the population growth, thus insuring adequate internal revenue receipts; and the increase in wealth led to large imports of foreign products, which further expanded the custom revenues.

During Cleveland's administration, the surplus grew to $422 million, and the $195 million of bonds which could be nullified by the treasury's power were quickly absorbed. Tax reduction could not be assured, and the administration would not agree on expenditures. One year's surplus revenue retained by the treasury meant a reduction in the monetary circulation of at least 12 percent, and such a reduction in business activity might easily hasten a crisis. The policy of depositing this government surplus with banks was unpopular, and for a time the treasury questioned whether it even had the authority to do so. If the Treasury Department bought bonds, it exposed itself to the charge of giving bonuses to bondholders by the payment of premiums and of promoting speculation in government securities.

Some thought that the authority to purchase bonds had been granted to the secretary of the treasury by the Civil Appropriation Bill of March 3, 1881, but Fairchild had been cautious in his management of treasury affairs, and had always waited until he had received legislative permission. After much bickering while the condition of the treasury needed instant relief, both Houses of Congress, through the passage of separate resolutions, gave their approval to the purchase of bonds.

The insincerity of the promises made by both Republicans and Democrats in 1884 about revising the tariff was clearly evident. Neither party had been precise as to methods, and between the two proclamations there was little actual difference. The Republican party pledged itself to correct the inequalities in the tariff and also to reduce the surplus, while the Democrats agreed to revise the tariff in all fairness to all interests and without injustice to domestic industries, and both extended support to the workingman. According to the Republican platform, tariffs should be so levied that capital and labor would get their due reward, and under the Democratic party's plan, every change must be regardful of the labor and capital involved. The only difference in the platforms was a Republican recognition of the wool industry as being adequately protected, while the Democrats made more of the necessity of economy and declared that sufficient revenue could be obtained from well-regulated taxes on fewer imported items, placing the higher duties on luxury articles.

During the campaign of 1884, the Democrats handled the tariff question in a cautious manner, apparently endeavoring to make it as easy as possible for dissatisfied Republicans to vote their ticket, and no change was made in their position until 1888 when they squabbled among themselves as to the methods of tax reduction. When the discord was finally silenced, the Republican-dominated Senate blocked the way with a plan of its own.

There was no real public demand for tariff rate reduction on the part of producers and consumers, and if the surplus had not continued to pour into the treasury with such speed, it was highly probable that the tariff discussion would have lain dormant. Although the president at all times favored a reduction of revenue, he was characterized as infatuated with his plan of remedy and even accused of allowing money to accumulate in the treasury, using the surplus to produce a condition creating a free-trade attitude. In his message of 1885, Cleveland placed the need of tax reduction exclusively on the grounds of excess revenue and declared that there was no reason for a discussion of the wisdom or haste for the protective measure. Yet he had followed the party platform insofar as to suggest that reduction be made upon necessities rather than upon luxury items.

The Democratic party suffered from lack of financial leadership in the House of Representatives. The chairman of the Ways and Means Committee, William R. Morrison of Illinois, had already lost prestige in an attempt to pass the so-called "Horizontal Reduction" measure in 1884, a bill which was so senseless in principle that it failed to satisfy either party. There was general concern that any tariff plan that might be proposed would not be consistent with the promises of the party platform, but to revise the tariff without damaging established industries was very difficult and required great knowledge of the industrial world and practical experience in the details of business.

On February 15, 1886, Morrison again introduced a tariff measure, in which lumber, fish, salt, flax, wood, hemp, jute and wool were exempt from the tariff. The country interpreted this bill as significant change toward free trade, but the proposal to place wool upon the free list disturbed the farmers, and there was suspicion that this was a trick to gain sectional votes. Later, it was felt, even metals and minerals might be surrendered to free trade.

On June 17, by a vote of 157 to 140, the House rejected even considering the bill. Thirty-five Democrats under the leadership of Samuel J. Randall of Pennsylvania joined the Republicans in opposition, and this disagreement within the Democratic party was further emphasized a few weeks later when Randall introduced a measure constructed on protection lines. He received little support from party members of the Committee on Ways and Means, who described the bill as increasing rather than reducing revenue and possibly placing the party in jeopardy of not redeeming its pledges. The Republicans argued that the measure did not correct inequalities, but even withdrew all protection from some industries. There were indications that the Republican party was drifting away from its platform of 1884, toward a policy of objecting to any tariff reform whatever.

In his second message to Congress in 1886, Cleveland referred to the extraction of revenue above the needs of government as "ruthless extortion," and laid emphasis upon the burden of taxation on certain classes, calling attention to the taxes paid by the farmers and questioning whether laborers were not placed at a disadvantage by the tariff. He recommended a reduction in taxes on the necessities of life and also on raw materials and declared that there must be a willingness on the part of some to make concessions for the public good. But the Congress which had refused to acknowledge Morrison's bill in June was still in power and could not be persuaded, even by the president's appeal; the House once again, by a vote of 154 to 149, declined to consider tariff bills. Cleveland was not daunted; there were rumors that the administration would present a more decisive plan of tax reform to the next Congress but that concessions might be made to Randall and his followers by removing tobacco from internal revenue taxes.

All hopes of party harmony were shattered by the president when, departing from all precedents, he devoted his entire message to Congress of December 1887 to revenue reform. Few documents issued by a president have attracted so much attention as did this paper, in which the president dwelt upon the "inexcusable extortion" in raising revenue beyond the needs of the government, by which money was needlessly taken from trade and the people's use. There was an overaccumulated National Treasury on one hand and a depleted monetary condition in the business of the country on the other. The president then entered upon discussions of taxation, the terms of which were vague and which could be interpreted as an endorsement of a free-trade policy. The existing tariff was denounced as "vicious, illegal and inequitable," but at the close of his argument he announced that the question of free trade was absolutely irrelevant in the discussion.

To many members of the president's own party, the unexpected essage seemed like political suicide. In the 1886 election, the Democratic majority in the House, which would occupy from 1887 to 1889, had been cut from forty to twelve. William Morrison was defeated and John G. Carlisle was returned by only a narrow margin. Fears were expressed that the Democratic party was rushing to destruction in placing so much emphasis upon tariff reform, but disagreements also existed within the Republican party. For years it had been dissatisfied with the existing tariff; some wanted a reduction in duties on sugar and a compensating reward to home producers, while others feared to open a single gap in the high wall of protection and thought it would be better to reduce, if not repeal, the tax on liquors and to make the general duties so high that imports would fall off. Still other members were not adverse to an excessive tariff, for huge plans were in the making for big governmental expenditures for ships, river and harbor improvements, and coast defenses.

The campaign of 1888 was devoted to the tariff at the expense of all other issues. Groups were organized to promote tariff reform and to defend protection; speakers covered the country explaining to farmers, laborers and artisans the significance of the tariff proposed by the Democrats; and the Finance Committee of the Senate prepared a bill which should solidify the newer Republican principle.

During the campaign the Democrats were at a disadvantage, as it was impossible to remove the impression that the Democratic party was headed toward free trade,

and further it was forced to defend a movement in which it did not sincerely believe. President Harrison, in his letter of acceptance, said that the struggle was not between tariff schedules, but between wide-apart principles. The Republicans won in the presidential and congressional elections of 1888 and interpreted their victory as a victory for protection. After the election, the Senate substituted its measure for the Mills bill and later passed it by a vote of thirty-two to thirty. All other action on the tariff was subsequently defeated by that Congress.

When the Republican party gained control in all branches of government under Harrison's administration, it began to formulate a new tariff. The chairman of the House Ways and Means Committee was William McKinley of Ohio. The basis of the measure was the Senate bill prepared in the previous session, and the purpose was to perfect the method of protection. No secrecy was applied: public hearings were held and special interests were won over for support. Discussions on the tariff had shown that the farmers were dissatisfied with a policy of protection which favored the manufacturer, and to be in harmony, President Harrison advised that the protective principle be applied to farm products as well as manufactured items. Duties on agricultural products were increased and especially important was the increase of duties on such commodities as woolens, dressgoods, carpets, linen goods and tin-plate, while on the other hand, the free list was enlarged to include products which did not compete with domestic production. The measure also recognized the principles of privileges and subsidies.

Over the reciprocity clause there was a long and annoying struggle. In October of 1889, before Congress assembled, a conference composed of representatives of nineteen independent nations of the Western hemisphere was held in Washington. This Pan-American meeting was first proposed by James G. Blaine, during his earlier term as secretary of state, but the plan had been discarded until the last year of Cleveland's administration. When it did convene, Blaine was again in office to welcome it. The main topics were methods of communication between North and South American ports, the establishment of a standard weight and measure system, the possible use of a common monetary system and a plan for settling all questions of dispute between the countries forming the conference. The reciprocal trade principle received favorable recognition at this conference, and interest was further stimulated by Blaine, who was deeply concerned with the doctrine of reciprocity. Blaine did not succeed in persuading the House to incorporate the measure into the McKinley Bill. The high protectionists regarded with suspicion any plan that was directed toward free trade in products in which the United States was concerned, for it was thought that South America, being predominantly agricultural, could easily compete with the western farmer. If trade agreements were arranged with South America, opponents of free trade held that it would be necessary to allow wool, leather, lead and copper duty free or at low rates.

Blaine carried the fight to the Senate. His argument was that the United States should retain certain duties until concessions were provided by the exporting countries. Eighty-seven percent of the products of Latin-America were already admitted duty free, with sugar being one exception. Blaine suggested a reciprocal arrangement, whereby instead of paying money for imported sugar, a large portion of this cost would be paid for in lumber, salt, iron, flour, beef, furniture and hundreds of other products. These proposals were favorably accepted by most Republicans, but although protection had been endorsed in the elections of 1888, it was feared that the Republican leaders in Congress were carrying the issue too far. Supporters of subsidies were also found backing reciprocity, for they reasoned: of what use would the establishing of steamship routes between the United States and South America ports be if trade were removed?

Reciprocity triumphed, although the Aldrich amendment, which incorporated it into the bill, differed from the proposal made by Blaine. Instead of permitting the president to reduce duties if reciprocal privileges were granted, the executive was authorized to impose discriminating duties in case reciprocity was restrained. Constitutional lawyers in the Republican party questioned the constitutionality of placing huge discretionary powers of taxation in the hands of the president, but this position was overruled by a majority of the party. It was argued that the influence of an optional power in executing the law did not transform the president into lawmaker.

In spite of energetic efforts of the House to secure an early passage of the tariff bill, it was held up for over five months, delaying the final enactment until October 1, 1890, a month before the congressional elections. Further protection was guaranteed by the enactment of a customs administrative law, by which new precautionary measures against undervaluation were established. Litigation was also decreased by making the decisions of the Board of General Appraisers final and decisive.

The Tariff Act of 1890 fulfilled all the hopes of its planners in reducing revenue. Customs receipts fell from $854 million in the four years 1885 to 1889, to $830 million in 1889 to 1893. Expenditures, including the interest on the public debt, increased from $1,052,000,000 to $1,382,000,000. The increase of internal revenue from $491 million to $603 million or over $150 million a year, helped to make good some of the deficiency, but the treasury was being pushed nearer the danger point; in 1892 the excess of revenue over expenditures was only $10 million and in 1893, $2 million.

The Republicans were sincere in their support of the principle of protection, and they were also frank in their advocacy of appropriations. The Democrats endeavored to accuse the Republicans of wastefulness and created popular prejudice by calling the Fifty-first Congress the "Billion Dollar" Congress—to which Representative Reed replied that the United States was a billion dollar country. In January of 1892, Representative Holman, a Democrat, proposed a resolution providing that no money should be appropriated except to carry on the departments in an efficient manner, and Dingley of Maine introduced a counter-resolution declaring that the functions of the nation and the duties of Congress extended to appropriations for projects of national importance, for the benefit of the country, and such are not likely to be obtained by private enterprise.

There were serious discussions over the adoption of a sugar tariff and of the income tax, and when it was first presented in a caucus of the Democratic members of the House of Representatives, there was a pledge that the income tax would be a separate bill. To insure its passage, however, it was afterward tacked upon the tariff measure. No such demand had been made in the Democratic platform: even President Cleveland, in his message of December 4, referred to the proposal, as yet unreported from the committee, as "a small tax upon incomes derived from certain corporate investments." It turned out to be more than this: a tax of 2 percent was imposed upon all incomes in excess of four thousand dollars.

The Wilson Bill passed the House by a vote of 204 to 110, and the Tariff Bill reached the Senate without the united backing of the majority party of the House responsible for revenue bills. The Finance Committee of the Senate tried to reshape the measure, and hundreds of amendments were made in the interest of protection, until it became so unrecognizable that it was referred to as the Gorman Tariff, because of the all-pervasive influence of Maryland's Senator Gorman, who modified not only the details but the principles.

In the end, the House yielded to the Senate, which was willing, if necessary, to accept the responsibility of no legislation. The president would not endorse the bill and allowed it to become law without his signature.

On December 19, 1893, the Wilson Tariff Bill was introduced in the House. In brief, the new tariff measure provided for the adoption, wherever practicable, of ad-valorem instead of specific duties, and the "freeing from taxes of those great materials of industry that lie at the basis of production." There was an extension of the free list, including such items as lumber, coal, wood and iron ore, and it was predicted that the Democrats would show their insincerity once again by protecting the iron and coal industries in the South, which proved false. However, many of the prohibitory rates of the McKinley Tariff were reduced, such as on silks, cottons, woolens, glass and chinaware. Since it was estimated that revenue would be reduced by $50 million additional taxes would be sought by increasing income tax and taxes on hard liquors.

Ever since this campaign opened, the Republican party managers have relied upon one great cry; that Mr. Cleveland is the friend of the English—that he desires Free Trade for England's sake; that he has made an ignominious surrender of our rights to the greed of the Canadians—for England's sake. Of course, this is a plain and simple lie, told only to catch the Irish vote, on the supposition, which seems to be a firmly rooted idea among the Republicans, that every Irishman is a fool. We draw this inference because we can not conceive it possible that any man, not a fool—we will go further and say not a born fool—could imagine a President of the United States so insane as to do any thing whatever for the love of England—or Germany or Portugal or Madagascar. A man who, in this country of free voters, would draw up treaties or in any way influence the policy of the government to favor another nation at the expense of our own—why, he would walk about the streets in his night-shirt, for he could not possibly know enough to put on his clothes in the morning.

This seems to us to be no more than common honesty and common sense. We do not know what the managers of the Republican party think of it—but we know what they do in such matters. They have had no scruples about calling Mr. Cleveland a friend to England and an enemy of his own country, and they have acted as if they seriously believed that the absurd accusation would obtain credence among American voters. They have not troubled themselves to explain *why* he should be a friend to England rather than a friend to Senegambia or the South Pole, or how he could possibly gain any thing by such a friendship—such questions have given them no concern. They have contented themselves, firm in the belief that they were following the rules of "practical

158

politics," with telling the country that when Mr. Cleveland urged the necessity of reform in the tariff he meant Free Trade, which would benefit the British; and that when he approved a treaty with Canada it was only in order to surrender American rights to foreigners. It was a silly lie; but after all, a lie is a lie. And now mark how plain a tale puts them down. For they had to back up their lie with action, and their action has killed the lie.

Let us state the facts briefly. Our relations with Canada have been "strained," as the diplomatists say, for many years. In our commercial intercourse we have given Canada many advantages, and she has returned our courtesy by harassing our fishermen. This state of affairs forced us to demand the termination of the treaty which governed that commercial intercourse. When this was done, by the vote of the Republican majority of the Senate, the President was called upon to protect our interests by such retaliatory measures as might be necessary to meet Canadian injustice. It was also his duty to negotiate a new, and more satisfactory treaty. To this latter task the President addressed himself, and, by the efforts of able commissioners, a treaty was drawn up with the government of Great Britain. About that treaty, its value, its character, its probable influence on our concerns, the voters of this country know no more than they know of the Book of Mormon. They know its bare terms, undiscussed and unexplained—that is all. It went to the Senate for ratification, and after months of waiting, the Republican majority in the Senate rejected it, alleging only that it did not do justice to the United States, and favored Canada at our expense—an allegation of which no proof was offered—of which the falsehood was shown by the bitter complaints of the Canadian press and

public. Every one in Canada cried out against that same treaty, and said openly that it involved a surrender of Canada's rights. But our people were allowed to know as little as possible of its character and its meaning. All they knew, in the end, was that it was rejected by the Republican majority in the Senate, and that its rejection was a slur upon the President.

And what did the President do? What did he do, this friend of England, this betrayer of American rights? Why, he did what he usually does, the simple, honest and manly thing. He asked the Senate to give him the *power*—which he had not—to put into force that same policy of retaliation which the Senate had recommended to him a year before. The Senate would not accept the treaty which, in his opinion, bound Canada to fair treatment of the United States. Then, he said, let the Senate give him the power to deal with Canada, without a treaty, so as to protect the rights of Americans, It may have been "bad politics" for the Senate to reject the treaty on a bare unproved and unprovable assertion, impeaching the good faith of its makers. It may have been "good politics" for the President to demand that the Senate should sustain its own judgement. We do not care to enter into the question. To us, the one significant fact of the whole business is that the President's action, in following the course of duty which he has always marked out for himself, has put an ever-lasting quietus upon a lie that was backed by the whole power and authority of the Republican party. Hereafter, nobody will accuse Grover Cleveland of betraying his own country to please the English. No American has so faced the British nation since Andrew Jackson fought at New Orleans. He has done only his honest duty—but see what short work Honesty makes of a Lie.

THE MAN WHO DARES—AND THE MEN WHO DARE N'T.

Sometime in the far future, perhaps a little this side of the millenium, a tariff law will be framed solely in the interests of the people and in the light of common sense. It is otherwise at this writing. Republican orators like to boast of the high morals of their party, but whenever it gets down to tariff-moulding it proves to be led by a lot of ordinary political tricksters, just like any old party. In the case of the new tariff the problem has been, not how the needed revenues could best be raised, but how many dollars the people would give up to the Trusts without kicking. It must have been this, for, when a duty is carried to the prohibitive point, the question of revenue is eliminated; and when it is carried away beyond that point it must be simply a matter of guessing how much the people will stand. We learned long since that a Republican tariff robs the citizen. We seem destined to learn this time that it can also be made to rob the government at the same time. Duty after duty has been pushed beyond the prohibitive point, and so beyond the revenue-producing point. The national treasury is thus being robbed for the benefit of the protected interests and the Republican party. With its same old over-confident fatuity the party is paying its campaign debts by taxing the people; only this time it seems to be more than customarily brazen and foolish. It can always find excuses for robbing the tax-payer, but it will have hard work to explain its failure to provide revenue by other means than direct taxation.

TRYING HIS PATIENCE.

Not the least interesting events of the season other than elections, the sweet notes of Nilsson, and the picturesque acting of Irving, are the numerous business failures which are daily taking place. Whether or not they are a prelude to a panic we cannot say; but they are certainly too frequent to indicate a healthy state of things. The peculiar feature of the statements made by the wrecked business-houses is the number of preferred creditors. A firm fails, and, of course, the men who are "let in" think that the assets, if there are any, will be fairly divided among those who are entitled to them. But this is where they make a mistake.

There is not the slightest intention of dividing the estate rateably among those who are justly entitled to a share of it. The mercantile swindler is too smart to do anything of the sort. He gives preferences to his relatives and friends, and the man who is neither a relative nor a friend, but simply an ordinary tradesman or merchant, has to suffer. There are preferences for grandmothers, and grandfathers, and uncles, and aunts, and sisters, and brothers. Anything, so long as the money is kept in the family. It does not matter in the least if these friends have any claims on the estate. The swindler who fails in business makes this all right, and comes out of his scrape better off than ever he was. When will Congress give us a proper bankrupt law to crush the preferred creditor fraud?

LET US HAVE A GOOD BANKRUPTCY LAW, AS A PROTECTION AGAINST THE "PREFERRED CREDITOR".

The great political parties are in a quandary. They would be willing to give almost anything to get rid of the tariff question. But, like Banquo's ghost or a young man who can't grow a moustache, it won't down. The truth is that neither the Democratic nor the Republican managers have any very distinct ideas on the subject of Tariff Reform. They don't know how to tackle the question, and they treat it as gingerly as possible for fear of making some terrible mistake.

There are many political magnates of both sides who are prepared to be either Free-Traders or Protectionists; but they want to be certain that, whichever way they turn, they will be on the safe side, and retain whatever they may have of power and patronage. The question has been treated in so unstatesmanlike a manner that it is now too late to make it a plank in either presidential platform. It must be reserved for a great and honest new party—an Independent party—to put the tariff on a basis suited to the wants of the community. The existing parties have had their chance, and have signally failed.

165

Consequently, when at Chicago it became necessary to appeal to this last class,—the workingman whom Protection fails to protect,—fearful of the effects of Tariff-Reform logic against Protective sophistry, the framers of the platform in desperation threw out a sop of free whiskey and tobacco, hoping thereby to divert the workingman's attention from his true interests in a whirl of enthusiasm for cheaper luxuries. It is in fact to ignorance, vice and prejudice, that the once "Great Party of Moral Ideas" is making its appeal in this year of 1888. But the intelligent American Workingman who is not deceived by the fallacious arguments of the high-protectionists is the last man to be led by the cry of "Cheap Liquor."

Even if the intelligent workingman could not plainly see that the Republican party in working for any tariff change is working first for the employer and secondarily, if at all, for the employee; even if the workingman did not know that the employer always first considers his own interests, and secondarily, if at all, those of the employed, and is ever ready to reduce wages when the importation of foreign laborers, by the natural law of competition, renders this possible, irrespective of any tariff laws,—is not a party which goes in for one set of principles one time, and for another set of principles another time, and tries to straddle two sets of principles at the present time, an unsafe party for him to pin his faith to? Such a party by its own policy proves itself to be not a body of loyal citizens united for the carrying out of a great theory of government, but an aggregation of individuals banded together to retain power for power's sake and the advantage that will accrue personally to them thereby.

THE REPUBLICAN IDEA OF PROTECTION.

A high tariff on the monopolist's wards, free entrance for pauper labor, and a lock-out for the American workingman.

We have spoken of "selfish ends." Let us make it clearly understood that a man may work for himself without working for selfish ends. We all are working for ourselves, in this hard-working country—that is, we are working for ourselves, our wives and our children; and such work is good work, good and creditable. It is good work, whatever honest form it takes. The manufacturer who invests his capital, his brains and his industry for the benefit of himself and his family does his duty as a citizen. In his legitimate efforts to make money no one desires to interfere with him; no one grudges him the wealth which he may acquire by producing and selling a good article at a fair price—and the laboring man and the farmer stand in the same case. Every citizen has the right to earn the best living that the natural advantages of the country afford. But if one citizen, not content with this plain law of equity, seeks to enrich himself by taking an unfair advantage of all other workers, *and is found out*, it is certain to go hard with that man. The laborer and the farmer are just now finding out that the protective tariff which so benefits the manufacturer is of absolute detriment to them. The over-protected manufacturer, who is very alive to the tendency of the times is also finding out that the laborer and the farmer are finding him out. Perhaps, before this campaign is over, the man who lives on the "protection" which his fellow-citizens pay for will come back to the doctrine of the Republican platform of 1884, and fall in line with his fellow-countrymen in demanding the consummation of a scheme "to correct the inequalities of the tariff and to reduce the surplus." This is a campaign of education, and the lessons of the past should not go unheeded.

HIGH-PROTECTIONIST HUMBUG VERSUS THE COLD TRUTH.

Protectionist orator.—Look around you, my friend, and
reflect that you owe the magnificent prosperity which you enjoy to our glorious protective tariff—Disgusted farmer.—Johnny, get your
gun, get your gun!

RESTORING PROSPERITY.

The Republican vandals damaged it badly; but it will soon be as sound as ever again.

THE REPUBLICAN PRESS is just now in a most embarrassing predicament. The task of explaining the bounteous blessings of a McKinley tariff becomes the soothing recreation of an idle hour, compared with the job that now confronts it. It is forced not only to soar into the realms of romantic fiction in portraying the imaginary calamities that should daily attest the decay of our prosperity under Democratic rule; but it must perform the infinitely harder feat of imparting an air of truth to its untrue tales. The money stringency of a few weeks ago made plain sailing for the Republican Press. Factories and mills and banks did close then. It was easy to insist, with a glittering show of plausibility, that the fear of a slump in money values cut no figure in the panic; and that it was wholly due to the fear that our scheme of tariff legislation was to be reformed. "It is silly to pretend," said the Republican Press, "that the present financial stringency is due to a mere scarcity of money, caused by fear that our standard of value may change; and it is the veriest nonsense to argue that a repeal of the Sherman Law will better our condition, so long as wicked Democracy is threatening to dig up the roots of our prosperity."

No sooner had a session of Congress been issued, with the known object of repealing the Sherman Law, than there was a perceptible halt in the succession of failures that formed the burden of the Republican dirge. With the actual meeting of Congress, and the reasonable certainty of prompt relief from a threatened silver basis, stifled confidence breathed again. Then came the prompt action of the House, removing the poison from the Sherman Law by an imposing majority. In sacrilegious defiance of Republican prophecy, the money market at once became easier, a premium on currency ceased to be demanded, and industrial and commercial interests on every hand found new life.

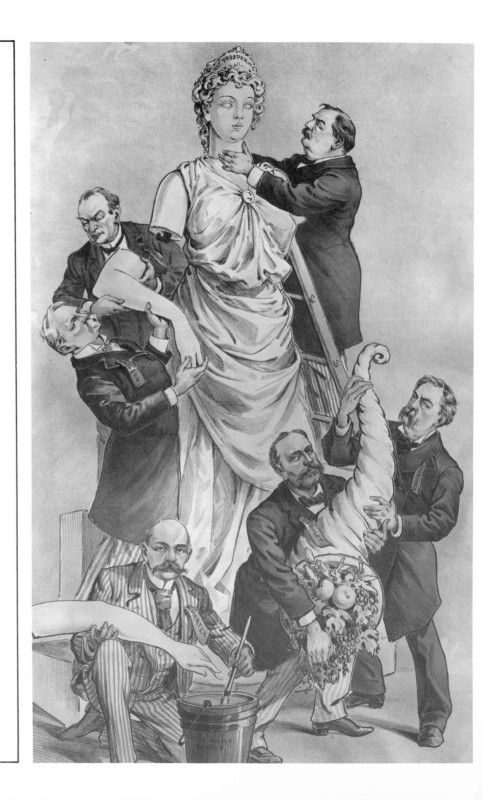

THE GRAND OLD GAME OF TIT FOR TAT.

Germany.—You vill not take mein raw sugar,—I vill not take your bork or beef or hay or noddings. Donnerwetter! France.—Sacre nom de dieu! You discriminate against my wine! Is it not so? I will not take your goods. Uncle Sam.—What do I care for commercial intercourse and prosperity? I've got my "home market" all to myself, see?

One of the most striking evils of the protective system is the manner in which other nations "get back" at us for the tariff-duties we impose upon their products.

Unlike most evils of Protection, this one reacts upon the protected manufacturer.

Fate has played a scurvy trick upon William McKinley, of Canton, Ohio. Five years and a half ago, by the grace of Chance, his name was put to a tariff-bill containing the highest duties that the manufacturers had ever been able to buy. The Republican party was wrecked by this bill two years later, but the name of "McKinley" had come to stand for Protection. Prior to 1890 McKinley had been a Congressman of admitted mediocrity. During a long political career he had earned no fame of any sort. He stood for no principle and was useful only to count in a quorum. He was just a plain hired-man on the Republican farm. Then a cruel accident made him chairman of a Ways and Means committee, and his name went to the tariff-bill framed by his abler colleagues. Thenceforth he was hailed as the chief sponsor of Protection. Naturally he began to cultivate some views on the tariff. This was not hard for him to do. He had lived so long with no particular views on any subject that it must have been a relief to be tied up to something in that way. He learned the stock phrases of Protection and rattled them off, parrot-like, whenever the chance came. By dealing in flowery generalities about "prosperity" he came to be regarded by a considerable element as one really endowed with power to make life easy. He preached always of a golden time when wages would be high, the necessaries of life cheap and money plentiful,—and the millenium seemed to be awaiting the crook of his finger. Had the tariff continued to be the chief issue of the day McKinley might have served a long term as a popular idol. Unhappily for him another issue came to divide the people, and the tariff is regarded with comparative indifference. See the result: McKinley, facing an emergency that demands a man of parts, shows himself to be a man of weakness.

There are more than seventeen million working people, of all classes, in the United States. Among these there are over seven-and-a-half millions who, in one way or another, are engaged in agricultural occupations. What are the other nine-and-a-half-millions—Knights of Labor? Not all of them. According to the census reports we must deduct four million people who are doing "professional" work, or the like—lawyers, doctors, clergymen, clerks, inventors, commercial travelers, musicians, teachers, and capitalists generally. Trade, transportation, mining, manufactures and mechanics employ the other five-and-one-half millions. No census report can tell us how many of the whole number belong to "organized labor," but last year the two principal organizations gave it out that they had 1,100,000 between them. We will let it go at that.

These few statistics, which the reader may easily verify for himself, are set down here merely as an illustration in simple proportion. It requires no profound study to learn from them that the farmers—that is, the people engaged in agricultural employments of all sorts, are, numerically, the greatest body of workmen in this country—that they have an enormous plurality over any one other class of laborers. They do not make so much noise as, let us say, one certain other class; but they can make presidents and congressmen, and through their representatives can make laws. These facts we sometimes forget; and to people in the large cities a howling "master-workman" on a street corner is a much greater figure than a silent farmer on the far horizon. Yet the master-workman has one million men behind him, while there are seven-and-a-half million persons doing work on the farm lands in the United States.

These things are undeniably true—yet it is equally true that there is no large class of men in the country whose interests receive less intelligent and sincere attention from either state or national legislators; and the reason is not mysterious. The farmers have not the means of ready inter-communication, the facilities for frequent meeting and for the discussion of public matters which townsfolk enjoy. They are hard-working men; their acquaintance with any but their own narrow world is slight; they have little time or opportunity to read the newspapers—and those that they do read are not the sort to give them broad views of human affairs and of the world's progress. They grow, naturally, in such a life, conservative, "hidebound," (in the good old country phrase,) and intensely partisan.

Thus it comes that their representatives in Congress or in the state legislature are often peculiarly *un*representative of the very men who elect them to office. The country member is, nine times out of ten, the smart man of a village or a country town. He gains his position in politics by his influence with the townspeople on the one hand and with the party managers on the other. Thus he is put forward as the candidate of his party, and when election-day comes, the farmers of his district drive in, from miles around, and vote for him, *because* he is the candidate of the party. He can rely on their vote, if he is a partisan in good standing; and he need do no more to keep in favor with them than to canvass his district in the orthodox fashion, and make a few empty promises. If, when he is elected, he has offices to dispose of, they go to the townspeople who worked for him; if he gets an appropriation for his "deestrick"—it goes to the local contractor for dredging some ten-foot-wide creek between a cheese-factory and a railroad station. As for the farmers—why, he will give them a brand-new speech when he comes up for reelection.

Truly, he appears sometimes as the champion of a bill to suppress the manufacture of oleomargarine, or some such measure. But it is doubtful if he is moved to this course as much by the prayers of the farmer as by a desire to make the oleomargarine men buy him off. And if he carries through a bill for the establishment of a state Board of Agriculture, it is safe to predict that two or three of his political workers will find employment on that board. It is much the same way if he be a member of the national legislature. You may hear him talk, in the House of Representatives, of the needs of the wool-growers and the sugar-planters; but you may be sure that the woolen manufacturers and the sugar refiners have made their especial needs more clear to him.

This may explain why, for a quarter of a century, the American farmer has had to pay a burdensome tax levied for the protection—that is, for the pecuniary benefit—of the American manufacturer. It is a tax of which the farmer gets no manner of good. The only rational excuse for asking him to pay it is to be found in the assertion that it benefits the country at large. This might be a good excuse if it were true. That it is not true the farmer may now find out; for such a discussion has been started on the subject that even in the furthest of the back counties a man can have small excuse for remaining ignorant of what has been said for and against a high protective tariff. He has never before had this opportunity. So stoutly, so ingeniously have the supporters of this system maintained the fallacies on which it rests that only the exceptional courage of one man availed to bring the matter into open court, and put the question before the people. It has now been fairly put; it is no longer a blasphemy to discuss it. The farmer can hear and read what reformers of the tariff have to say for themselves—and for him. When he finds out what the tax really is, and that it is for him to say whether or no it shall be levied hereafter, we believe he will find it cheaper to do his thinking for himself, instead of leaving the job to his party leaders.

THE TARIFF COW.—THE FARMER FEEDS HER—THE MONOPOLIST GETS THE MILK.

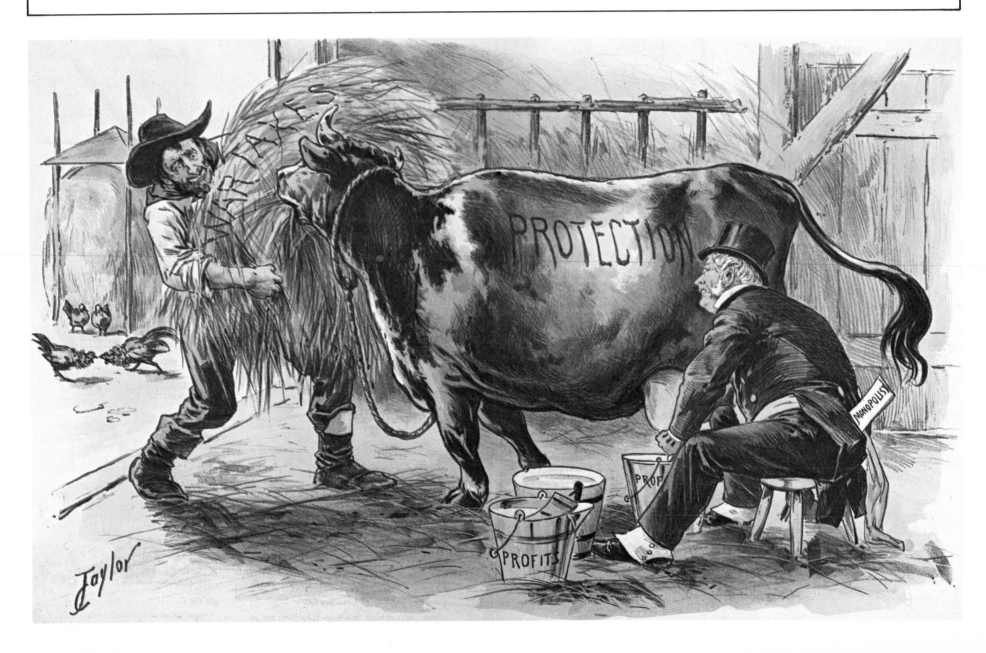

TARIFF
CIVIL SERVICE
LABOR
SILVER COINAGE
MONOPOLIES

The civil service reform movement gained popularity after President Garfield was assassinated by a disappointed office seeker, a tragedy which brought to the public's mind the need for a method to replace the "spoils" system, generally attributed to Andrew Jackson, in which appointments to office were granted for political service to the party and not for experience and fitness for the job.

Congress passed an act in 1883 authorizing President Chester A. Arthur to appoint civil service examiners, who should procure qualified persons by fair examinations without regard to party. From those passing the civil service examinations, appointments and promotions were to be made. In accordance with this act, during the next twenty years 100,000 officeholders were put under civil service rules, and succeeding presidents added to the number of government officials who were examined before receiving their appointments. Officeholders appointed by this system held their positions, assuming satisfactory service, regardless of the party in power.

The civil service reform met resistance during Grover Cleveland's first term of office. He increased the effectiveness of the system, however, and his concern for doing the right thing earned him the respect of the public, and the Democratic party reluctantly nominated him for a second term. He was defeated by Benjamin Harrison even though he had the larger popular vote by nearly 100,000, for he lost the electoral vote.

Civil service suffered again during the Republican administration and the system probably would have been destroyed had it not been for Theodore Roosevelt, a young Republican, who was on the civil service commission.

The Democratic platform of 1884, in its reference to civil service, used only the equivocal phrase, "We favor honest civil service reform." The Republican platform was more explicit in its phrasing on the subject of reform, demanding that it be extended, and it openly recognized the corruptness which existed in the power of official patronage. If either party could be called a friend of civil service it was the Republican party, but it had just been defeated at the polls. Grover Cleveland, as governor of New York, had been friendly toward the movement, so the independent friends of civil service put their confidence in the president-elect rather than in the Democratic party. In reply to a letter from George William Curtis, president of the National Civil Service Reform League, Cleveland pledged himself to the civil service law, "because my conception of true democratic faith and public duty requires that this, and all other statutes, should be in good faith and without evasion enforced, and because, in many utterances made prior to my election as president, approved by the party to which I belong, and which I have no disposition to disclaim, I have in effect promised the people that this should be done" (from *Cleveland Writings and Speeches*, Parker, ed.). Cleveland also implied that he would not remove any man from a nonpolitical office during the time for which he was appointed. This statement was afterward supplemented by oral declarations that when the term of office of a Republican expired under a definite tenure, the position would be filled by a good man of the Democratic party, if one could be found, and further confirmation of these principles was given in his inaugural address when he said, "Merit and competency shall be recognized instead of party subserviency."

Public interest was also aroused as to the number of appointments the Democratic president would make from the South. Southern whites had been practically omitted from executive appointments since before the Civil War. The leading men in the South were Democrats for the most part, and many had served in the Confederate Army. People anxiously waited to see if Cleveland would recognize his party following from the South, and in what spirit Southerners who still may have held theories of government opposed to national unity would perform the obligations of government office if they were appointed to positions of trust.

Cleveland's appointments met with general approval, though not all were of a high order. Cleveland gave the South its fair share by not taking a half-way action, for Senator Lamar of Mississippi was appointed secretary of the interior and Senator Garland of Arkansas made attorney-general, and Senator Bayard of Delaware, whose name had been presented in three national conventions for the presidential nomination, became secretary of state. Daniel Manning of New York was chosen for secretary of the treasury and William C. Whitney, also of New York, was appointed as secretary of the navy. Whitney had served as a corporation counsel for the city of New York, while Manning was chairman of the Democratic State Committee of New York. Only on grounds of personal friendship could the Whitney and Manning appointments be accounted for, and it was with much public dismay that these two men were intrusted in such positions. It was at once noticed that the secretarial appointments from the Northern states were not experienced in national affairs and that several were completely unknown outside their locality. Appointments to the diplomatic service also received much criticism because of the inclusion of many Southerners, for of the seventy men appointed to the diplomatic and consular service, thirty-two were from the South.

Cleveland's appointments to minor offices were made under several disadvantages. Being the head of his party he had embarrassed his independents by setting high standards of conduct to which the people would refer when his performance fell short of accomplishment. On one side he would be charged with indifference to party claims; on the other, of insincerity. The Democratic spoilsmen accused him of disloyalty and the Republicans charged him with hypocrisy, while the independents, encouraged by his firmness and aroused by his short-comings, were soon left in bewilderment. It was an impossible task for Cleveland to satisfy the demands of office seekers, though many changes had been made, but even critical reformers were inclined to be tolerant in regard to removals from the higher offices of trust and confidence. Some officeholders, protected by the long dominion of Republican success, were incompetent and corrupt. One advocate of civil service reform declared that a clean sweep throughout the South was needed. "The federal service had been thoroughly corrupt for twenty years, especially in the Mahone (Va.) areas. To purge it completely was one of the reasons for which Cleveland was elected."

The civil service could not be placed on a satisfactory and sound basis until it included both Democrats and Republicans, and how to accomplish this without a case for complaint was a difficult problem. A considerable number of officeholders, such as customs collectors, internal revenue collectors and postmasters, held their offices under the four-year rule, and the Republicans under this tenure would soon be forced to stand aside. The object of the four-year rule was to pave the way for politicians to make changes and it was incumbent upon Cleveland to appoint Democrats to replace Republicans upon the expiration of their terms of office, no matter how well they had performed their duties. Cleveland made no apology for this, for he believed, as did many reformers, in the policy of equalization.

In pledging himself to civil service reform, President Cleveland had served notice that one class of officials would be removed from office: the postmasters who had used postoffices as headquarters for committee work, for distribution of party literature and the display of "irritating placards." Many were officials who had neglected public duty to do private work. Stirred by these acts, Cleveland suspended over six hundred officials before he completed his first year in office, including postmasters, district attorneys, marshals, consuls and internal revenue personnel, all serving under the four-year term.

These removals led to a clash between Cleveland and the Senate. When Congress met in December of 1885, the Republican senators held a caucus and laid down a policy to be followed in the matter of appointments; they determined that there should be no rejections of nominations except for causes which would insure the rejection of nominees of a Republican president under like circumstances; and secondly, that information called for in cases of removal must be furnished. When this information was refused by several cabinet members, under the authority of the president, on the grounds that public interest would not be promoted thereby or because the reasons asked for referred to executive acts only, the Senate therefore held up nominations when suspensions were involved, and intimated to the president that if he would abandon all charges against the officials who were suspended and admit the removals were based on the spoils system, all opposition would cease and the confirmations would follow. The committee on the judiciary proposed a resolution, which was passed by the Senate, January 26, 1886, directing the attorney general to submit all papers in the Department of Justice touching the suspension of the former United States District Attorney for the Southern District of Alabama. Attorney general Garland refused this order, in a special message to the Senate, and the president made an address in which he expounded his interpretation of executive power. He declared that the Constitution gave him sole right of suspension or removal; he himself was responsible to the people: "I regard the papers and documents withheld and addressed to me or intended for my use and action, purely unofficial and private; not infrequently confidential, and having reference to the performance of a duty exclusively mine." The clause of the tenure of office act which required reasons for suspension had been repealed in 1869.

The success of the civil service reform was greatly endangered by the indifference of some of the cabinet members and the high officials of large and important bureaus. Many of these men were primarily chosen for reasons unrelated to loyalty to the new civil service policy, and it was impossible for the president to supervise the entire expanse of appointments, since so many interpretations of the reform could be used in the different divisions of the civil service. The "policy of equalization," as adopted by the postmaster general, was surprising—many postmasters were dismissed on the ground of offensive partisanship. Democratic congressmen sought newspaper articles or affidavits to prove partisanship, and fourth-class postmasters were released by the hundreds. The changes took place so rapidly that it was evident that practically wholesale changes would be made in two years instead of four.

The law governing the classified service became a mockery, as shown by evasion and deception in many offices. Postmasters in Indianapolis, Philadelphia, Milwaukee, and Baltimore made drastic changes in the clerical workers and embarrassed the administration by their speedy removal of job holders. The postmaster of Baltimore cleared his office of Republicans and took "pride and pleasure in advising that the new appointees were selected because they were Democrats." Henry Watterson of the Louisville *Courier-Journal* declared that "officially every man is offensive who is not in sympathy with the party in power, that is the meaning of the Democrat idea of representative Republican government based upon party responsibility."

In the railway service, nearly three-fourths of the employees were removed, and in the Indian service and patent office, extensive changes were made. It was impossible for the president to be duly informed in regard to the qualifications of the seemingly infinite candidates for office.

Spoilsmen of the old order, such as Senator Gorman and Vice President Hendricks, were in high standing with party councils and their advice could not be slighted. Cleveland came to the White House but with little acquaintance with congressmen except those from his own home state or those met during his tours of campaigning, and whether he was deceived by bad advice or whether his attitudes toward improved political service were of too high standards to be practically imposed is still questionable. Yet with many evidences of partisanship the president showed an independence of party pressure which rekindled the hopes of doubting reformers. President Cleveland reappointed Pearson for the important office of postmaster of New York, a man who had worked up from the lowest grade of the postal service until he was made postmaster by President Garfield in 1881. Likewise, Burt was restored to his position in the Naval Office in New York, although he had been removed by his own Republican party leaders because of this fidelity to the merit system.

In the confusion of all the conflicting policy, the confidence of the civil service reformers was grievously tried. In the turmoil of reappointments, removals, bad appointments, sneers at reform and sometimes hearty commendation, the reformers found their only encouragement in their crusade.

The National Civil Service Reform League, in August 1885, resolved that President Cleveland had proved "amid perplexities and difficulties his fidelity to the patriotic principles asserted in his letter of December 24, 1884" beyond the requirement of the law, for important administrative officers of the party, opposed to the administration, had been appointed and retained in positions commanding large patronage. The interference of congressmen with executive action had been notably repressed, and reasons for suspensions and removals had been stated to the people. Later on, when the principle of equalization was lost, Curtis complained that "in the survey of the whole civil service there has been about as complete a change as was practicable." In 1885, federal employees numbered about 120,000 of whom only 14,000 were protected under civil service rules and of this entire group of federal officeholders two-thirds were changed during the first half of the administration.

Of the chief officeholders, including Internal Revenue and custom collectors, also fourth-class postmasters, numbering around 58,000, over 45,000 were replaced.

Many reformers recognized the burden which the president would have to carry, if he continued an inflexible loyalty to reform as he continued to promise. When elected he would have broken his party apart, alienated the Democratic majority in the House of Representatives and isolated himself politically so that he would have been unable to serve reform or any other good cause.

Many Democrats complained about the retention of Republicans in the unclassified service regardless of the drastic changes that had been made. Early in 1885, Tammany Hall had resolved that the civil service law was an infringement upon the privileges bestowed upon officials of the government. The Democratic State Convention also passed unsatisfactory resolutions on civil service and openly scorned the merit system by renominating David B. Hill for governor of New York. Democrats at the same time endorsed President Cleveland and censured the civil service law as a substitute for personal and party responsibility. Randall of Pennsylvania, chairman of the House Committee on Appropriations, led an effort to have the civil service law repealed in May of 1886, and again the Democrats argued that the law was unconstitutional, while the Republicans were told by their own leader that they should refuse to serve their country under a Democratic administration. No leader in either House of Congress was aggressively engaged in the reform movement, and while Congress reluctantly increased appropriations, at no time were the funds adequate for the normal development of civil service during Grover Cleveland's first term in office.

The confidence in civil service was again restored in July of 1886 when the president warned officeholders against the use of their positions to control political activities either at primaries or to secure delegates to political conventions. "Officeholders are the agents of the people, not their masters." (Richardson, *Messages and Papers*). Two district attorneys, one a Republican and the other a Democrat, were dismissed for disobedience to this order, but when protests were made against the injustice of these removals, the cases were reopened. The Democrat was restored to his office, while the Republican was condemned. *(New York Tribune*, November 25, 1886). The president was accused of insincerity and the hopes of the reformers were once again shattered.

Unfortunately, the Civil Service Commission did not show strength—it feared the politicians, and would not support a firm adherence to the law, nor did it try to suppress unfriendly criticism. The commission made a few weak investigations only after many protests and complaints had been made by the reformers; their findings were always inconclusive, and the spoilsmen had blittle to fear from these inquiries. Two of the commission's members, Oberly and Edgerton, were political hacks, and in 1887 one of the members brought scorn to his office after making campaign speeches in Maryland. The commission did show some activity in the latter part of Cleveland's administration, however, and in May 1887, under its suggestion, the executive expanded civil service rules by extending the competitive principle to promotions.

Glowing promises had been made in the Republican platform of 1888 not only that the merit system should extend to all grades of civil service reform, but that the reform should be observed in all executive appointments. These pledges President Harrison accepted: "In appointments to every grade and department, fitness and not party service should be the essential requirement, and fidelity and efficiency the only tenure of office." Harrison found his intentions frustrated by the demands of unsatisfied office seekers and charges of inconsistency were the end result. President Harrison reorganized the Civil Service Commission, bringing it up to the standard which had been set by Eaton, its first chairman. He appointed Theodore Roosevelt, a

Republican who had achieved a reputation as a vigorous campaigner for reform measures in the New York State Assembly from 1881 to 1883, and Thompson, a Democrat, previously selected by Grover Cleveland.

The merit of these selections was generally recognized, and the friends of civil service reform were not disappointed in the serious efforts of the commission to enforce the law, so far as it affected the Classified Service, and in the persistent recommendations for further extension of civil service rules to departments not yet brought within their influence. Two years elapsed before the president could be persuaded to redeem the pledges of the Republican platform of 1888 by an extension of the Classified Service. In 1891 further progress was made by adding a portion of the Indian Bureau, a year later the Fish Commission was added and in 1893, the Clerical Force of free-delivery post-office personnel. The merit system was then adopted for laborers in the navy yards, and steps were taken to close admittance to the Classified Service by abolishing the rule whereby promotions could be made from the Unclassified to the Classified service. The regulations of the Civil Service Commission were gradually improved to make the eligibility list public and by securing appointment on local examination boards of men whose tenure of service was independent of the heads of the offices for which appointments were to be made.

Theodore Roosevelt put new life into the commission and made many vigorous speeches in answer to critics of civil service reform. Roosevelt asserted that much of the money contributed by office seekers for political assessments was retained for private use by those who collected it, and he was especially active in clearing up falsehoods concerning the character of civil service examinations. The misrepresentation was so malicious that it was believed that all questions asked were from the ridiculous to the sublime.

President Harrison, on the other hand, was accused of surrendering to such party bosses as Quay of Pennsylvania, Mahone of Virginia, and Platt of New York. Quay was believed to have used corrupt methods, binding Harrison hard and fast in the dispensing of patronage and burdening him with the selection of J. Wanamaker for postmaster general. The selection of Clarkson of Iowa as first assistant postmaster general aroused suspicion which was duly justified: he earned the distinction of being named "Headsman" by changing thirty thousand officials in a single year. Within eighteen months, more than half of the twenty-six hundred officials, then directly appointed by Harrison, were changed and of the sixty thousand fourth-class postmasters, another one-half were replaced, and Pearson, the New York postmaster originally appointed under a Republican administration and reappointed by Grover Cleveland, was relieved at the expiration of his term. (*Harper's Weekly*, July 18, 1891.) To the Republican spoilsmen he was a fugitive, as to the Democratic spoilsmen he had been an intruder.

The wrath of civil service reformers was greatly aroused. Being less charitable to Harrison than to Cleveland, because Harrison had assured the people with explicit pledges to maintain a rigorous role in enforcing a strong reform, they accused the Republican party with a ferocity unequaled since Grant's administration. Harrison was accused of favoritism to a long list of relatives receiving political preference, and another criticism was that the press was subsidized as never before by appointment of editors to public service.

Public opinion was slow to change, yet the spoils system didn't go on without being criticized sharply. So much ill feeling was generated that this dissatisfaction, along with the independent vote, was responsible for the defeat of the Republicans in state elections in the fall of 1889. The Democrats even won in Iowa, a state whose loyalty to Republicanism had never been under suspicion. Pressure on the part of Republican publications demanded that Matthew S. Quay and W. W. Dudley should resign from the National Republican Committee, and President Harrison became so alienated with these bosses and campaign leaders that they would not support his bid for renomination in 1892.

Take down from the shelf that Roman History of yours, dust it, and turn to the chapters about the Tarquins, and then look at our centre cartoon. But perhaps you are well read in history, and know more about them than we can tell you? Perhaps, on the other hand, you never heard of a Tarquin? But, whether you have or not, lend us your ears, and we will tell you a little story about them. The Romans got tired of the goings-on of the Tarquins, especially of the particularly bad behavior of Mr. Sextus Tarquinius, the son of the delectable Tarquinius Superbus. A revolution followed, which put an end to monarchy in Rome, and established the Republic.

It must be remembered that this is all mythical history, but it has quite enough truth in it for our purposes. When the Tarquin family and their adherents discovered that no persuasion would induce the Romans to have them for rulers, they resolved to have harmony at least among themselves, in order that they might recover what they had lost. With this end in view, they swore an oath of harmony over the body of a victim sacrificed for the purpose. Now this is the precise position of the Republican party. It has been practically kicked out of office for its crimes, and it is split into factions. The only way to reach harmony and power is to sacrifice the victim, Civil Service Reform.

The picture will doubtless be looked upon by many of the Republican leaders as a pleasing fancy; but as nothing else. The suggestion can never be acted upon, because respectable Republicans—we mean the patriots and honest men—will have Civil Service Reform, while the corrupt and tricky ones will not have it. They will not have it because it would take away all their power and patronage; and it is of much more importance to most Republican politicians to be able to influence the appointment of a postmaster or a consul than to devote themselves to legislating for the good of their country. The members of the Roman House of Tarquin, having been driven from power by the people, called together their adherents, and swore an oath of harmony over the body of a victim sacrificed for the purpose. They then undertook to get back to Rome, and History records that they Got Left.

THE TRUE MEANING OF REPUBLICAN HARMONY.

The members of the Roman House of Tarquin, having been driven

from power by the people, called together their adherents, and swore an oath of harmony over the body of a victim sacrificed for

the purpose. They then undertook to get back to Rome, and history records that they got left.

It has been remarked that there is now no great issue before the country, and there is a great deal of truth in the statement. Yet, if one reads the newspapers they will be found filled with columns upon columns of the opinions of different politicians, and the proceedings of their organizations. What do we want of all these politics? Is this country any better off because a corrupt Congressman or more corrupt Senator expresses his view on this nomination or that appointment? These views mean nothing else but spoils, money, knavery; there is not one grain of patriotism, honesty or common sense in a barrel of them. After the monstrous exhibition of swindling and trickery displayed in the passage of the River and Harbor Bill, it is evident that there is little or no hope for the improvement of the political condition of the country so long as parties are constituted as at present.

We want a new party. A party that has the interests of the country at heart and the confidence of the people. We have no longer any use for a gang of Republican knaves, thieves and tricksters, any more than we require Democtratic tricksters, thieves and knaves. They have shown that they both meet on the one common ground of robbery. If the worst elements of the two parties would combine and form one grand corruption party, Uncle Sam would know precisely how he stood, and would be able to get rid of the impudent loafers at very short notice. But they will not afford him the opportunity. They have his farm in their hands, and do little more than spend their time in quarreling and stealing. In these two accomplishments they have both proved themselves adepts.

Who is this frank, sturdy, handsome youth who offers his services to the much-exercised Uncle Sam, who sits on a fence-rail watching the disputes of his worthless help? It is the Independent new party, who, with his Civil Service Reform hoe and other honest equipments, is prepared to carry out the necessary work which Republicans and Democrats have so shamefully neglected in their struggle for plunder. The job will have to be given ultimately to this young man. It is too bad that it should have been for so long a time in the hands of incompetents. Bundle them off at once, Uncle Sam; kick them out, voters, when you get a chance of doing so at the ballot-boxes. Honest Democrats and honest Republicans must combine and manufacture the new party, whose principles must be a reformed tariff, a reformed civil service, no monopoly and honest government.

UNCLE SAM'S NEGLECTED FARM.

New and independent party:—Look here, Uncle Sam, isn't it about time you got rid
of those two quarrelsome fellows, and gave the job to me?

TARIFF
CIVIL SERVICE
LABOR
SILVER COINAGE
MONOPOLIES

The decades from 1870 to 1900 were turbulent years with conflicts between labor and business. Labor began seeking a collective bargaining instrument that would provide protection for the individual workingman. Mass production was causing labor to lose its class-consciousness and pride. Production line work made the old craftsmen obsolete. The need for labor organizations was imperative. As industry spread, labor spread with it, making working conditions a national problem, rather than a local one.

After the Civil War the National Labor Union was organized but failed to weather the depression of 1873. Another labor movement, the Knights of Labor, a semisecret society under the leadership of Terence Powderly, hoped to establish one union for all. The Knights of Labor battled for public ownership of cooperatives, utilities and other popular reforms. In the mideighties they won a strike against the railroads, but lost others. After a bloody and unsuccessful attempt to organize the McCormick Harvester Company in Chicago in 1886, the Knights of Labor declined. They never recovered their influence after the Chicago riots.

The American Federation of Labor, founded in 1886, followed a more conservative policy than the earlier labor unions. The AFL built a federation of separate unions, leaving untold thousands of unskilled workers unorganized. Avoiding third party politics, the federation grew to its present-day position, using collective bargaining techniques. They employed the strike only as a last resort.

Labor continued to receive tremendous opposition from industry, and business formed its own protective associations and organized political lobbies. Labor had other problems besides combating the hostility of industry; hundreds of thousands of immigrants provided an abundance of unskilled labor. At the same time thousands of freed Negroes migrated to the northern factory cities. The immigrant and Negro were difficult to organize, since they were uneducated and willingly accepted low wages, long hours and poor working conditions. Labor problems were also tied to politics and law under the jurisdiction of local and state courts. Labor unions scored victories in the eastern section of the country while losing in other sections.

The attempts of labor and various other movements to change the economic organization of our society caused more widespread discontent than at any other point in the history of our country. Protests against factory conditions spread to other areas of our industrial life, especially to the railroads that were being built across the vast expanses of the West. Organized labor struck and boycotted; legislatures passed laws and established boards of arbitration. Strikes were not a new weapon, but not until this period were they recognized as a part of the routine of industrial life. Most of the workingmen in individual trades had been organized into national unions, but not until 1881 was any permanent progress made in combining different trades and classes of workmen to support a common platform. The Crisis of 1883 and the depression that followed seriously affected the railroads. Management was forced to reduce wages and to make other economy moves that provoked employees. In 1885 the workmen for the Missouri Pacific Railroad struck for a higher wage scale and won. Overjoyed by this victory, they pushed their demands even further.

In this dispute, the Knights of Labor became involved. This organization, with apparently the most peaceful intent, was based on the principle of alliance of all classes of workmen of every trade within one big association.

Its printed declarations emphasized mutual help and cooperation; its purpose was "the organizing and directing of the power of the individual masses," in order "to make industrial and moral worth, not wealth, the true standard of individual and national greatness." (Preamble of Knights of Labor, in Ely, *Labor Movement*, 1886.) Their principle that "the injury of one is the concern of all" provides the explanation for the disturbances in which the Knights of Labor were involved in 1886. The organization had grown so rapidly that workmen who did not have the remotest knowledge of its principles were joining by the thousands. All were eager to find a means of industrial reform or to gain new concessions from their employers. Between 1885 and 1886, the membership grew from 111,000 to 730,000. Its growth was so rapid that the executive board attempted to check the initiation of new members. A lawless element comprised of rowdies and vagrants gained admission into the Knights of Labor.

The movement had now reached a crucial period: in 1886 the number of strikes had doubled from the previous year. In the opening months there were nearly five hundred labor disputes. These disputes centered on demands for wage increases and shorter hours.

Terence V. Powderly, the leader of the Knights, was regarded as an intelligent, honest, and conservative man. Powderly, however, did not have complete jurisdiction over strikes, and his influence was not strong enough to control the loosely organized assemblages scattered over the country.

These signs of weakness were evident in the Southwestern Railroad Strike. In 1885, District Assembly #101 of the Knights of Labor, which had its headquarters in St. Louis, hastily extended the number of local chapters from five to thirty. Officials of the Knights interfered with shop management of the railroads until the railway labor expenses for work became unrealistically high. In December, the Texas and Pacific Railroad went into bankruptcy, and its receivers notified the railroad workmen that the previous agreements for their labor contracts were no longer obligatory. Labor leaders claimed the receivership was unnecessary and

was merely an excuse of the company, whose real intent was destruction of the labor union. In February 1886, a mechanic at Fort Worth, Texas, who was a prominent member of the labor organization, was legitimately discharged. The shopmen went out on strike when management refused to reinstate him. The strike spread until it affected all the Jay Gould system in Texas, Kansas, Missouri and Illinois, tying up six thousand miles of railway. As the situation became more acute, trains were held up by force; violence and destruction of property spread, and in some states the militia was called out. In Illinois, the governor remained aloof and left the maintenance of law and order to untrained deputy sheriffs. On April 9, 1886, a squad of special deputy sheriffs fired upon a crowd in the railyards of East St. Louis, Illinois, killing several bystanders. The strike ran its course, after seven weeks, and finally ended in a complete failure.

This strike brought severe criticism upon the entire Order of the Knights of Labor. It was difficult to judge the merits of the original dispute, but the public was prompt to denounce labor violence. Ironically, Jay Gould was held in low esteem by the public and he lacked the qualities of sincerity and honesty of Terence Powderly. The result of the strike against Gould's Missouri Pacific Railroad showed the inability of state and local authorities to control mob violence and rioting. An investigation was made by Congress but its conclusions were of dubious value, since the congressmen were biased in favor of management. While the St. Louis strike was in progress, another was taking place by the employees on Third Avenue Street Railway in New York City. This strike was not sanctioned by the executive board of the Knights of Labor. It lasted for many months and was characterized by intense violence. Every streetcar had a police guard.

One of the most reasonable demands of labor during this period was the eight-hour day. The appointed date for this to go into effect was May 1, 1886, but many employers would not agree to it. As a result strikes erupted throughout the country. Particularly hard hit were the building trades. The most serious disorders were in Chicago; the strike of freight handlers caused interruptions in other industries and involved over sixty thousand persons. On May 3, a confrontation at the McCormick Farm Implement plant took place between strikers and the police. Several were seriously wounded. On the following day, a meeting was called in Haymarket Square to condemn the actions of the police in shooting the workmen. Addresses by several alleged anarchists became so violent that police were ordered to disperse the gathering. A bomb was hurled from the crowd and the police fired upon the crowd, wounding sixty and killing seven. (*Encyclopedia of Social Reform*).

The whole country became panic stricken by this incident. Few persons in this country had believed that the labor movement would be accompanied by mob violence. They feared that anarchism of the European type would invade the United States. The wrath of the American people was directed toward the foreigners who they thought were responsible for these outrages. Prompt action for the punishment of these anarchists was demanded. In July 1886, eight of the anarchists were arraigned. During the trial, the prosecution disclosed that the anarchists had planned to use bombs should there be a confrontation with police. Seven of the eight brought to trial received sentences of capital punishment.

A conflict in Milwaukee between a mob and the police was quickly ended by action of Governor Rusk. The militia dispersed the mob by standing firm and firing over their heads. Another strike hit Chicago in November, this time at the stockyards. It was the largest strike since the railway trouble of 1877. Twelve thousand men participated in this near-riot and again the militia was called out to restore order. President Cleveland was disturbed by the seriousness of the situation, and in April of 1886, he sent a special message to Congress. This message was the first on labor since the founding of the government. In it, he proposed the formation of a Labor Commission, composed of three persons who should be regular officials of the government. These men were appointed to settle all disputes between management and labor. Cleveland expressed a preference for a permanent commission rather than temporary

arbitrators who were chosen during the heat of a conflict. His recommendation was generally praised by all parties, bringing comment that it was a big step toward centralization. It committed the Democrats to the doctrine of federal intervention. Congress had already acknowledged the new labor claims in 1884, when it established a national Bureau of Labor for statistical inquiries. The House had created a standing committee on labor as early as December 1883. A bill was introduced in Congress designed to establish a board of arbitration for each industrial dispute as it arose, a plan less extreme than that of the president.

Neither recommendation was acted upon. President Cleveland again pursued the need for industrial peace in his message of December 1886, demanding that labor be aided by more positive and direct methods. Congress was not willing to go as far as the president suggested; but in October 1888, a law was enacted for the settlement of differences between railroads and their employees. Arbitration was subject to agreement of both sides, and settlement was to be based on investigation, for there was no governmental legislation to enforce the judgment. The measure was of little value but was considered a sign of good will, despite the fact that arbitration was not compulsory.

During 1886 and 1887, four states—Massachusetts, Iowa, Kansas and New York—passed legislation establishing boards of arbitration. However, in no case did these new boards not have compulsory power. In Massachusetts the decision of the board was obligatory for a limited time, but only when both parties applied for board action.

The Knights of Labor movement began to wane in 1886 when public sympathy was lost after the organization passed resolutions appealing for mercy for the seven condemned anarchists of the Chicago riot. Terence Powderly and his conservative element had worked hard to suppress the extremist group which had gained control within the order, and in the following year, succeeded in voiding the resolution of sympathy for the condemned anarchists.

The growing opposition to the Knights of Labor came

from the trade unions which placed emphasis upon self-government and demanded that each trade should promote its own causes. Many workmen were members of both organizations, making them subject to dual authority. The Knights organization was accused of admitting "scabs" and of aiding unfair employers in their dealings against the unions. The Knights were also accused of ordering men to work for wages below the union scale and of engaging in boycotts for which trade unions had little compassion.

A federation of ninety-five trade unions had been formed in 1881, but it gained little influence until it was reorganized in 1886 under the name of the American Federation of Labor (AFL). The serious mistakes that the Knights made in that same year (1886) gave this new organization its opportunity to thrive at the expense of its rival. The Knights had been involved in too many disorders and schemes. Later they became involved in political entanglements: in 1896 they endorsed free silver coinage; in 1898, they condemned our expansion policies; and in 1899 they called President McKinley a bitter opponent of labor.

Organized labor caused distrust and antagonism, not so much from the occasional violence which accompanied their struggles, but mostly because of their use of the boycott and sympathy strikes. Many friends of labor were gradually alienated by their methods which seemed to be forming an established policy of terrorism. Boycotts were endorsed by the National Federation of Labor against many businesses employing nonunion labor. In a single year, newspapers, breweries, cigar factories, and coffee importers were targets of this organization. The public became alarmed at such practices and would not admit the reasonableness of some strikes.

An agent who ordered strikes was called "the walking delegate." He was a new factor in American industrial life and was regarded as inconsistent with the independent concept of business which was traditional. It was considered absurd that a cigar-worker should have the power to give strike orders to a brewery worker.

One of the great and marvelous mysteries of American politics is the Friend of the Workingman. As far as we know, he has always existed—at least ever since the formation of the Republic. And it is a strange and startling fact that in all that time he has never contrived to ameliorate the condition of the workingman. In spite of his heroic struggles, that is, apparently, the one thing that he can not do. He can ameliorate his own condition; and he generally does. As a rule, you may know the friend of the workingman by his diamond stud, which is like unto a locomotive head-light for size and shine. But by his works you will never know him. Search his record as you may, you will never find that he has kept wages at a just and remunerative figure; that he has opened profitable avenues of employment; that he has done anything to bring about a better understanding between labor and capital. But you will pretty surely find that he has amassed a fortune for himself; that he is living on the fat of the land; that his associates are monopolists and money-grabbers of all sorts, and that he himself has never done an honest day's work in his life.

Mr. James G. Blaine is at present very anxious to have it understood that he is a Friend of the Working-man. Let us see exactly what sort of Friend he is to anybody except himself. When this campaign began, there where certain vague rumors in circulation, to the effect that Mr. Blaine was interested in certain enterprises in the Hocking Valley, Ohio. Now at that time the Hocking Valley was full of underpaid, overworked, desperate miners, who, later, were driven into a strike which became, in the end, a riot. Now it was not advisable that a candidate for the Presidency should be even suspected of being one of the greedy monopolists who

190

had driven these unfortunate men to the last refuge of despair. So some blainiac was found to write a letter to the Republican nominee, asking him if the rumors were true. The Republican nominee answered with promptitude and a lie, which is what he has been known to do before. He wrote: "I am not and never have been the owner of any coal lands or iron lands or lands of any character whatever in the Hocking Valley or in any part of Ohio. Nor have I at any time owned a share of stock in any coal, iron or land company in the State of Ohio."

The "Hope Furnace" and the Standard Coal and Oil Co. were two of the Hocking Valley enterprises, consolidated. On September 30th, 1884, there were printed in the *Evening Post* of New York this receipt:

"NEW YORK May 25, '82.

Received of J. Henry Brooks, Fifty thousand dollars of the First Mortgage bonds of the Standard Coal & Iron Company on account of James G. Blaine, numbered from 351 to 400 inclusive.

[Signed.]
S. B. ELKINS."

And a letter from Mr. Blaine to a business agent, which commenced:

"SENATE CHAMBER
WASHINGTON, Dec. 30th, '80.

Dear Sir—Find inclosed my draft for $25,000 in payment of my subscription to the Hope Furnace enterprise—"

and which was signed by J. G. Blaine.

The authenticity of these documents, and of various others of the same purport, is admitted by the Blaine

organs. They have made a feeble attempt to show that the transaction was a sort of complicated, extraordinary, mysterious loan; but no fantastic theories, no reckless sophistry can get around the clear testimony of Mr. Blaine on this subject. Mr. Blaine has called it, over his own signature, "my subscription to the Hope Furnace enterprise." Very often Mr. Blaine is not to be believed. His organs tell us that he is a truthful man. Let us then believe him—on this occasion only. Why? Because he would have had no object in lying.

This is the Friend of the Workingman. The owner of a hundred-and-fifty-thousand-dollar house in Washington, which he holds to-day. The owner of a fifty-thousand-dollar share in the Hocking Valley monopoly, which he shifted—for he got out of his investment at a profit—before the crash came that ruined the hapless wretches who had been lured into the enterprise because "smart Jim Blaine" was in it. In—yes, in on the ground floor, and out at the back door. And now, to-day, the only way he can find of repudiating his partnership with the men whose short-sighted avarice brought about the bloody riot in the Hocking Valley, is to represent himself as a stool-pigeon, used, with his full knowledge and consent, and to his own profit, to lure others into an enterprise which he himself crawled out of.

In Hocking Valley lies the record of Mr. Blaine's friendship for the workingman. Let Hocking Valley's starvation, riot and murder tell the tale of his affection for those who toil for their daily bread. Let his palace at Washington tell the tale of his affection for a tricky and dishonest politician, who has systematically used his public office for his private profit.

THE FALSE "FRIEND OF THE WORKINGMAN."

Hungry miner.—You call yourself our friend! You ask for our votes! Why,

you are the ally of the monopolists who starved us out in Hocking Valley, and imported cheap Italian laborers to take our place!"

Protection is a dam. It protects the pond behind it; but it doesn't protect the watercourse below. Of course, a little water percolates through, and there is a nice mill-race that carries the flood to the favored mill; but the bed of the stream below is dry and bare. That is what Protection means to this country. It protects Mr. John Roach, and monopolists of his kind. They feed the manufacturers, who bolster up the system. But the money that they dam up and distribute among themselves is the money that ought to be in the pockets of the poor devils who work for them. And it never gets there. If the underpaid workman and the underpaid clerk want to find out why the laborer cannot get the hire of which he is worthy, they would do well to send their own man to Congress, with instructions to find out what Protection is doing for them and to use his discretion in voting. And then, probably, the monopolists would buy him up.

THE PROTECTORS OF OUR INDUSTRIES.

Have we protected and nurtured this animal so long only that it may become the prey of foreign huntsmens? Look out for the hounds!

There is a crisis in the affairs of labor which no man who works for other men can look upon with indifference. However worthy the purpose of the general organization known as the Knights of Labor may be—and Mr. Powderly says the purpose is merely to reconcile and harmonize capital with labor for the amelioration of the hardships of the latter and to the advantage of both—the local organizations are led in large part by unwise and reckless men, and some recent action of theirs has robbed the general as well as the local orders of much of the public sympathy which they commanded a few weeks ago.

Labor is to a large extent the victim at this moment of its own foolishness. Undoubtedly the railroad men of the southwest system had much to complain of, but they began their fight on trivial grounds and so gave the enemy an advantage which need not have been conceded. The fight on the Third avenue road was begun because of the use of "insulting words" by employes opposed to labor unions and the refusal of the company employing them to discharge them. The tie-up of other roads capped the climax of this foolishness, and of course had to be abandoned. Every step made by these local organizations has been to the rear, and that at the very time when labor needed all the conservative wisdom it could command.

The other night Herr Most harangued a gathering of socialists, apparently under the impression that they were workers, and advised them to arm, incidentally offering to sell them guns at ten dollars apiece—which would probably net the generous soul a large profit. About the same time some workers in Greenpoint left the sugar refineries in which they were employed and immediately proceeded, to inaugurate a riot, and for days were busily employed in beating such men as dared to take their places in the deserted works. For weeks two women bakers have been boycotted by individuals who have apparently nothing better to do, and the result is that the women are making more money than ever before, public sentiment giving them money very liberally and likewise a larger trade than they have heretofore enjoyed.

Between its unwise friends and its open enemies labor is having a very hard time of it, and the worst of it is that there is small prospect of an improvement. As the days go on the feeling between labor and capital grows more bitter, and men like Mr. Powderly have partially ceased to control the organization which without their wisdom might easily become dangerous and so lose vastly more than the progress it has made. It ought to be enough for labor to do to fight the general enemy, and in order to do this effectually it must be more thoroughly disciplined and controlled than it has yet been. The monopolists are very strong, and to fight them well there must be a compact, thoroughly commanded force, at peace with itself and given to no recklessness or disorderly conduct. The labor element ought to have more friends in congress than it can possibly have as long as it acts unwisely, the better to ensure protection against foreign contract labor. Happily, the free traders remain timid, as a matter of prudence or conscience, and are likely to do nothing very dangerous at present, but there can be ample protection in due season by providing for it at the polls.

For the present look out for the hounds, ye Knights of Labor! They are in your midst as well as at your front and heels. They represent anarchy. They fly the banner of incendiarism. They threaten riot and murder. They outrage freedom of opinion with their boycotts. They provoke public sentiment with their childlishness. Take care of the enemies within your gates and you can fight free trade and monopoly with a fair assurance of final and complete success.

"AT BAY."

TARIFF
CIVIL SERVICE
LABOR
SILVER COINAGE
MONOPOLIES

In 1837 Congress provided for the free and unlimited coinage of silver on a basis of approximately sixteen to one as compared with gold, referring to the respective weights of a silver dollar and a gold dollar.

Before 1870, silver was produced only in small quantities, and its mintage was negligible. In 1873 the Coinage Act was revised, the provision for silver coinage was removed, and silver was abandoned as money. The advocates of free silver referred to the particular act of Congress as the "Crime of '73" and declared that silver was dropped because of the use of fraudulent methods. In fact, the Coinage Act had been discussed at length both in and out of Congress before being passed, and there was only a slight interest in silver at the time.

Hardly had the Coinage Act passed before many western states were producing silver from new mines, in such quantity that the price of silver began to fall rapidly. The mine owners started a movement to restore free and unlimited coinage, but the conservative elements within the political parties fought the free silver movement on the assumption that cheap silver, if coined, would upset values and eventually lead to inflation.

The leader of the free-silver force in Congress was Richard P. ("Silver Dollar Dick") Bland, a Democratic Representative from Missouri. In 1876 Bland succeeded in getting a bill for the free coinage of silver through the House, but it failed to pass the Senate. The following year, a compromise known as the Bland-Allison Bill passed both Houses, calling for the purchase of silver for coinage purposes. The treasury was to buy from two to four million dollars worth of silver per month, and Congress passed the Bland-Allison Bill over President Hayes' veto.

The infrequent discussions as to the suspension of silver purchases under the Bland Act, or for providing a freer coinage gained little attention from 1879 to 1888.

The Republican platform of 1884 ignored the issue and the Democrats had little or no particular enthusiasm for it.

Even before his inauguration, President Cleveland urged suspension of further purchase and coinage of silver, and later with persistent regularity, he repeated the warning of crisis because of the increasing burdens placed upon the gold reserve. In 1887, Cleveland allowed a bill providing for the exchange of trade dollars into standard dollars to be coined outside of the limits authorized by the Bland Act of 1878. A further devaluation of silver during his administration gave weight to his criticism against the existing policy.

From 1878 until 1884 there had been little change in the sixteen-to-one silver to gold ratio, but by 1885 depreciation had changed the ratio to nineteen-to-one, and by 1889 to twenty-two-to-one. Even then the warnings of the president had little effect, other than to anger the silver faction of the Democratic party, which denounced the cries of alarm uttered by the previous Republican administration. The opponents of the Bland-Allison Act were at a disadvantage, for the earlier warnings of disaster had not been fulfilled. Year after year the silver coinage increased in volume, while the country grew in prosperity and the gold balance was not adversely affected.

Some financial experts admitted the favorable condition while others foresaw a dim future. *The Financial Review*, a competent authority, declared in 1885 that there was no "friction or breakage in the financial machinery"; that "the year 1886 closed no less hopefully than it opened"; that "1887 was a great year of industrial activity"; that in 1888 "the financial machinery of the country worked well" with "hardly a ripple of excitement" in the money market; and that 1889 "surpassed all its predecessors in the general volume of trade movements."

Farming interests in the West and South, however, did not share this enthusiasm, for farming prices were steadily dropping during this period. This lower level of prices was attributed to an inadequate supply of money, for the volume of government legal-tender notes had been fixed at a stationary position, and since 1870 the world's gold production for each five-year period had shown a decline, and national bank circulation was steadily shrinking. The activity in industry and commerce was rapidly expanding and the Boards of Exchange by which enterprise and trade were carried on were in greater demand. Their value was enhanced and lower commodity prices were the result.

A majority of both Houses of Congress was in favor of silver, but the conviction was not yet so strong that they were willing to adopt free coinage. In the closing days of the Forty-Eighth Congress, February 26, 1885, the House refused to suspend the further purchase of silver, by a vote of 152 to 118. The Democrats were hesitant to go too far in making radical changes which might possibly cause a temporary coinage disturbance, provoke a crisis and frighten away new members of the party. In 1886 a bill for free coinage was defeated in the House by a majority of thirty-seven. The Democrats were about evenly divided, ninety-six in favor and seventy against; only thirty Republicans voted for it as compared with ninety-three against it.

Although Congress remained loyal to silver, the country did not welcome the use of silver dollars. In the East they were regarded as a nuisance and were sent back to the government vaults, and the mints were loaded with unused silver dollars. Provisions were made in 1886 for the issue of silver certificates in denominations of one, two and five dollars. While the suppression of the treasury notes of smaller denominations about the same time made room for a larger use of silver or its certificate, a more important factor in enlarging the circulation of silver was the decline in the volume of national bank notes, because of the scarcity of bonds available as a guaranty for circulation.

The plentiful revenue which the government enjoyed led to wasteful schemes of expenditure. As the president complained, "It attracts the gaze of states and individuals with a kind of fascination" (Richardson, *Messages and Papers*). The Republicans, as a whole, were in favor of liberal appropriations, because they warded off the day of tax reduction and were consistent with the general economic policy of national development. It also afforded an opportunity for establishing a system of coast defenses, building up the navy, constructing new communication lines across the country and for furnishing a merchant marine by subsidies. Millions could be spent on education. Senator Dolph said, "If we were to take our eyes off the increasing surplus in the treasury and stop bemoaning the prosperity of the country, and trying to make the people dissatisfied with an alleged burden of taxation which they do not feel, and to devote our energies to the development of the great resources which the Almighty has placed in our hands, to increasing the products of our manufacturers, of our shops, of our farms, of our mines and our forests; to cheapening transportation by the improvement of our rivers and harbors, and to restoring our foreign commerce, we would act wiser than we do." (*Congressional Record*, Fiftieth Congress, December 21, 1887).

For a period of six years, beginning in 1890, the dispute over free coinage of silver outweighed all other questions of public interest. The silver question did not seriously disturb Congress during President Cleveland's first administration, nor was silver coinage a notable political issue in the presidential campaign of 1888; the Democrats discreetly avoided all reference to the matter in their platform. The Democratic House of Representatives, in dread of endangering the success of Cleveland as a candidate for reelection, thought it wise to suppress a bill which passed the Senate in April of 1888, providing for a slight increase in the coinage of silver to make up for the decrease in national bank circulation.

The Republicans determined to make party gain out of Cleveland's strong opposition to silver coinage by favoring the use of both gold and silver as money. Silver, however, was steadily falling in value, and by 1887, the ratio of silver to gold had dropped to twenty-two-to-one. It was necessary to take quick action if this decline was to be stopped. The supporters of silver, irrespective of party, were encouraged by Harrison's selection of William Windom of Minnesota, as secretary of the treasury, for Windom was believed to favor plans for currency expansion. New importance was given to the question in September of 1889 by the support of Mr. St. John, president of a national bank in New York City, when he advocated the gradual retirement of United States notes along with an increase in silver coinage.

The administration regarded the situation to be exceedingly serious and expressed fear that a free-coinage bill might be passed. The free-coinage majority in the Senate would become larger with the admission of the new states in the Northwest, as many were in favor of silver. However, the Republicans had regained control in the House, and there was the possibility that President Harrison would be successful in checking any efforts this branch might undertake, as he was as staunch in his denunciation of silver coinage as his predecessor. However, he did not adopt a policy of determined opposition, and this new turn in the attitude toward silver took the country by surprise—doubly so when Secretary Windom, in December 1889, presented a complicated scheme for the larger use of silver for monetary purposes.

This sudden change was ill-advised, for even President Harrison, in his message to Congress, confessed that he had given Windom's plan only a hasty examination. Windom's scheme, in brief, was the issue of silver certificates against bullion at its market value. As a compromise measure, it was not acceptable to the silverites or to the supporters of a gold standard, for the silverites complained that the plan was a noxious scheme whereby silver was degraded to the position of the baser metals whose value was determined by gold, and the opposition objected because they felt it put the government in the role of a speculator in metals, and because no fixed limit was placed on the amount of silver which the treasury might be required to absorb by law. Congress lost no time in taking up the issue and many more free-coinage silver bills were added to the proposed bill submitted by Secretary Windom. So many schemes were devised to help silver without going to the extent of actual coinage that it seemed impossible for there to be agreement on any one proposal.

The Senate Bill, as finally written, made provision for the purchase and coinage of silver bullion by the treasury to the amount of $4.5 million per month at the market price, as well as of all gold bullion which might be offered. Against this metal treasury, notes were to be issued, redeemable on demand in lawful money of the United States without recognition of either metal. This plan was opposed in the House, and for some time no progress was made, until finally the Republican Senators and Representatives agreed upon a compromise bill which followed closely to the provisions of the Senate measure. It called for a monthly purchase of 4.5 million ounces of silver instead of $4.5 million worth

and gave the secretary of the treasury the responsibility in the payment of the notes in silver bullion at the market value on the day of redemption. This measure was finally agreed upon, June 7, 1890, by the House. For the extreme silverites, it was too conservative, and they renewed the struggle in the Senate—all compromises were set aside and a free-coinage measure was passed June 17 by a vote of twenty-eight Democrats and fifteen Republicans against three Democrats and twenty-one Republicans (*Congressional Record*, Fifty-First Congress). Upon a renewal of the fight in the House, the advocates of free-coinage lost by a vote of 135 to 152. After further quarreling and conference, yet another compromise was reached on July 7, 1890, with a provision made for the monthly purchase of 4.5 million ounces of silver by the treasury, and for the issue of notes based thereon, which were to be legal tender for debts, and redeemable in gold or silver at the treasurer's decision. It was also announced that it was to be "the established policy of the United States to maintain the two metals on a parity with each other upon the present legal ratio or such ratio as may be provided by law."

"Gold Republicans" were now in a dilemma, as their party was the one that had resumed the question of silver coinage. They knew that many among their group favored free and unlimited coinage by the results of the voting in both Houses, while some feared that if they should allow the silverites to have their way, and then rely upon the president to veto it, the success of the Republican tariff measure would be in peril. It had been rumored that certain western senators were withholding their assent to the extreme tariff measure then pending until they were assured that the party would support silver. Senator Platt of Connecticut complained that a veto would serve to break up the Republican party and pit the West against the East. Others were not so sure that the president would feel free to veto a free-coinage measure, for since his message to Congress in December he had remained silent. Mustering to party harmony, the doubters determined to take no chances: a bill for the remedy of silver passed both Houses by narrow party votes and became law July 14, 1890. The provisions and the wording of this measure of 1890 are credited to Sen. John Sherman, who, though he did not agree with the bill, gave the act his endorsement in fear of a worse measure, and supported it only in order to save the credit of the country. Once passed, the Republicans happily assumed full responsibility for the law. The confidence of conservative businessmen in the Republican party had again been justified, and they declared the statute a "safe silver act."

No incident in our national history up until that time demonstrated such a lack of determined statesmanship. If President Harrison, supported by senators and representatives from the East opposed to free coinage silver, had fought the silver proposals on every occasion, it would have been impossible to pass the silver coinage bill. Antisilver representatives had more than one-third of the votes in the House and could have prevented the passage of the measure even over a veto. The responsibility for the Sherman Act must therefore be placed upon President Harrison and his political advisors from the East.

Under the earlier Bland-Allison Act of 1878, the treasury had stuck to the policy of purchasing and coining silver at the lower limit of $24 million per year, which was permitted under the act. Now there was no discretion granted: 54 million ounces of silver bullion must be purchased each year, an amount equivalent to the total silver production of the United States in 1890. Against this bullion a new form of treasury notes was to be issued: the monetary circulation, already a mixture of legal tenders, gold certificates, greenbacks, national bank notes and silver certificates, as well as gold and silver coin, was still further confused by the addition of treasury notes whose terms of redemption were left loosely defined, "in coin," instead of specifically in gold or silver. Bland denounced the act as a "masterpiece of duplicity and double-dealing" (*North American Review*, September 1890).

The silver party did not give up the agitation. Farmers' organizations in the South and West adopted free coinage of silver as part of their platform of reform. The demands of these various organizations did not vary greatly: they called for the abolition of national banks, the free coinage of silver, a large issue of treasury notes, an income tax, and the public ownership of transportation companies. In order that farmers might borrow money more advantageously, they also favored a subtreasury plan, involving the issue of treasury notes to be loaned at a low interest rate upon the deposit of nonperishable goods in warehouses established under governmental direction. These expanding farmers' organizations became a controlling force in political elections; in some states more than half the legislators were pledged to the farmers. Alarmed by these evidences of the strength of the silver movement, the conservatives

prepared to make further concessions and within six months after the passage of the Sherman Bill, the Republican majority in the Senate agreed to support a measure for the purchase of an additional 12 million ounces of silver bullion during 1891; for the purchase of more if the national bank circulation dropped below $180 million; and for the free-coinage of all silver whenever the market price of silver should have remained for a year at or above the coinage rate. The free-silver segment in the Senate, however, would not yield to any limitations and carried a free-coinage clause by a vote of thirty-nine to twenty-seven on January 14, 1891. In the House the coinage committee reported against the measure but no direct vote was acquired on the bill.

During 1891, debate was minimal, for all energies were devoted to preparations for the coming presidential campaign. As soon as the Fifty-Second Congress was organized, in December 1891, bills were introduced to repeal the Silver Act, and even John Sherman acknowledged that the law had proved ineffective. However, these efforts were unsuccessful and it was impossible now to undo the damage. The free silver party nearly achieved a victory when the free-coinage measure was introduced in the House by Richard P. Bland, by then chairman of the committee on coinage, in March 1892, but the opposition resorted to filibustering to kill the measure and the bill was dropped.

The 1892 platform of each party demanded the support of the party of the values of both gold and silver. The Democrats still denounced the Sherman Bill and all the Republicans who supported the act were from the western states. A number of Democratic representatives who before had been friendly to silver now opposed the bill, justifying their opposition by the assertions of the party platform and in view of the outward oppositon of Grover Cleveland, now renominated for president.

The government, by limiting the coinage of silver, was deliberately depreciating its value, and as the treasury had already loaded itself with an enormous volume of of silver, it was concluded that wise financial policy demanded that the value be maintained by giving further opportunities for its use. The United States alone produced more than half the world's supply of silver, and so had the responsibility for working out a financial policy of its own by independent action, not feeling it necessary to wait for international agreement. As the president said "We are large producers of silver, and should not discredit it." (Harrison, in Richardson: *Messages and Papers*).

THE GREAT UNKNOWN.

As REASONS multiply why all Presidential aspirants should put out their money views in plain words, the silence of William McKinley deepens. And such reasons do multiply with bewildering rapidity. The latest big reason is furnished by the Senate of the United States,—the body which the Constitution intended to be a safeguard against hasty and unwise legislation. Not only do avowed Silverites control the Senate Finance Committee, as the result of a deal with Republican Senators, but a majority of the whole body is in favor of the fifty-cent dollar. It has shown this by passing a free-coinage measure. Yet the people have not been terrified by such treacherous assaults upon the national credit, knowing that there were two good reasons why they could not succeed. Grover Cleveland furnished them both. They knew he would eagerly veto any free-coinage measure that might reach him; and they knew when national bankruptcy threatened, because of the criminal negligence of their lesser servants in the Senate, that he would use the full power of the executive to avert it. This he has done more than once, and the people have learned to look upon him as their real safeguard.

Now the Senate, on the eve of adjournment, has struck down the only law that enabled the President to protect the national credit and the public honor during the next six months. This will increase the anxiety and impatience of the people until something definite is known of the men who will seek the Presidential chair. In response to the question, "do you stand for sound money or the 50 cent dollar?" put to him the other day, Mr. McKinley replied: "Public office is the people's honor. Public service well done is its own honor." This reply has been criticised as being no reply. We do not think, however, that the vulgar rules of logic should apply to the infrequent orations of this man, since he is clearly one favored of heaven, who can speak only in terms of omniscience unintelligible to earthlings. A Mahatma, according to them, is one who has attained the fullest wisdom and has become a perfected part of the great universal soul. Mr. McKinley is either that, or else he is something very much less impressive.

THE SILVERITE has long sought to dignify his metal by pretending that the matter of its use as money is a great principle, like representative government or individual liberty. Yet, for all his work, "free silver" is still a cause without a party; and attempts to engraft it formally upon other parties have always been warmly resented. Other parties have given it secret encouragement and help, but no party of importance has openly espoused it. This long-continued failure of its partisans to unite under one banner is the strongest proof that "free silver" is not a principle, but a mere "special interest." Being nothing more than this, no great party will ever form about it—just as no great party will ever form solely to secure a tariff on musical instruments or a bounty on sugar. Nevertheless, the Silverites are always pretending that they are just on the point of getting together to fight for and by themselves.

Each campaign year, especially, the air is full of these rumors. Having at last become convinced of the wicked treachery of both Democratic and Republican parties, these earnest souls resolve to form a party by themselves, to the standard of which all true Silverites will rally from every quarter. This year the report came to us in February. Under the leadership of Senator Stewart a sure-enough "free-silver" party was to be formed, and this party was to draw so many votes from all the other parties that it would carry the next election with great ease. Although these reports were of the most positive character they did not find much belief among the people. We expressed our own disbelief in them at the time;—adding that we did not believe the Silverites were honest men fighting for a great cause, but simply bounty-grabbers trying to have the government buy their product at twice its market value. That was four months ago.

To-day no silver party is talked of and the Silverites are back at their old trick of trying to scare the old-time parties into giving them something. Now, if all this silver agitation, especially during the past four years, has failed to stir a silver party together, is it not pretty certain that there is not enough vitality in the silver question to support a party? And if "free silver" can not stand by itself, in what particular scheme of legislation may it properly find a place?

William McKinley of Ohio is still busily saying nothing, but he has answered this question with all desirable clearness. Bright lovers learned long ago that "silence gives consent,"—and not the coyest maiden in all the lore of Love was ever more suggestively silent than the Canton statesman. The Silverite has made his proposal in plain terms, and William, blushing prettily, looks down and says no word. His modest silence might be taken to mean something else than consent, perhaps, but for this fact: that when the Sound Money man approaches him he is driven away by William's guardians, who declare with strange warmth that William shall not be made to speak his mind. This is the significant thing about it: the Sound Moneyman is dissatisfied and suspicious about this silence, while the Silverite finds in it a warm affirmative to all he proposes. Nor can it be otherwise so long as the wooed one stays coy; for just so long will his record be taken to indicate his present views—and his record is unquestionably in favor of "free silver" as against sound money.

If the Republican party declares formally for "free silver," under the leadership of Mr. McKinley, it will be a grand good thing for the business interests of the country, because it will for the first time put silver in the open, where it can be fought to a finish. Also Mr. McKinley will be doing a graceful act in compelling the Republican party to recognize its own much-abused but legitimate offspring. For the "free silver" idea is clearly a child of Republican paternalism. Its birth-marks are too plain to be mistaken. The party of Protection can not consistently refuse to show to the silver-miners of the West the same consideration it would show to the wool-growers of the East and the cotton-growers of the South. It is quite as just and logical to pay a bounty on silver as to pay a bounty on sugar. "Free silver," then, belongs by right in the Republican platform, and Mr. McKinley will make a great record for consistency if he succeeds in putting it there.

Of course, the chances are that he will not succeed. At best, he will have to submit to a straddling version of his silver faith by his party's platform; and, of course, it may be wholly repudiated and a declaration for gold put in its place. But a President is more than a platform, and if Mr. McKinley is elected, on whatsoever platform, he may be relied upon, if his record means anything, to complete the ceremony of installing "free silver" in its rightful place. That place is on the list of articles entitled to the fostering care of Republican legislation. And so the voters of the country may assume that the principal candidate of the Republican party to-day stands for "free silver." His past record and his present silence both say it. Under this condition all Silverites will naturally flock to his support; while the voters in favor of sound money will be drawn to his opponent—providing that opponent is sound himself. Here is a chance for Democratic leaders to do a little thinking, along with the business men of the country.

THE SKELETON AT THE FEAST.

Sundry Republican newspapers are constantly apprising the country that it is in a fair way to be ruined by the machinations of President Cleveland and his Secretary of the Treasury. They affect to regard the present financial complication as the natural result of a sinful Democratic policy. The ability of a Republican editor to ignore something much plainer than his nose is almost superhuman. Here we are struggling under a Republican law which demands that we pay out our gold for silver, in the face of the financial law which requires us to keep our gold; and these papers gravely warn us to watch the President closely, because he is likely to do something wicked with our credit. They also foster the impression that Secretary Carlyle, by some occult process, can enable us to go on defying the laws of finance with impunity. We have the assurance of President Cleveland that "The purpose of the Government to preserve its own credit unimpaired, and to maintain the parity of the two metals by all lawful means, will not be abandoned under any circumstances." We must be content with this until the Sherman law is repealed. Secretary Carlyle's measures to tide over the intervening period have shown a genuine regard for the welfare of the people. He has acted less like a banker than like a man of good common sense who seeks his end by unconventional but practical means. An issue of bonds or any other measure to replenish our gold reserve would not make the repeal of the Sherman law one whit less imperative. Despite the straits we are in, it is best that this law continue in force until the silver idol is shattered beyond the possibility of repair by Republican cement. In the meantime, any fear about the safety of the public credit should be allayed by the reflection that the present administration, if it tried, could not commit an act of greater folly than that from which we are now suffering.

THE POLITICAL SAFE-BREAKERS FOILED.

TARIFF
CIVIL SERVICE
LABOR
SILVER COINAGE
MONOPOLIES

After the Depression of 1873, corporations began to replace individual or partnership businesses. American genius and enterprise displayed itself in endless activity and invention. It shared commercial organization and the rapid development of the establishment of large transportation systems. Large industrial establishments began to grow. In many instances a small number of factories and mills increased production. In 1880 there were about two thousand mills producing wool; but ten years later the number of woolen mills was reduced to thirteen hundred. The number of iron and steel mills was also decreased but the production yield was nearly one-half greater. Farm implement manufacturing plants in 1880 numbered around nineteen hundred; they were reduced to less than nine hundred in 1890, although the capital outlay had more than doubled. In the leather industry, three-fourths of the factories disappeared in a ten-year period, but the volume of leather products increased fivefold. Large-scale production was the by-word; specialization of tools, machinery and labor added a new dimension to industry. The large-scale production of big companies led to reckless and intense competition, resulting in overproduction and waste.

In order to correct these newly created industrial problems, efforts were made to establish mutual agreements between rival companies, both as to production and price. The ideal solution was the establishment of one overall management for each branch of business. If this could not be attained, the common goal was for a few large corporations to work in harmony. This principle was first carried out in transportation, when many small lines were consolidated into a few huge systems. Later, other industries followed the same methods. The change was most noticeable in the manufacture of bulk commodities of a standard uniform quality. Freight charges constituted a large expense to the product and the ultimate cost was foisted onto the consumer. Favorable shipping contracts with the railroads gave a decided advantage to many large manufacturers and proved to be an important factor in advancing consolidation.

This principle of strength through consolidation was evident when the railroads acquired and gained complete control of the anthracite coal mines in Pennsylvania. By 1888, seven coal-carrying railroads were owners and controllers of nearly all of the anthracite coal in the United States.

Another example of the trend toward industrial consolidation was the Standard Oil Company. Prior to 1879, a small group of men were stockholders in various companies of the oil industry, scattered in many cities throughout the country. This mutual ownership of stock made it possible to secure policy arrangements between the owners of these respective companies. This bond was not strong enough, and a new method of organization was adopted in 1882. For easier control of management, the Standard Oil Trust was formed. All the stock of the many companies was assigned to the guardianship of trustees, who issued certificates showing the amount of each owner's investment in stock held in this trust. The complete operation was then managed by nine trustees, the chief being John D. Rockefeller of Cleveland, Ohio. In this scheme of centralized control, new legal procedures had to be devised to avoid unfavorable publicity.

Other industrialists faced the same problem. Eagerly they followed the example of Standard Oil Trust. The American Cottonseed Oil Trust in 1884 and the National Linseed Oil Trust of 1885 were striking examples of this type of management. The movement spread so quietly that the public was hardly aware of the significance of these newly formed corporations. In 1887 these new arrangements spread to the sugar, lead and whisky industries. A curb was put on the movement during 1888, owing to the uncertainty of the elections, but in 1889 it was again revived with vigor and rapidly brought manufacturing of other products under this centralized control. In addition to these newly created arrangements for centralized management, there was an effort to establish secret agreements or contracts between separate corporations. Many companies legally incorporated in accordance with state charters. The public showed little concern over the rise of trusts.

The first trusts did not create a favorable public impression, however. The Standard Oil Company, the first trust, had a corrupt record. Its corrupt practices had been attacked for ten years in the states of Ohio, Pennsylvania, and New York. It was charged with building its huge monopoly by fraudulent methods and by entering into secret unwritten agreements. The charges against Standard Oil included securing illegal and discriminating rates and rebates from the railroads, obtaining protection money from independent producers, spying on business rivals, threatening to ruin competitors, and corrupting legislative bodies. These charges, of course, were difficult to prove, for evidence was difficult to locate. Standard Oil claimed ignorance of the operations of its thirty-nine subsidiary organizations. The subsidiaries, in turn, claimed ignorance of the actions of the nine trustees who controlled Standard Oil from the New York offices. Standard's officials, when summoned for questioning in court or legislative committees, evasively answered charges put before them. Standard's failure to open its books for public inspection resulted in public resentment.

Standard Oil received unfavorable publicity from the election of Henry B. Payne, senator from Ohio. In 1886, the Ohio Senate investigated charges of bribery in connection with Payne's election, in which Standard Oil was implicated. The Senate Committee on Elections refused to make the investigation. Senator Payne remained silent and many people believed him guilty. It was rumored that the Standard Oil Company had taken over the Senate. Furthermore, the presence of Secretary Whitney in the cabinet gave the trust an added advantage. Senator Frye implied that the Standard Oil Company was the greatest monopoly in the United States: "A power which makes itself felt in every inch of territory in this whole republic, a power which controls business, railroads, men and things, shall also control here?" (*Congressional Record*, July 22, 1886). Whitney and

Payne later denied being influenced or bribed by Standard Oil. However, suspicion still lingered.

The trend toward monopolies had great economic significance but was barely understood at the time. The public saw the monopolies as trade conspiracies, as hydra-headed monsters, constrictors, giant robbers and destructive tyrants. Under their "iron heel" the individual was trampled to death. (Richardson, *Messages and Papers*, 1886).

The goal of the trusts was economy of administration and reduction of manufacturing cost, thus enabling them to keep the price of commodities at a low level with reasonable profit. Theoretically, quality was improved and the cost reduced. The public correctly believed that the trusts were responsible for the raise in prices of commodities.

Trusts attracted the speculative promoter, who had found an easy method for deceiving purchasers of securities. Many employees were discharged from their jobs as trusts reduced expenses by consolidation. After the formation of the Sugar Trust in 1887, a number of refineries were closed or dismantled. This caused elimination of jobbers and salesmen. These factors added to public reaction against trusts. There was no clear distinction made between large-scale production and monopolistic procedures, because the two were so closely intertwined.

The tariff question became confused with the trust issue. Democrats argued that in reality the tariff was a super trust. The Republicans did not accept the Democrats' interpretation. They argued that those industries which prospered under tariff protection could do equally well without it.

Proponents and opponents of the trust did not hesitate to vocalize their opinions. Opponents charged that the trust was an alien economic structure, that it was a European invention. They accused trusts of dealing in foreign goods to the detriment of American industry. Many persons believed that the phenomenal growth of the trusts would not last long; that it was impossible to defy the law of competition which governs our economic structure. Proponents of the trust contended that it stimulated economic growth. Every factory bought by a trust was likely to create another one. James G. Blaine of Maine declared that trusts were largely a private affair with which neither the president nor any private citizen had any particular right to interfere. (Blaine's Portland speech, August 15, 1888). Thomas B. Reed, Republican leader in the House spoke in favor of monopolies. "I have listened," he said, "to more idiotic raving, more pestiferous rant on that subject than on all the others put together." He declared that there were no monopolies in the country, and there never could be; "There is no power on earth that can raise the price of any necessity of life above a just price and keep it there." (*Congressional Record*, 1888).

The Republican party added its voice to the antitrust outcry and occasionally sponsored legislation designed to protect the consumer against excessive prices exacted by monopolies. President Harrison in his message of December 1889 gave warning that trusts in the nature of conspiracies should be made prohibitory and even penal legislation (Richardson, *Messages and Papers*, 1888). In 1888, an investigation of trusts was performed by the Senate Committee of New York and by the national House of Representatives, but in neither case were the results useful. Meaningless laws regulating trusts were passed, but these laws lacked enforcement mechanisms. These laws made it a criminal conspiracy for two or more persons to agree to limit the price or production of any article. In actual practice it was difficult to prevent such agreements or to obtain proof of their existence. Trusts therefore continued to enjoy the laissez-faire position of the government.

In Congress, more serious constitutional difficulties thwarted governmental interference. The federal government had no control over corporations created by state charter. After two years of debate, Congress passed the Sherman Antitrust Act. (Senator John Sherman of Ohio actually had little to do with the preparation of this bill. See George Frisbie Hoar, *Autobiography*). Under terms of this act, there could be no combination of business which restrained trade and commerce between the states. Persons who acted in restraint of trade were subject to a fine of up to $1,000 and up to one year in jail.

The courts, both state and national, found it difficult to deal with the trust litigation. It was plain that this new form of management tended toward monopoly and malpractice. The spirit of the age demanded freedom of contract. The courts held that agreements to raise prices were invalid. However, clever attorneys for the trusts found legal loopholes and many trusts escaped restraint.

At one time it was hoped that a solution had been found by insisting upon corporate reliability. In 1890 the highest court in New York decided that the North River Refining Company had violated its charter by illegally surrendering the responsibilities of management into the hands of the Board of Trustees. The transfer of the stock of the Standard Oil Company by the shareholders to the trust was also condemned by the court.

In Illinois, the state court held in 1889 that the Chicago Gas Trust Company, a charter corporation, by buying the controlling shares of stock of all the gas companies in the city had created a monopoly. Furthermore, its action was illegal, since the power to buy stock was not granted in its charter.

These decisions did not stop the movement of trusts, for a new form of conglomeration was created: the holding company. Even before the Federal Antitrust Act of 1890 was passed, the American Cotton Oil Trust, the Distillers and Cattle Feeders Trust, and the Sugar Trust had transformed from combines under a trusteeship into separate corporations with responsible men as directors. The Standard Oil Trust was terminated, but a common and centralized policy was continued through the authoritative control of the separate principal corporations by the same board of management. However, holding companies did not always have legal immunity from prosecution.

One problem in dealing with trusts, monopolies, and holding companies was lack of uniform state legislation. What Illinois would not permit, New Jersey, West Virginia or Delaware would protect. States had to allow the corporations to participate in interstate commerce. Nor could a state stop the purchase of securities of local corporations by corporations residing in any other state. It was therefore difficult to locate the origin of monopoly or to apply an effective cure. In 1892, the chancellor of New Jersey ruled against the Anthracite Coal Railway Corporation on the basis that leases made by the railroad were illegal. As far as the price of coal was concerned, the decision was of no significance. Out of eight opinions handed down by the federal Court during President Harrison's administration, under the Antitrust Law, seven of them were unfavorable to the government. In 1895, the Supreme Court of the United States decided that manufacturing and production were not related to interstate commerce and that an attempt to monopolize manufacture was not necessarily an attempt to monopolize commerce. "Only when the natural and direct effect of an agreement is to restrain interstate commerce can the Antitrust Act be invoked" (Addyston Pipe and Steel Co. vs U. S., opinion rendered in 1899).

The penalties imposed for violation of the Sherman Antitrust Act were inadequate: corporations were not frightened by the fines mentioned. Congress could not regulate some monopolies, since they could not be brought under the interstate commerce provisions of the existing legislation.

Public grievances against the railroads covered a wide range and there was an increasing hostility toward organized capital. The economic power of the railroads was staggering. For example, the actual earnings of a single railroad company were greater than the revenue of a state, and the salary of an official was many times larger than that of a judge or governor. Public opinion clung to the idea that the federal government should regulate railway rates.

Another method was employed by business: the pool. Great rail systems such as the Texas and Pacific, Union Pacific, Northern Pacific and the Atchison, Topeka and Santa Fe entered into pools. A considerable amount of cotton in the South was shipped under this arrangement; and in the North and East, there were two great pools which controlled the transportation. Such agreements increased the cost of shipping to such an extent that the farmer suffered greatly.

To the grain grower, the railroad (or its agent, the elevator company) appeared to be the chief price fixer. The farmer did not understand the concept of supply and demand. Nor could the Western farmer be convinced that the railroads were engaged in an unprofitable business even if the rates of dividends were low.

In many parts of the country, subscriptions for railroad construction were easily obtained. Later, it was found that the securities were rendered worthless by a blanket of preferred mortgage bonds issued to complete or equip the new rail line. It was believed that the subscription money was usually turned over to construction companies in alliance with railroad promoters. By some trick of finance, the builders became rich.

Another problem was discrimination in the form of preferential treatment for some favored shippers. There was both personal favoritism and local discrimination. For example, rates on bulky products for long-distance hauling were reduced and the efficiency on cross-country hauls was greatly improved. The average annual freight rate for hauling wheat from Chicago to New York by rail was lowered from forty-two cents per bushel in 1868 to fourteen cents in 1890. Local rates were not cut in a corresponding degree, making gross discriminations against the short haul shipper. Farmers and manufacturers who did not live at competing terminal points complained that they had to suffer losses from higher freight rates. The railroads declared these claims were exaggerated and avowed that the low rates on grain

and other products which entered the Eastern markets reduced the cost of living. If there were evils, the railroad management was sure they could be corrected by competition. Under the law of supply and demand, the freight rates had shown a steady decrease. Management considered anything that reduced the forces of competition to be detrimental and discriminatory. They also fought special legislation directed against them, arguing that existing laws were sufficient.

Huge amounts of capital were diverted into railway securities. Many companies were organized on grossly inflated bases. The eastern promoter and builder turned to the speculative investor, rather than to the shipper, for his immediate profit. The stock exchange gave greater opportunities for making money than did railroad management. The corporation laws of the states placed no restriction upon reckless financiering.

Stockholders had little if any control over boards of directors. The West Shore Railroad was built in 1882 in New York State for the sole purpose of "holding up" the New York Central Road. Railroads established on the weakest of bases sought business at any price. Local rail agents entered into all sorts of schemes to attract business. These schemes were unchecked by higher management, causing a most chaotic situation. Pooling arrangements to maintain or divide traffic were broken. Many railroad officials had to admit that the transportation business had developed so rapidly that it was beyond their capacity to manage the affairs. Some even welcomed government regulations, believing that all other devices had failed.

Attempts to secure regulation by Congress were sought. Two bills were introduced in Congress. One, supported by the conservative group of the Senate, provided for the establishment of a commission to collect information, hear complaints, and exert a general advisory power. The other, a more radical bill introduced earlier, was favored in the House. It laid down fixed rules for the regulation of railway charges; declared what common carriers could and could not do; and made them liable for damage suits brought by persons injured through their actions. (McPherson's *Handbook of Politics*, 1886). It was objected that a commission would be powerless to correct these injustices because railway corporations would influence the appointments of commissions, just as they had bribed state legislatures, corrupted courts of justice, and influenced governors of states. There was also difference of opinion on the part of the supporters of regulation as to whether pools should be permitted. Some disapproved of them, not on any logical ground, but because "the mere fact that the railroads wanted pools was sufficient reason for prohibiting them." (*Quarterly Journal of Economics*, January 1890). Others feared that if discriminations in rates were forbidden there would be an agreement to raise rates.

During several sessions of Congress, no compromise could be obtained by the supporters of either of the rival bills. In 1885, the House passed one bill and the Senate the other. In 1887, an interstate commerce law was enacted in both Houses. This act provided against discriminations, prohibited the pooling of traffic, made it illegal to charge more for a short haul than for a long haul over the same line, and required the railroads to file their rates publicly. It provided for a commission of five members, none of whom could be selected from the ranks of railroad men or could own any railroad securities. The commission was given power to investigate, order violators to refrain from their illegal deeds, provide a uniform system in railway accounting, and obtain from each road an annual report of its operations and finances. During the first years of the commission's existence it remained conservative. At the end of the first year it was admitted that the act had cured several abuses.

However, the cure proved to be merely an illusion. Rebates and special concessions continued to be secretly agreed upon. Gentlemen's agreements and traffic associations took the place of pools. The powers of the commission were in dispute and often rendered worthless by the court decisions. The railroads would not remain at peace with one another. Many, forgetting the cutthroat competition which existed before 1887, believed the division of business by pooling was responsible for the constant warfare. Instead of being a panacea, the Antipooling Clause actually accentuated some abuses by placing railroad lines at the mercy of the most reckless companies.

In 1888 the strife, bitterness, competition and rivalry of rail lines in the West knew no bounds. By 1890, the practices of giving cut rates to favored shippers was completely unrestricted. Special privileges of yardage, loading, and cartage were granted. Freight was underbilled or carried under a wrong classification, and secret notification of an intended reduction of rates was made to favored shippers. The ingenuity of rail officials in breaking the law knew no limit and was a discouraging commentary on the dishonesty which penetrated the center of business enterprise.

Many of the railroads were anxious to stop the ugly practices, since investors demanded reforms. Personal agreements were made by railroad presidents to secure harmony and uniformity of rates. In January of 1889, an Interstate Railway Association was organized under the guidance of John Pierpont Morgan, a banker, for the purpose of preventing rate-cutting on Western and Southern railroads. Most of these efforts failed. The personal agreements were pushed aside and rate wars followed in rapid order.

Gradually, the commission expanded its activities and legal jurisdiction. It not only endeavored to correct existing discrimination but in some cases fixed actual rates to be charged. In 1887, the commission was accused of misinterpreting the original intent of the legislation and of trying to supervise the railroads. The influence of a federal board in exerting advisory powers had been underestimated in some ways. However, the commission labored under several handicaps. It was understaffed and unable to investigate all complaints. The commission was also overloaded with administrative work; during the first two years, 270,000 railway rates were filed.

In 1889, the commission ordered that rates on imported products should be the same as on other goods. The Supreme Court overturned this ruling by declaring that foreign competition constituted a dissimilar circumstance, and this should be taken into account. The Court blocked all efforts of the commission to fix rates and advised it to confine its activities to investigation of violations of the long and short haul clause and to the prevention of discriminations. Such decisions, handed down from the Court, rendered the commission a useless body. Not until 1897 was it possible to secure a decision from the Supreme Court, and then the decision was based on a provision of the Antitrust Law of 1890, rather than on the Interstate Commerce Act.

Is it not beautiful to see how many totally different disinterested friendships the good Mr. Blaine is capable of? The down-trodden Irish are the dearest friends of his bosom; the colored man is not only his brother but his uncle and his aunt and his pretty cousin; his soul yearns to be at peace with the hardy Briton and all other foreigners; he respects the rights of capital to such an extent that every monopolist in the country is his devoted ally, and if he has one single preference for any human being in this beautiful world, it is for the workingman. Great Scott! how he loves the workingman! How he wallows in affection for him! And what a deep-seated distrust he has of that cruel Governor Cleveland who vetoed the bill permitting the laboring classes to ride at five cents a head on the Elevated Railroad, between the hours of nine and five—when, it is well known, the laboring classes always take their pleasure! We really believe there is nothing—nothing until next November—that Mr. Blaine would not do for the workingman.

And yet we scarcely believe that Mr. Blaine understands the workingman. It strikes us that, not to put too fine a point upon it, he takes the workingman for a fool. He and his followers raise the howl of "Protection to Labor—Down with Monopoly!" and they all seem to think that they have only to howl loud enough to make the workingman believe that they mean it. It is our opinion—and we claim to know a little more of what real work and real workingmen are than can a lobbyist like Mr. Blaine or a stock-gambler like Jay Gould, or a tuft-hunter like Mr. Field—it is our opinion that the workingman is likely to know his natural enemies when he sees them. And he has only to open his eyes to see what manner of men are Mr. Blaine and his supporters.

"STOP THIEF!"

Level-Headed Workingman.—"Too thin! That trick is very stale. I guess we know a monopolist when we see him!"

For instance, it is doubtful if Mr. Monopolist Gould could get along at all without the advice and sympathy of ex-Senator Conkling, who, perhaps, knows more about the power of the political machine in proper hands than any man in the country. Where would Mr. Shipbuilder Roach be , if he were not in perfect accord with the celebrated naval economist, Mr. Robeson? Like a ship without a rudder would be the great Mr. Vanderbilt, were it not for the wise counsel given him by Mr. Depew, who tells him how to manage New York Central, Lake Shore and other little investments.

Mr. Russell Sage is not as conspicuous a monopolist as some of the tribe, but he holds his own very well with his put-and-call specialty. Mr. Jones is on very good terms with Mr. "Beauty" Hoar, and Mr. Corbin propitiates a powerful favorite who attempts to hide her identity. Of course Senator Miller and the Standard Oil Monopoly are inseparable, while Mr. Cyrus W. Field makes himself solid with Senator Cameron. Thus are all these people striving to be happy, while a clamoring crowd outside the grounds, and cut off from the festivities, fill the air with groans.

Oh, yes, the monopolists are having a very nice time at this garden party, or *fête champéire*, thinking only of their own interests and utterly regardless of what is going on among the great body of the people who are not monopolists. There was a well-known historical character, who behaved very much in the same way as these gentlemen are behaving, and his successor suffered for it by losing his head, and there was a general break-up of the Government. The man who lost his head in the French Revolution was Louis the Sixteenth—the sensual, reckless, degraded fellow who pursued the policy of our monopolists, was Louis the Fifteenth, of France. The orgies of the *Parc aux Cerfs* and his gross immoralities were not worse in their way than the methods pursued by our monopolists in securing special legislation to protect their ill-gotten gains.

THE GARDEN PARTY OF THE MONOPOLISTS—LOUIS XV. STYLE.

RICH MEN, in spite of what the socialists and anarchists would have us believe, are, under proper social and political conditions, rather a blessing than a curse to the community. They are the financial mainstay of the government in time of war; in peace they encourage the arts and the higher handicrafts, and they keep money in circulation in a way that is especially convenient to many trades and professions. A man who has a five-hundred-thousand-dollar house built does not, perhaps, give employment to so many men as would be employed by five hundred different builders of one-thousand-dollar houses; but he stimulates all the building, house-fitting and decorating trades by giving them larger profits, and by putting his money in more quickly, and in larger sums. Thus, indirectly, he may benefit more men, and the benefit is lasting. And there are a good many other ways in which a rich man is peculiarly useful to the community. He has been found to be a handy thing to have around, on more than one occasion.

Even when he goes a-fishing, he is not utterly useless. For instance, in this very state, he has done more to preserve the Adirondack Forests, and to keep up the average of the rainfall, than any other citizen. Of course, he has no higher motive than to preserve the forests for his own fishing; but certainly that is not a bad motive. There is no harm in fishing—no sin in even a rich man's fishing. But while we are willing to maintain this proposition, which may appear somewhat bold in an age which takes the Socialist uncommonly seriously, we must admit that in its practical application it is subject to a question of conditions. A man may be wrongfully rich, and may go fishing in an iniquitous manner. These are facts which we must not lose sight of, however anxious we may be to assert as an abstract principle the right of the human being to accumulate double-eagles and cast flies for trout.

The great dam disaster at Johnstown points the moral attached to one of these facts with painful force and directness. The rich men—we call them rich for purposes of argument; as a matter of fact, it seems they were rich only in the sense of being able to spend jointly a few thousand dollars for their annual pleasures—the rich men who built and maintained the dam got their fishing at the cost of other men's safety. Perhaps they can not be held legally responsible for the damage they have caused. Certainly, as we said last week, every citizen of the Conemaugh Valley should have felt it his individual duty to fight tooth and nail against their monstrous invasion of the public right to the safe enjoyment of life and property. But wherever the real burden of responsibility may lie in this sad affair, every man of that fishing-club must feel that he is not guiltless—that his right to make the most of his money, and to catch fish for his own pleasure carried with it no right to endanger the lives and fortunes of his neighbors.

The reader may remark that this is a self-evident truth. It is evident now; but it was not evident a month ago, and it was not evident in all the years that it has been open to discussion. It took the bursting of the dam to make it evident—even to the intelligent, practical, educated men who had built up great and flourishing towns right under the leaking wall of that lake of death. Let us not despise the humble logic of common-sense. It may be tedious; but it is useful. We are willing to accept one proposition as proved, in this instance. May we not save ourselves from another costly demonstration by applying the same proposition in other instances, and by reasoning out kindred propositions by simple analogy?

Is it safe for a nation to dam up its total industrial product by law, shutting out the buyers of all the rest of the world? Is it safe for a nation to sacrifice its whole carrying trade, to prohibit its citizens from buying ships and then to put a prohibitive tax on ship-building materials, so that they can not build for themselves? Is it safe to suspend the wholesome laws of free competition and to encourage monopolies and combinations to fix and raise prices? Is it safe to allow a few men to grow rich by these means, when the increase in their wealth must come directly out of the pockets of all their fellow-citizens? If these things are safe, then it is safe to let fishing clubs build mud dams where and in whatever manner they please—and those who protest are idle theorists and alarmists.

217

Uncle Sam is rich enough to give us all a farm, of course. But he is neither strong enough nor foolish enough to allow monopolists to import pauper labor to compete with laborers who come here of their own accord to cast their fortunes with him. Capital combines to control the price of labor. Then Labor combines to counteract cutting down and protect its interests. So far, honors are easy and all is fair.

But when Capital sends abroad and buys muscle at its own price to uproot American labor, it is time to cry, Halt! The trouble in the Pennsylvania and Ohio coal mines and in the Cleveland Iron Mills, grew out of this industrial procuration to debauch American labor.

There is no "Know-nothingism" in this, either. Any European who has the industry and saving-virtue to accumulate money enough to bring him to America and the courage and enterprise to pull up and strike for a new home here, is welcome. He will make a good citizen. Assisted emigrants are an enemy to American labor, native and naturalized, and a peril to the country.

And the capitalist who assists or profits by such an importation is a more dangerous and unprincipled enemy of public peace than the importer of infected rags and small-pox patients.

THE TWO PHILANTHROPISTS.

"Don't fret, Uncle Sam, we only want to make a bigger man of you!"

The consolidation of the telegraph companies is an accomplished fact, in spite of efforts at injunctions and other abortive attempts to stop the consummation of the business in the legislature at Albany. As we prophesied, nothing could be done, and Mr. Jay Gould is master of the situation. How could it be otherwise? Was it to be supposed for a moment that Mr. Jay Gould would enter into such a gigantic transaction without laying his plans accordingly? Mr. Gould had carefully anticipated everything that could possibly be said or done against him, and all the attacks that have been made fall like split peas against an ironclad. Mr. Gould is not the kind of man to leave such things to chance. He knew perfectly well that the scheme which has successfully carried out would not be popular with everybody, and he has consequently met all the troubles half way, and can let all newspaper abuse and the protests of the Chambers of Commerce pass by him as the idle wind which he regards not. It was well that Mr. Vanderbilt was so ready to lend him a helping hand.

THE WALL STREET HELL-GATE.

Measures ought to be taken at once to blow up this obstruction to legitimate trade.

The most painful feature of the recent failures in Wall Street is the heavy loss that General Grant has experienced. It is impossible not to feel sympathy for him. Of course, when he risked his fortune among the rocks and shoals of the Street, he could scarcely expect to fare better than others of his fellows who pursue the same hazardous calling. But still, however, it has not been shown that General Grant had any knowledge of the queer and reckless kind of business that his sons and their very original partner, Mr. Ward, were carrying on. We do not think that General Grant ever aspired to the position of an enormous capitalist. He probably desired to increase his means, as most men do; but certainly he would not countenance such knavery as the firm of Grant & Ward seem to have practised. We don't want General Grant in politics, but we don't want him to be beggared through no real fault of his own.

WE ARE not sure that our Republican friends care to discuss the tariff question. They seem to be more deeply interested in private matters of their own, in which outsiders can hardly take an intelligent interest. It is not for us to say whether the Republican party belongs wholly to Mr. James G. Blaine or whether it owes any duty to Mr. Benjamin Harrison, as its regular nominee. This delicate question of party etiquette we must leave for the party to settle; and if Republicans have no time for other questions, far be it from us to obtrude unwelcome topics upon their consideration. So perhaps it is not a bad time for people whose interests lie in other directions to talk among themselves of the things that concern them. While the Republican party is determining the ownership of its own house, let us who hold the good of the nation more than the good of any one man or any one set of men—let us try to find out who owns this country; whether it is the property of one class or of all its citizens.

Still, whether the politician knows it or knows it not, this class exists, and rules the country on the final arbitrament. It does not always appear in its strength; it is not readily roused to action; it is conservative and deliberate; it represents the solid judgement of the people. It was this class that decided, when the issue was once fairly presented, that the Union should be preserved—and the mere politicians had nothing to say about it. It is this class which will, sooner or later, decide whether the financial system of this country shall be arranged to make millionaires of a few men who are willing to "fry out fat" for the politicians, or whether it shall be made to meet the needs of the majority. It is to this class that we appeal, leaving the "fat"-seeking office-mongers to their private squabbles.

To men of this class we say, in plain English: You are paying an unnecessary price for all the necessaries of life, for no other reason than that it profits certain men who support and sustain certain of the legislators who are supposed to represent you at Washington. These men could earn a good living as well as you can, without government protection. With a protection that is accorded to them only, they make much more than a good living. By the grace of the government, a tax is levied upon the whole country for their special benefit—a tax that is to-day far in excess of any possible need of theirs. The day has long gone by when this tax was necessary to put them on an equality with the other manufacturers of the world. To-day its reduction to a reasonable figure will deprive them of nothing but unreasonable, extortionate and illegitimate profits; and will restore to you, the tax-payer, a sum that you can ill afford to pay and that they can well afford to lose.

In thus addressing the great class of which we speak, we do not forget that it is a class of all classes. It includes the doctor and the lawyer, the mechanic and the farmer, the day-laborer and the clerk, the merchant and the shop-keeper. Every one of these men is this day paying more than is necessary or right for the common things of life, by way of tribute to a favored class that makes no adequate return to the nation for the nation's protection. In the weeks to come we mean to show to the unprotected voters of this country exactly how great a burden the present tariff lays upon their shoulders; and we think they will find our showing more worthy of their consideration than the dissension in the Republican party over the relative importance of Messrs. James G. Blaine and Benjamin Harrison.

PROTECTION FOR CAPITAL ONLY.

The protective policeman won't see the robbery over the way. . . . it's off his beat.

The
Pen,
Not
The
Sword

SPANISH AMERICAN WAR
FOREIGN RELATIONS

A half-century of Spanish misrule and broken promises of reform culminated in the Cuban revolution of 1895. The revolt began when José Marti landed on the eastern coast. The revolt swept westward, soon enveloping the entire island. The patriots proclaimed a republic, and Tomas Estrada Palma became provisional president. Rebel generals, such as Maximo Gomez, Antonio Maceo, and Calixto Garcia employed guerilla warfare tactics against the two hundred thousand troops sent from Spain to quell the revolt. They cut off a Spanish detachment here and there, then vanished into the jungle. The insurgents were never maneuvered into a pitched battle as they were militarily inferior to the better armed and trained Spanish soldiers in the field. In time, the war developed into a system of terrorism; the insurgents destroyed crops, burned sugar refineries, tore up railroad tracks, and exacted forced loans from merchants and bankers.

Under Governor-general Martinez Campos, the Spaniards conducted the war in accordance with European tactics. When these methods failed, Campos was recalled. His successor was General Valeriano Weyler, whose brutal policy was to starve the people into submission. Weyler built barriers of wire entanglements across the island to prevent the rebels from crossing from one place to another. Hopefully, the rebels would be driven into restricted areas where they would be captured or killed. Militarily the strategy was sound, if the plan could be sustained. In Spanish-held areas, suspected rebel sympathizers and their families were herded into concentration camps. Throughout the island, lack of food and poor sanitation caused disease and starvation, and the mortality rate among these unfortunate people was appalling. Though the United States government maintained a policy of neutrality, public opinion solidly supported the insurgents. Despite neutrality laws, Cubans in the United States and American sympathizers frequently managed to send war material and arms to the insurgents. A considerable number of American soldiers of fortune made their way to Cuba.

By early 1896, American public opinion against the war became so intense that both Houses of Congress passed a joint resolution favoring the recognition of Cuba's hostile rights. Secretary of State Richard Olney offered to mediate, but Spain turned down the offer. President Cleveland, who refused to be bound by congressional resolutions, asserted that the time was not propitious for the recognition of hostilities, much less for independence. The president did manage to secure the release of some captured Americans and accepted a congressional appropriation for food for the starving insurgents. In 1897, Secretary of State John Sherman requested abolition of Weyler's concentration camps. On August 4, Madrid sidestepped the issue by replying that the situation was not as serious as it was pictured.

When Gen. Stewart L. Woodford succeeded Hannis Taylor, the American minister in Madrid, on September 13, 1897, he once more expressed the wishes of the United States for ending the war and announced that American patience was growing thin. Within a few days the ministry of Spain resigned and a new one was formed under the leadership of Señor Sagasta. General Weyler was soon replaced and Cuba was granted self-government. On December 6, 1897, President McKinley expressed his desire to give the new policy a fair test.

Self-government pleased neither the Cuban loyalists nor the insurgents. The loyalists rioted in Havana on January 13, 1898. Frightened by loyalist denunciation of Americans, Consul-General Fitzhugh Lee advised the president that it might become necessary to take drastic steps to protect our interests in Cuba.

As a result, the battleship *Maine* was ordered to Havana. In retaliation, the Spanish cruiser *Vizcaya* was ordered to visit New York Harbor. Ostensibly, the *Maine* was anchored in Havana Harbor on a so-called goodwill mission. There was nothing concerned with goodwill about it. The battleship was there to protect the American residents and American owners of Cuban property. In February, the *New York Journal*, a Hearst newspaper, published a stolen letter written by Señor de Lome,

Spanish minister in Washington, to a friend in Cuba. Señor de Lome labeled McKinley a "cheap politician who tries to leave a door open to himself while on good terms with the Jingoes of his party." Highly embarrassed, de Lome admitted the letter's authenticity and resigned.

Jingoist papers had a field day with the affair and were still exploiting it when news of the *Maine* explosion hit the wires. Two hundred and sixty of her officers and crew lost their lives in the February 15 disaster. Captain Sigsbee of the ill-fated battleship asked the public to refrain from judgment pending investigation. Most Americans assumed that the loss was due to Spanish treachery, that the explosion was caused by a submarine mine. The Spanish Court of Inquiry reported that the explosion might have been caused by combustion in the ship's magazines. Historically the explosion will remain a mystery. However, it was no mystery at the time to the board of American naval officers who were appointed to investigate the disaster. They reported that the explosion was caused by a submarine mine, which, in turn, set off an explosion in the ship's bow.

Throughout the United States, the words "Remember the *Maine*" became a vengeful sound. President McKinley still tried to prevent a war, largely because the country was unprepared for a conflict. A presidential spokesman, Minister Woodford, reported on March 29: "The president instructs me to say that we do not want Cuba. He also instructs me to say, with equal clearness, that we do wish immediate peace in Cuba. He suggests an armistice, lasting until October 1, negotiations in the meantime being had looking to peace between Spain and the insurgents, through the friendly offices of the President of the United States."

Spain made many counterproposals, and the road to peace was cluttered with obstacles. Many men of influence advocated war; some were outspoken while others were more subtle in their words. Senator Thurston of Nebraska said, "War with Spain would increase the output of every American factory, it would increase the business and earnings of every railroad, it would stimulate every branch of industry and domestic commerce." War was to be promoted as a commercial enterprise. Warmongers hid behind no democratic rhetoric. They didn't say they wanted to make the world safe for democracy. They were frank in saying we would take Spain's possessions because we were strong enough to do so. Thurston was not alone in favoring war; Henry Cabot Lodge, Theodore Roosevelt, and others were as war-mad. An attempt on the part of Germany, France and Austria-Hungary to intervene on Spain's behalf was

blocked by the friendly attitude of Great Britain and by President McKinley's own diplomatic skill. In April, the president sent Congress a special message favoring war as a means of ending the conflict. Eight days later, on April 19, Congress declared "that the people of Cuba are, and of right ought to be, free and independent," demanding that Spain withdraw from the island and directing the president to use our forces to carry the resolutions into effect. It was formally stated that the sole purpose of American intervention was to liberate the Cuban people from Spanish rule.

Before the outbreak of hostilities on March 8, 1898, Congress had appropriated $50 million as an emergency fund for national defense. Three weeks later, Congress added $39,000,000 more for the navy. The War Department had been slow to rise to the crisis. Our military posture was alarming; our regular army consisted of 28,183 officers and men. A larger force of poorly-trained state militia could not be assigned to federal service without the consent of War Department Secretary Alger. Weapons were scarce—a few good Krag-Jorgensen rifles and carbines, a larger number of antiquated 45 caliber Springfields, which used black powder, and a limited supply of smokeless-powder cartridges. There was more coast artillery than field guns. Congress authorized the president to call for 200,000 volunteers, and about 182,000 were actually enlisted. Many of these troops were militiamen.

The Spanish army had about 492,000 men under arms. Of these, 10,000 were in Puerto Rico, 51,000 in the Philippines and 278,000 in Cuba. Many of these soldiers were poorly trained and equipped; others had been forced to enlist and their hearts were not in the cause. Spain's best soldiers were no match for the American regular army. Though the United States army was small, it was composed of well-trained and disciplined men. Most of the officers were West Pointers. Many had seen service in the Civil War or in the taming of the West.

When the war was declared in April, Admiral Dewey, then a commodore, was in command of the Asiatic fleet. The Americans had been concentrated at Hong Kong in readiness to strike at Spanish forces in the Philippines. However, Dewey was forced to leave Hong Kong by a British proclamation of neutrality. Dewey's fleet, consisting of a cruiser *Olympia*, three smaller cruisers, two gunboats, a revenue vessel, a collier and a supply ship rendezvoused at Mira Bay on the Chinese coast. On April 25 he received orders to destroy the Spanish fleet which was anchored in Manila Bay. The fleet waited for the arrival of Williams, the American consul at

Manila, before departing. Then, in the late afternoon of April 26, the ships steamed across the China Sea and entered Manila Bay on May 1.

The Spanish fleet at Manila, commanded by Rear Admiral Montojo, was no match for Dewey's force, and the Spanish shore defenses proved useless. In the early morning, the Americans bottled up Montojo's fleet near the Cavite Base and annihilated it during a five-hour siege. American casualties were light: eight men were wounded and no ship was lost.

The action in the Philippines abruptly came to a standstill. The Americans were without troops to garrison the city of Manila. Dewey decided there were neither enough sailors or Marines to serve as an effective police force. He waited until the arrival of ground troops from the United States before entering Manila. For months Dewey's ships were anchored in the bay. On June 30, a small contingent of American troops arrived. It was not until August 13 that enough land forces, with the aid of Filipino insurgents, were able to rout the Spanish and occupy the city. In the Philippine campaign and elsewhere during the almost bloodless war, the navy showed great achievement in contrast to the inefficiency of army leadership. In two major naval engagements in which the Spanish navy was destroyed, American losses were less than twenty men.

The new United States navy, small in comparison to that of Great Britain, contained some powerful vessels manned by skillful officers and men. The main strength was in four battleships: the *Oregon*, *Indiana*, *Massachusetts* and *Iowa*. The *Texas* was rated as a second-class battleship. Numerous cruisers of various classes, gunboats, torpedo boats, and many antiquated monitors were used only for coastal defense.

The navy had been prepared for war. John D. Long, head of the Navy Department, was a very capable man. Theodore Roosevelt, his assistant, was even more capable and possessed a keen knowledge of naval requirements. He understood the importance of preparedness for war and lightning first strikes.

The weakness of the Spanish navy is attributed to inadequate and unskilled seamen. Spain had only one first-class battleship, the *Pelayo*, but she was smaller than the American battleship in the same class and in need of repair. The Spanish naval strength lay in numerous armored cruisers and destroyers, of which the United States had none. Most Americans feared that Spanish sea power was much more formidable than it really was.

At the outset of the war, the North Atlantic fleet, under the command of Rear Adm. William T. Sampson,

was dispatched to Key West. Immediately after the declaration of war, Sampson's fleet moved into Cuban waters to blockade the northern coast. Commodore Winfield S. Schley's force was lying in readiness at Hampton Roads while Commodore J. A. Howell's northern patrol was guarding the eastern seaboard of the United States from Maine to Delaware. Capt. Charles E. Clark brought the battleship *Oregon* from the Pacific Coast around Cape Horn to the Florida coast, a voyage of some fourteen thousand miles. The battleship arrived on May 26 in fine condition and ready for duty.

Rear Admiral Sampson was anxious to get into action and proposed attacking the defenses around Havana. The Navy Department, fearing further international complications, especially with Germany, ordered him to conserve his strength by restraining from unnecessary activity. Intelligence reported that the Spanish Atlantic fleet of four cruisers and two destroyers had been sighted sailing from the Cape Verde Islands under the command of Rear Admiral Cervera. A waiting game followed. Sampson steamed toward Puerto Rico, thinking that Admiral Cervera would refuel at San Juan. Not finding him there, he turned toward Havana on May 12. On the previous day, Cervera had engine trouble near Martinique and had proceeded to Curacao, where he took on a supply of coal. When the news that the Spaniards were near Martinique reached Washington, Commodore Schley was ordered to sail to Cienfuegos. On the south coast of Cuba, Cienfuegos was thought to be the likely place for Cervera to patrol. However, Cervera had taken shelter in Santiago Harbor, and it was days before the Americans found him. Cervera was fairly safe in the bottle-shaped harbor; the narrow entrance to the harbor was well-fortified by guns and mines. He maintained communication with Havana even though the railroad line was cut. Neither troops nor supplies could be sent to his aid.

By the end of May, Schley's force was able to blockade the harbor. Soon afterwards, Sampson's fleet arrived and Sampson assumed command of the whole operation, which involved the greater part of the American navy. Long range bombardments soon reduced some of the resistance. On June 3, an attempt was made to block the harbor by sinking an old collier, the *Merrimac*, across the narrow channel. The effort failed, but the attempt won world-wide applause.

Previously, the United States government had decided not to use large landing forces in Cuba until after the hot summer months. The generals feared deadly tropical fevers which took high tolls during the summer. But

Cervera's plight offered an opportunity to strike a fateful blow. Seventeen thousand ground troops embarked from Tampa, Florida, in the middle of June, bound for Santiago under the command of Maj. Gen. William R. Shafter. Another force consisting of soldiers of fortune, ranchmen, big game hunters, cowboys, Indians, and other adventurers was commanded by Col. Leonard Wood, an army surgeon who had been active during the Indian wars. Architect of this operation was Lt. Col. Theodore Roosevelt, who had resigned his office in the Navy Department to organize an expeditionary force. Roosevelt was offered the top command, but he insisted that Colonel Wood should retain it because of his experience. The regiment was nicknamed "Roosevelt's Rough Riders," or "Teddy's Toughs," as they were called initially.

The army landed at Daiquiri, east of Santiago, on June 22, under cover of barrages from naval guns. Despite inadequate landing equipment, about six thousand men reached Cuban soil by nightfall. The following day, General Lawton's men captured the village of Siboney and the rest of the army landed there.

General Young and the Rough Riders scattered a Spanish detachment at La Guasima and pushed the Spaniards into Santiago. The next week was spent in regrouping the army at Sevilla, bringing up supplies, and making contact with the remnants of General Garcia's insurgents. By this time the United States soldiers were beginning to feel the ravages of fever, poor food and inadequate shelter from heat and rain. General Shafter became ill and was unable to conduct the campaign. Despite Shafter's illness, an attack was planned for San Juan Hill at the end of June. Major General Wheeler's division, which included the Rough Riders, and Kent's division of infantry were to advance on the hill. Major General Lawton was to command 6,500 men to storm the fortifications at El Caney and to protect Wheeler on the right.

On the morning of July 1, Lawton's men attacked the Spanish at El Caney; by late afternoon El Caney was theirs. The fighting at San Juan hadn't gone well; heavy losses were sustained while troops were crossing the San Juan River. Lack of organization and authority caused doubt and hesitation; for a time the troops were trapped under intensive firing. Finally, Brigadier General Hawkins, a Civil War veteran, and Colonel Roosevelt, who was now in command of his regiment, led courageous charges against the Spanish defenses. The fighting remained intense and the battle moved toward Santiago. Some of the rear soldiers wanted to withdraw from the action, but the men and officers at the front protested and refused to retreat. The victorious Americans dug in on the captured hills. On July 3, General Shafter, in serious condition, cabled Washington that he could not take Santiago by a sudden attack and that he had considered withdrawing about five miles to hold a better position. American losses for the battle were 1,100 men.

On the day that General Shafter sent his cable to Washington, a turning point dispelled all thought of retreat. The Spaniards believed that the capture of Santiago was imminent. General Blanco in Havana ordered Admiral Cervera to leave Santiago Harbor. On July 3, Cervera steamed out of the harbor and attempted to escape westward. Admiral Sampson, on the cruiser *New York*, was not with the fleet but had left strict orders to pursue Cervera if he should break out of Santiago. His orders were immediately executed and the American fleet quickly overtook Cervera. In the ensuing battle, Cervera's entire fleet was sunk. The *Cristobal Colon* was the last Spanish ship to go down. No American ships were lost and there were two casualties; one sailor killed and one seriously wounded.

Admiral Sampson, on the cruiser *New York*, did not take part in the action. Commodore Schley was the senior commanding officer during the engagement. A bitter controversy later arose over the question of who was in command.

Santiago was vulnerable from both land and sea but held out until July 14, when General Toral agreed to surrender, thus ending Spanish rule of the island.

McKinley appointed Leonard Wood as provisional governor in Cuba. Although many Americans wanted United States annexation of Cuba, the vast majority stood by our pledge to help establish a free and democratic Cuban government.

Meanwhile, festering internal problems were developing into open sores in the Philippines. As in Cuba, many of the native people had long been dissatisfied under Spanish rule and had revolted frequently. The last of these revolts occurred in 1896. In this Catholic country, the Dominican Order held vast areas of land in the islands and consequently wielded considerable political and economic power. To protest church excesses and civil misrule, a revolt was organized by the Patriot's League under the leadership of Emilio Aguinaldo. The insurgents suffered such privation that Aguinaldo and other top leaders accepted an armistice called the Treaty of Briac-No-Bato on December 15, 1897. Primo de Rivera, the Spanish governor-general, promised to correct certain abuses and to pay the leaders $800,000 if they would stop the revolt and go into exile. The Spaniards never honored their agreement.

Before Commodore Dewey left Hong Kong, he was informed by the American consul at Singapore that Aguinaldo was anxious to continue his struggle against the Spaniards. Dewey therefore arranged a meeting and an American boat brought Aguinaldo and thirteen comrades to Manila Bay. The Americans gave them needed support and soon the Filipinos started a new revolt that ended Spanish domination over much of the Philippine Islands. Aguinaldo's insurgent forces even laid siege to Manila.

Another incident complicating the Philippine situation was the appearance of five German warships in Manila Bay. They had been dispatched to protect Germany's small commercial interests there. All other foreign warships observed neutrality. The Germans ignored the American blockade and interfered with the movements of the insurgents. They openly expressed their sympathy with Spain. Dewey's patience became exhausted and he sent word to the German commander, Vice-Admiral von Diederich, that if he wanted trouble he could have it right now. The import of the message was increased by the presence of the British naval forces in the harbor. Commanded by Capt. Edward Chichester, the British force would have joined the Americans if armed hostilities had broken out between Dewey and Diederich.

Great Britain and the United States had maintained a close friendship during this period; much of it was due to the personal influence of John Hay, the United States Ambassador at London.

Reinforcements arrived late in June. A force of twenty-five hundred troops commanded by Brig. Gen. Thomas M. Anderson landed at Cavite outside of Manila. Brig. Gen. Francis V. Greene and Maj. Gen. Wesley E. Merritt both arrived with additional men before the end of July, making a total of eleven thousand troops. The plight of the Spaniards in Manila became critical. On August 13, the American forces quelled all resistance after a short fight in which only a few Americans were killed or wounded. The day before Manila had surrendered, Secretary of State William R. Day signed a document providing for an armistice, for relinquishing all Spanish claims to Cuba, and for cession of Puerto Rico and Guam to the United States. All Spanish troops were to evacuate Cuba and Puerto Rico. The disposition of the Philippines was to be decided at the peace conference.

The Philippine question was a touchy one; public opinion was divided as to what should be done with the large archipelago. Some wanted to retain it as a fueling base; others wanted to withdraw from the Philippines altogether. In the end, President McKinley decided to annex all the territory. Opponents of annexation contended that the remoteness of the islands would prevent eventual statehood status for the Philippines. However, expansionist views prevailed and on February 6, 1899, the treaty was signed. Approval by the Queen of Spain was delayed by internal politics until March 19, 1899.

The drama which Spain is playing in Cuba continues to be a grotesque and incongruous mixture of tragedy and farce. From Madrid come magnificent Castilian threats, and, after them, pompous Generals to explain, with a voluminous embroidery of words, why they are not carried out. And from Havana come tales of fact to refute these explanations. The Spanish soldier sails from home with high ideals of military valor, and, a few weeks later, robbed of his pay and his rations by haughty, gold-laced Hildalgos, he is begging in the streets of Havana for the price of his dinner, the victim of a sickly attempt to preserve 17th century traditions in the Western Hemisphere. Manifest destiny never promised anything more surely than it promises the failure of this attempt. Whether it will come out of the bare inferiority of Spain to the Insurgent forces, or whether it will be hastened by help from us, tactfully described as "good offices," is a problem that the best diplomats of both countries seem unable to solve. It will have to work out itself. On our own side we have the satisfaction of knowing that the Jingoism which would have had war for war's sake regardless of its justice, has been held in check by the very caution which itself begot; and that armed intervention will never come until it shall be deemed unavoidable by cool heads. For once the Jingo has been of service to his country by inducing a conservative deliberation which will, whatever may come, forbid all questioning of our motives.

The near future promises to enlarge our understanding of the Insurgent. As yet we have had little chance to know him. The press portrayals of his character have been based upon long-range observation or pure fancy. It was impossible that there should exist any class of human beings endowed so exclusively with noble traits as this character in daily newspaper fiction. He was so sternly patriotic, so vehemently self-sacrificing, so hungry for privation. He was never happy except when he was being butchered or starving to death. He would get up in the night if there was a chance to suffer. He was just too good to be true. Coming face to face with him it was inevitable that this ideal should be bruised. Trustworthy reports from the front disclose that the Insurgent is strangely human. He does *not* devote his spare moments to dying in great agony; he has placid moments when he confesses a disinclination to build roads under a blistering sun; and he is of so carnal a habit that, after doing without food a couple of days or so, he hails the appearance of a casual meal with signs of the liveliest satisfaction. Some of the reports on these hitherto unsuspected traits of his character are meant to be discouraging. Yet, in justice to the Insurgent, we should remember that the severest of them show him as common-sense would have expected him to be. Having gone to one extreme let us avoid going to the other. The Insurgent is neither an angel nor a fiend. It is true that he has a stomach and a liking for life, but in spite of it he *is* a fighter and he *is* a patriot.

SOME TIME IN THE FUTURE.

When insurgent and Spaniard have worn themselves out fighting for Cuba, Uncle Sam may

step in and comfort the fair damsel.

Peace comes with a halting gait. It will doubtless be held up a few times along the road. We are conducting our side of the negotiations with candor and celerity. The work consists chiefly in taking those things that are left untaken; and we have learned to be deft at it. Spain goes at her share of the work with less spirit. Every one knows she can have peace any day she chooses to ask for it. But, instead of asking for it bluntly, she betrays a tendency to hint. The intimation that she would like to know our peace terms, preferred through the French Ambassador, can hardly be considered more than a hint. True, it is significant of an awakening to wisdom on Spain's part, but it also signifies that she still clings to her tattered hope of European intervention. If she could but show her sister monarchies that our peace terms are such as to be a menace to other welfares beside her own, would they not combine for her in this last hour? Some such hope must be back of this first essay of hers. It pleases her to pretend that she has been shamefully abused. A study of her attitude suggests that Don Carlos is not the only pretender in Spain—not by an overwhelming majority. But, wriggle and pretend as she may, it is clear that peace is on the way, and on the route mapped out by our own Government.

WAR.

Hamlet McKinley—To be, or not to be; that is the question: Whether 'tis nobler in the mind to suffer the slings and arrows of outrageous fortune, or to take arms against a sea of troubles, and by opposing end them? Shakespeare.

235

Our studies in the science of applied Expansion go on in various parts of the world with a pleasant freedom from interruption by "incidents." We are learning our lessons well as we go. Presumably we had no need to take up the study. Our curriculum was already large enough. But it was forced upon us—in spite of a few chronic newspaper grumblers to the contrary—and we are making the best of it, very gracefully, as has been indicated. Our Cuban friends are behaving with unexpected moderation, perhaps because they have comprehended that their political fate is to be entirely of their own making. The Porto Ricans, needless to say, are showing themselves worthy of their new government. Porto Rico might have been taken by mail. In the Philippines there may be higher hurdles to jump. The conduct of our new acquisition with the gold collar now and then suggests the propriety of a little outspoken criticism. As our Mr. Dewey has ample facilities for making it, however, to be augmented presently by the *Oregon, Iowa* and *Buffalo* and a few more troops of regularly authorized disputants, it is not unreasonable to hope that our demonstrations in and around Manila will be completed ably if not peacefully.

A GOOD-NATURED HINT.

Uncle Sam.—Say, young fellow! You've behaved pretty well; but some of your antics are suspicious.

Just remember that I've got my eye on you!

War makes strange diversions. Having provided soldiers, rations, arms and ammunition, our war officials may have believed that they had reached the last of their duties. They did not suspect that they would be compelled to look after the general comfort and transportation home of the Spanish army in Cuba. Yet they are now facing these obligations, and they are doing quite as well as could be expected. Accommodations have been provided for such of the foe as it has been thought desirable to keep among us, and from all reports they seem to be not inferior to the accommodations of the average Summer-resort. As a Summer hotel-keeper Uncle Sam will probably do so well that his at present unwilling guests will revert fondly to the memories of his hospitality when another Summer comes. It is probable, also, that he will be obliged to inaugurate a series of popular excursions between Santiago and Cadiz. Doubtless they will be made both instructive and pleasant for the twenty-five thousand or so passengers. The latter may have preferred to remain in Cuba, but it is best for them to go home. They would only get into trouble if they staid there. Let us hope that Uncle Sam will do as well in these novel occupations as he has in others more familiar to war.

A TRIFLE EMBARRASSED.

Uncle Sam.—Gosh! I wish they wouldn't come quite so many in a bunch; but, if I've got to take

them, I guess I can do as well by them as I've done by the others!

SPANISH AMERICAN WAR
FOREIGN RELATIONS

Russia embarked on a great program of industrial expansion in 1880. Much of this was artificial and unnatural, but it succeeded with remarkable results. By the turn of the century, Russia possessed a well-expanded industrial sector. Such development required vast sums of money, and Russia had exhausted her capital resources. Both France and Belgium, on the other hand, had surpluses of capital to invest in any enterprise that would make a profit for them. Diplomats on both sides set to work to make satisfactory financial agreements. The Russians needed capital for their infant industries and were quite willing to pay a high interest rate. The French and Belgian people were simply looking for a sound investment and the French government sought to tie Russia with an alliance for political advantages.

Franco-Russian relations grew friendlier, while Anglo-Russian relations remained in open hostility, mutual dislike, and suspicion. Enmity existed between England and Russia because of their rivalry in Turkey and the Balkan states. Each time Alexander II of Russia tried to restrain the Turkish Sultan from his inept methods of governing the Balkan people, England backed the government of the Turkish Empire and helped them evade Russian demands. This gradually brought about the armed conflict of 1877-1878, known as the war of liberation of the Balkans.

Pan-Slavism as a national movement was little understood at the time; the Russians themselves did not quite realize the purpose of the movement. The concept of racial and cultural cohesion was the central theme of the movement. It was the racial element that created strong feelings of unity and of mutual bonds. There existed a big difference between the Russian and the Balkan peoples, both in numbers and in culture. Russia was many times larger and stronger than all of the Slav countries. The small geographical area of the Slavic nations made them very cautious and suspicious in their relations with Russia. The political system of Russia was such that it did not create confidence among the Balkan nations. They feared Russia's interference. Their independence was constantly threatened by Russian expansionism. In addition, Russia's centralized monarchy disapproved of the constitutional developments in the Balkans. Under such conditions, Slavic nations avoided the friendship of Russia.

During the 1880s Anglo-Russian relations strained under a serious crisis in Central Asia. England did not want to see Turkey become a stronger power. England feared the unity of the Ottoman Empire; she herself had occupied Egypt and intended to retain it. England wanted to weaken Turkey. As Russia seemed to have a tight control over Bulgaria, it was there that England planned to challenge her authority. Britain had the willing support of Austria.

Bulgaria was having troubles of her own. Her people were struggling for liberty and freedom from Russian control, which took the form of a tyrannical military rule of a few generals. With the advice and help of England, Alexander of Battenberg sided with the people and advocated a constitutional government. This aroused the ire of the Russians. Russia threatened to sever relations with Bulgaria. The people succeeded in holding their own with the support of England and Austria. This caused strained relations between Russia and England.

Germany tacitly supported the Anglo-Austrian alliance, for it served to counterbalance Russian strength. Otto von Bismarck miscalculated the situation, however, and eventually destroyed relations with Russia. The German attitude helped cement Russian and French relationships. Russia was steadily gaining influence in central Asia, conquering and annexing new territories. She gradually approached the frontiers of India. The British government became alarmed by this Russian expansion. The one hope of Britain was to establish a sphere of influence over Afghanistan and try to create a buffer-state between Russia and India. In counterpoint, Russia attempted to spread her influence in the countries surrounding Afghanistan. Much enmity arose over the situation. Great Britain's central Asian policy wasn't very successful. Their plan was fiercely resisted by the Afghans, who in no way wanted to lose their independence. They refused to have any diplomatic relations with the British and murdered some English officials. The Afghan War followed. The English conquered them, thus firmly establishing British rule over the little country.

Meanwhile, Russia began occupying such central Asian places as Khiva, Samarkand, Kokand, Merv, Bokhara and Tashkent. In 1885-86 the tension between Russia and England became very great, and it seemed as if war would erupt at any moment. The situation finally blew over, but it left a feeling of mistrust and hostility on both sides. The Anglo-Russian tensions during the 1880s strengthened the bonds between Russia and France. England and France were by no means friendly, so it was only natural that Alexander III of Russia, in order to support his own anti-British policy and to oppose Ottoman aggression, turned to France. Their alliance was a marriage of convenience, for Alexander III disliked the French political policies.

One of the most entangling problems of the European situation was the Russian relationship with Austria-Hungary. The complex policies in the Near East, with their parallel alliances, intrigues, and mutual distrusts made the political situation almost incomprehensible. From 1878 to 1897, tension existed between Russia and the Hapsburg monarchy. It was caused by Russia when she achieved a brilliant military victory near Constantinople.

Just prior to that, the Turks had signed the Armistice of San Stefano, which liberated the Balkan Slavs in 1878. The Russian guard regiments had already received their orders to march into the Turkish capital, but the British intervened to put a halt to the plan. The Berlin Congress that followed negated nearly all of Russia's advances. Only the freeing of the Slavs was accomplished.

The constant interference of England and other powers was one of the complicating factors in the Balkans. Particularly involved were England, who had kept Russia out of Constantinople, and Austria, who exerted great force to gain control over the Balkan people. The appearance of Germany on the scene caused a drastic change in the British policy, for it put her unexpectedly on the side of Russia. An agreement was signed between the two in 1893. Russia recognized the British influence in Afghanistan and for a time it seemed that the two powers would be able to maintain friendship in that region. Very soon, however, the old hostility flared up again.

Britain depended on her alliance with Germany after Austria-Hungary's defeat in 1867. The Austria-Hungary empire was governed by a Hungarian by the name of Andrassy, who was eager to collaborate with Bismarck. In 1879 Bismarck arranged a meeting with Count Andrassy to discuss their mutual problems. First, Bismarck suggested an alliance between the two empires against France and Russia. The count, realizing the dangers that were created in the West by Germany's annexation of Alsace-Lorraine, remembered France's hostility. Instead of an alliance, he proposed an agreement that would be aimed against Russia. The chancellor did not agree to this proposal, as he knew that his Emperor William would hesitate to antagonize the Russian Czar, a cousin and close friend. Bismarck compromised as he so often did during his years of service. He agreed to the conclusion of the alliance with Austria, which had been ratified on October 15, 1879. The destiny of the Austrian Empire became absolutely dependent on the policies of the German government. The two monarchies were bound to stand or fall together.

Bismarck's dealings with Austria were based on military motives. He wanted his southern borders neutralized, leaving only the east and west frontiers to defend in case of war. He left the Balkan disputes entirely up to Austria. Germany still had plenty of room for national expansion. Austria was left to deal with Russia and the Balkan Slavs as best she could.

The German chancellor now directed his attention toward making amends with Russia. In this respect he used a former alliance, the so-called "entente of the three emperors." He wished it restored in spite of the new alliance with Austria. Finally he persuaded Russia and Austria-Hungary on June 18, 1881 to sign an alliance renewal with him in Berlin. This pact stated that if one of the three countries should be at war, the other two would remain neutral. If war broke out with Turkey, a special agreement was signed by the three powers regarding neutrality. The alliance was renewed again in September of 1884 at Skierniewice, with a demonstration of monarchical friendship. In 1887 at the renewal conference in Berlin, Russia was treated coldly; but after long negotiations a treaty of "reinsurance" was finally signed. There remained a feeling of suspicion and distrust on both sides. The treaty provided for maintenance of the status quo in the Balkans, for continued control of the Straits, and for the secrecy of the treaty. The Germans also agreed to help restore order in Bulgaria and to remain neutral should Russia have to defend the Straits. The alliance was extended for three years.

By 1890, many changes had taken place in eastern Europe. Bismarck no longer guided the destiny of Germany. When William II ascended to the throne he refused to allow himself to be guided by the chancellor. Bismarck was faced with either becoming a tool in the emperor's hand or arguing with him. He chose the latter and he was soon dismissed. While Bismarck was still in power, the clique that was endeavoring to supplant him told the young emperor that the chancellor was too timid, that he relied too much on treaties and conciliation, that he needlessly feared a Franco-Russian alliance, and that he did not realize that German strength could conquer aggressors. Bismarck's very last act as chancellor was to keep William II out of trouble with Russia. The "Iron Chancellor's" aggressiveness reached its height about the time Emperor William died, March 9, 1888. Emperor Frederick III's brief reign brought about no great change in the situation in Germany, even though as crown prince, Frederick had been more sympathetic toward the liberals than his father had been. He was a confirmed believer in the Bismarckian system. On June 15, 1888, Frederick died, having been on the throne only a few months. The crown prince had no place or part whatsoever in the government of the empire. During his chancellorship, Bismarck had strongly resisted every attempt made by then Crown Prince Frederick III to interfere in political affairs.

In June of 1888, William II ascended the throne. From the standpoint of constitutional law his reign started in 1888, but in reality two years must be deducted. From 1888 to 1890, Bismarck governed in the name of William II. At the very outset and throughout his whole reign, William II felt himself competent to formulate imperial policy. Why was Bismarck unable to retain his position, which he held for thirty years, against a young man who had nothing in his favor other than his royal title? The answer was the Prussian army. The Prussian corps of officers was indebted to the chancellor; yet it felt itself bound by loyalty to the king, not to Bismarck. The chancellor had never taken direct responsibility over the military. The Prussian army was a political body within a political body, commanded by the emperor through the intermediary of his military cabinet and the general staff without any regard for the government. The professional jealousy of the generals was so great that no civilian, not even Bismarck, could gain control over the army. William I had never considered himself to be a rival of Bismarck over the conduct of foreign affairs. Instead, he wholeheartedly supported Bismarck. William II was a more aggressive man and was determined to be his own chancellor. As a result, Bismarck was forced to turn over the reins of power to him.

At the outset of his reign, William II hoped to prepare for a defensive war against Russia and France by formulating an alliance with Austria and possibly with England. Bismarck disapproved of both domestic and foreign policy laid down by William II before he was dismissed.

Throughout his life, the "Iron Chancellor" had a sincere liking for the American as an individual. Some of his cherished friends were Bayard Taylor, William Walter Phelps, Andrew D. White, ambassador in Berlin, and many other cultivated Americans. While the United States had a certain fascination for him, he nevertheless avoided any agreement with the United States during the thirty years he shaped Germany's foreign policy. It was during Bismarck's regime that relations between the two countries became strained for several years. At this time, our most important export goods were forbidden entry into the empire. The main reason for antagonism lay in the United States' efforts to become a world power at the expense of German influence.

When Bismarck was removed from the chancellorship, Germany was by no means a world power. In a military sense she was considered superior in Europe. By triparte agreements she gained a leading political position on the Continent. It was just before the Spanish-American War that the United States was projected into the international political arena. There had seldom been so many radical changes of far-reaching importance as during that period of time. Germany used her opportunities well during and shortly after the Spanish-American War when she seized Kiaochou, thus securing a sphere of influence in China. She then purchased the Caroline

Islands in the Pacific; and by amicable arrangements with England and the United States, she obtained the main portion of the Samoan Islands. In Africa, her sphere of influence was weak; her domains there were undeveloped and small. Germany gained nothing from England's Boer War.

William II was very anti-British at the time he ascended to the throne. He also knew that Alexander III of Russia had had many disputes with England over the years. Although William II wished to have a close relationship with the Czar, he was not adverse to the hostilities between Russia and England. Such a possibility would be advantageous to the young kaiser, as both the countries would be weakened by such a conflict.

European relations had been strained by the harshness and aggressiveness of the "Iron Chancellor," and Russo-German relations had entered a period of marked tension. Russia was seemingly inextricably bound to France. France's capital advances and loan arrangements, in which Germany had no hand, had firmly tied the Czar to France. The real break between Russia and Germany came when Germany increased tariff duties on Russian goods. The Russian government retaliated by raising her tariffs against German goods. The high tariff lasted about three years, from 1892 to 1894, as neither side would give in. It was evident that the young emperor of Germany had failed to establish a strong German influence in Russia. The Czar had spoiled his plans and to save the situation, the kaiser was forced to sign a new treaty in 1894. Germany thus abandoned all hopes of exploiting the Russian market in getting raw materials.

William II determined all German foreign and domestic policies after 1890. While the new emperor displayed no lack of enthusiasm in dispatching his duties as head of state, his technical knowledge was lacking. Although he permitted his ministers to oppose him in small matters, William II never allowed anyone to pursue a definite course in domestic and foreign affairs. Political chaos resulted from this method of government and nothing of great importance was accomplished during his reign.

The United States was on the verge of territorial expansion when Grover Cleveland assumed the office of president again in 1893. Relations of this country and Hawaii had been close for a long time. American industry and missionary work among the natives had had an important part in developing the islands. A reciprocity treaty had been negotiated in 1875 whereby lower grades of sugar were admitted duty free to this country. In 1884, Hawaii granted the United States a naval base at Pearl Harbor. The unstable government in Hawaii gave grave concern to planters who had commercial interests in the Islands. They directed their efforts toward the establishment of a protectorate, if not annexation, by the United States.

A political revolution took place in January of 1893. Queen Liliuokalani was removed from her throne and a provisional government established. The provisional government assumed, in the name of the United States, "protection of the Hawaiian Islands" and raised the United States flag over the government buildings. This action was not acknowledged by Secretary Foster, for fear of impairing the independent sovereignty of the Hawaiian government.

Strong pressure was applied to secure ratification of the treaty in the Senate. Current opinion was favorable for immediate annexation. Those who supported annexation pointed to the commercial advantages and military strategy the United States would gain. It was feared that if the United States did not take over Hawaii, England or some other power would do so. The Senate also had to consider constitutional problems in annexing distant territory. With these detailed questions the action was consequently delayed. After the facts were investigated, Secretary Gresham concluded that a great wrong had been done to a defenseless and independent state, and advised that amends be made by restoring the legitimate government. The United States was the first to recognize the independence of the Islands.

RIVAL SUITORS.

Courting Miss Congo.

THE centre of Africa is the centre of a good deal of attraction just now among the potentates of Europe. Uncle Sam, whose distinguished citizen Henry M. Stanley threw so much light on the secrets of the dark continent, not having the colonizing instinct very much developed, looks on as a comparatively disinterested spectator; but Germany, England, Italy, Portugal, and other nations are wooing the dusky maiden of the deserts most assiduously. It is all a matter of business. The Congo drains and opens up a vastness of territory containing many natives; these natives have wants which it is the ambition of civilization to supply. Civilization is quite prepared to furnish bibles, beads and rum in exchange for ivory, palm oil and gold-dust. The rivalry arises from the commercial industry of a lot of traders, who are all anxious to be first in a new field, and to control it. And so it goes.

England's experience in Africa has not, of late, been of so pleasant a nature as she could wish. Still, the "grasping islanders," as someone calls them, are never content to see any portion of the inhabitable globe occupied by others. Under Bismarck's influence, Germany has recently developed an astonishing *penchant* for colonization, and poor little Portugal claims that she was the first, and ought, in common justice, to be allowed &some finger in the pie.

Amongst them all THE JUDGE is inclined to let his sympathies go to Miss Congo. Whichever wins, she is pretty certain to get left, eventually.

"Too many lovers puzzle a maid."

European diplomacy in the East continues to preach a high and humane morality and to practise a steady devotion to its own selfish ends. There are some discordant notes in the concert of the Powers just now, but they only repeat a discord which has been periodical since the Powers first took the direction of Turkish affairs, and which must continue so long as their real object is to keep a jealous watch upon one another. Because of their interested support of the Ottoman Empire they were directly responsible for the Cretan troubles of thirty years ago; they must be held accountable for the Bulgarian atrocities of twenty years ago; the blame is theirs for the frightful Armenian massacres of last year and the year before; and, now, for the trouble in Crete. While professing to have interfered only from motives of lofty disinterest they have, in effect, encouraged and protected the Sultan in his misgovernment. Indeed, it is hard to see how the unspeakable Turk could have been any more unspeakable had he been left to his own sanguinary devices. He has received ultimatums until he must feel hurt and neglected when he can not begin his day by reading a fresh one, stern and final in tone. And then there is the British Blue Book. Whenever the cries of outraged Christians have become unusually piercing the British Foreign Office, nerved to desperation by their suffering, has rashly and wrathfully issued a Blue Book. But even this desperate remedy has not availed to make Armenians in Constantinople good life-insurance risks. There is a lesson in this situation for our own legislators. Let them review these futile efforts to answer the Eastern question, and see how all real patriotism and decency are sacrificed to base and selfish ends when a nation goes out of its way to interfere with the affairs of another.

THE QUARRELSOME EUROPEAN NURSERY.

Madam Peace—goodness gracious! Were there ever such troublesome children? They were always promising to be good, and yet they were always squabbling.

General Boulanger is enjoying his apotheosis in France to-day, and he will do well to get all the enjoyment he can out of it. No doubt it may be what Bismarck would call a "pleasant memory" for him, in later and darker days. But he should keep in mind the fact that when France dethrones an idol, she does not lift him gently to the ground; but slumps him down uncommonly hard, and dances on the resultant fragments. And it would be well for General Boulanger to bear in mind, as he recalls the fate of Napoleon III, that a Boulanger is not even a Napoleon III.

THE SITUATION IN GERMANY.

Peasant Hans.—You needn't trouble yourself to blow up that French bugbear, Prince Bismarck;

when the time for fighting comes, I'll be on deck!

The war cloud which has been hanging over Europe, on account of the recent difficulty between Turkey and Greece, has passed away for the present. Russia will now be able to devote her whole attention to throttling her Nihilists, England to keeping the turbulent Irish in order, and Germany to settling her domestic and imaginary Jewish troubles. But the European atmosphere will only remain clear for a time, for this Greek question is of such a nature that it is liable to be revived at any moment, and cause more exchanges of notes, and threatening talk by the newspapers of the respective countries, dispatches, envoys, protocols, preparations for war, then concessions on the part of either Turkey or Greece, and then peace again, until the next inevitable dispute arises. Americans don't really care whether Greece annexes Turkey or Turkey annexes Greece, or whether Russia or Austria annexes them both. Neither nationality demands any sympathy from us. American night editors are the only individuals who suffer by these troubles, because they have to look in Gazetteers to see how to spell the jaw-breaking names peculiar to South-Eastern Europe. Greece has no longer anything to howl about, and will cease, it is to be hoped, for some time to come, to disturb the neighbors.

The Anarchists and Socialists, and the turbulent and vicious among our German-American fellow citizens, were more or less miserable over the celebration of Kaiser Wilhelm's ninetieth birthday, last week, but decent Americans of German origin or free-born may well have taken pleasure in drinking the old gentleman's health. No earnest republican can unreservedly admire even the best of emperors—or, indeed, wholly understand the imperial idea. But, since there are emperors, it is desirable that they should be good of their kind; and there is no kingly ruler in the world to-day who is a better man, after his own pattern, than the white-haired old soldier who has just ended his ninetieth year. His traditions, his ideas of government, of social rank and caste, bind him closely to a time long gone by; his theories are the theories of the last century. But if he has old ideas, he has also old ideals, and his daily life is an endeavor to realize them or at least to live in conformity with them.

In Kaiser Wilhelm's eyes a monarch is a man who has duties, as well as privileges. He holds it incumbent upon himself to lead a life that shall be an example to his subjects; and he lives such a life as thoroughly as a man may. His private life is a model of dignified and austere virtue. He makes his whole family amenable to the rigorous code which he imposes upon himself. In public he fulfills every description of imperial etiquette; and he encourages in those about him a spirit of honesty, honor, activity and patriotism. We want no Kings or Kaisers in this country; but the highest and the humblest American citizen may well learn a lesson from the dutiful, self-restrained, conscientious life of this old-fashioned monarch, left over from the last century.

And even the Anarchist who would not drink the old Kaiser's health ought to reflect—if an Anarchist can reflect—that he has little right to complain of the good old Kaiser when he cries out against the government of Germany. Wilhelm is Emperor, in truth; but in Germany there is to-day a higher than the Emperor—the Emperor's humble servant; the Chancellor of the Empire, a stern, shrewd, stubborn, overbearing, foxy, sinister, loyal, fearless old man, named Bismarck, who holds the government of Germany in the hollow of his hand, and is the one arbiter of peace and war in all Europe. It is this original and powerful man who practically stands for Germany in her dealings with other nations; and it is he who to-day holds the balance of power in Continental Europe. His fame will outlive that of the honest old Emperor. Kaiser Wilhelm will figure in the school text-books with Henry the Fourth of France and Elizabeth of England; but Bismarck's name will live forever in the literature of politics; and even in fiction, as a type more strong, deep and subtle than any in the annals of statecraft. We use the name of Machiavelli in familiar comparison—but whom shall we ever compare with Bismarck?

THE EUROPEAN EQUILIBRIST.

If the French Republic does go under in the present time of trouble, it will be, not because of the great scandal, but because of the noisy scandal-mongers. Prophesies of disaster, widely circulated and long persisted in, may in the end undermine the credit of almost any institution. No doubt a great many of the newspaper correspondents who are so freely asserting that the last days of the Republic are at hand, have every reason to wish that their predictions might come true. All is fish that comes to their net; and the downfall of the Republic, while it may mean the suffering and danger of a great people, must surely mean columns upon columns of salable news for the journalistic adventurers who have thronged to Paris. But none the less is their conduct sordid and mean. The French Republic is in sore straits enough without the malign assistance of the newspaper harpies who are trying to stir the populace up to mischievous frenzy. Nor has the Republic, in spite of its misdoings in the Panama business, deserved this treatment. It has been a Republic in good faith, and not a temporary make-shift designed to keep the people quiet while some pretender's scheme of usurpation is undergoing a process of clandestine coddling. For this record it deserves loyalty from its friends, and consideration from all who are not its avowed enemies.

The truth is that the crisis through which the French Republic is passing at present is only one of those severe object-lessons by means of which a people is sometimes forced to learn the inevitable result of recklessness in public affairs—affairs governmental, commercial or financial. The Panama affair is no worse, morally, than England's South Sea Bubble; it differs in degree only, and not in kind, from her railway scandals of half a century ago, and from our own Crédit Mobilier iniquity. A nation that is not inherently rotten and vicious can live to learn such a cruel and bitter lesson, and to profit by it. There can be little doubt that the revulsion of feeling following the explosion of Law's Bubble brought about a healthy, if somewhat narrow, spirit of conservatism in business affairs, by which England is the gainer to this day and hour. Nor is it to be questioned that the exposures of the laxity and corruption that disgraced the Federal government during Grant's Presidential period were the direct cause of an awakened popular sensitiveness in regard to such matters which has gradually led to the purification and elevation of the government service in many of its branches—certainly we have every reason to pride ourselves on the steady improvement in personal character and general calibre of the House of Representatives, ever since that unhappy epoch.

The Panama scandal will doubtless cost France a great deal, but it may pay her more than it costs her if it stirs her to certain movements of reform and reconstruction. It may teach the lovers of the Republic that they can not guard their honor too jealously; and that they put her good name in all but fatal jeopardy when they permit colossal schemes for public investment to be floated without the strictest and most carefully safeguarded provisions for wise and faithful management. It may show the thrifty Frenchman, whether he be a workingman or a shop-keeper, that sure and small profits are the best and safest thing the small investor has to look for; and that when he reaches down into the blue woolen stocking, which stands as the type and symbol of French thrift, it should be to buy realties, and not to speculate in rainbows. And, perhaps, what is best of all, it may teach the whole French people that their whole judicial system is unpractical, unfair, unreasonable, undignified and inadequate beyond anything known in the civilized world.

What with the queer law of our Government lawyers, and the ridiculous inadequacy of our precautions against warlike attack, foreign or domestic, we do not cut a very dignified figure in the eyes of the world at large; and Europe may well add two more items to the list of points on which she loves to twit her younger sister. The European of to-day firmly believes that all Americans live in hotels or boarding-houses; that their children all drink mixed drinks and smoke strong cigars; that the raw Irish "servant-girl" is exported to America in large numbers, only to be blown up with kerosene, misused for kindling the fire; that the Fifth Avenue swell and the Wall Street banker walk about our metropolis with revolvers in their hip-pockets, that, in short, our habits are awful, and manners we have none. Probably, if our transatlantic friends could trace the sources from which they derived these impressions, they would find that a good many of them sprang from the one Yankee Nation of which our friends on the other side have really no idea—the Great American Joke—used too often, we fear, to the mystification of a literal-minded world.

Germany is ruled to-day by a man walking in a dream. The German Emperor, by those who have observed him closely since he became an emperor, has been denounced as a madman, a headstrong boy, a bigot and a tyrant. But, although his conduct has certainly invited each and every one of these accusations, they are all unjust. He is simply an anachronism: a man of the middle ages, a reversion to a type elsewhere extinct; a man who in the last decade of the nineteenth century lives, moves and has his being in a dreamland that was a reality to his remote ancestors. It is always a hazardous task to attempt to forestall history, or to make criticism upon the character of a public man until it has gone through its final trial; but the young Emperor has sat upon the throne of Germany long enough to justify those who have watched his career in passing certain positive judgements upon the man and upon his ideas. And it seems to us that no one who has conscientiously kept track of his doings and sayings can doubt that the man is as honest as his ideas are fantastic.

There can be no doubt that he believes in himself; and the size of Himself to Himself is something astounding and almost incredible in these days of cold, scientific realism. He has re-created for himself a world that to other men is lost in mists of historical romance. His fancy has evoked a pageant of the middle ages—of armored knights, of flashing swords and gleaming lances, of silken banners and sounding trumpets; of all that pomp and panoply that attended the monarch who went forth from his castle gates clad in the divine right of kings, to make war or peace on earth, as it pleased him.

258

To us of democratic America to conceive of such a picture requires an effort on the imagination; to the rulers of modern Europe such a conception represents a tradition of very little vitality. Theoretically, no doubt, the first Emperor of united Germany believed himself divinely commissioned to reign. Practically he was quite content to leave the working out of the will of Providence to his great Prime Minister. His son's brief reign, from beginning to end, was under the shadow of imminent death, and gave no indication of a definite policy; but there can be little doubt that the late Emperor assumed his duties in the true spirit of a constitutional monarch, and that he would rather have cultivated loyalty to the national idea than devotion to the personality of the sovereign. But in the mind of the present Emperor of Germany the whole German empire is buttoned up inside of his military coat.

Of course, there is something comic about this attitude, view it as you will; and it is comic., and nothing else, to Americans who regard it with nothing more than a curious interest. It is amusing to read from time to time of the fulminations of this chipper and self-complacent young deity in spurs and helmet; as he swaggers before the battle-scarred veterans whose prowess established the Empire over which the accident of birth has called him to rule, and instructs them in their duty, not to the great nation which they have welded together out of a chaos of disrupted elements, but to *him*—to him, the pitiful stripling whose only title to respect is that he is the son of his father.

But to the people of the German nation the serious

aspect of the situation must have an increasing importance with every year that increases the divergence of their path and that of their Emperor. For those two paths are separating day by day, and in the nature of things they can never meet. Since the year 1848, popular education has been steadily building up a new Germany. The spirit of modern culture has spread from the highest classes to the lowest. That great body of the proletariat which the German cartoonists figure as "Michael the Peasant" has grown most amazingly in knowledge and understanding. Originally this figure stood for a loutish clown, great in strength and endurance, ignorant, slow of apprehension, but wise with a certain mother-wit and native shrewdness. To-day the "German Michel" is a thinking man with a sound though rudimentary education. And the education that he has acquired is of the most materialistic and rationalistic sort. He has freed himself from the romantic traditions of feudalism, and he has learned to look upon the spread of science and civilization as the ultimate hope of the poor. With every step of his new education he draws further and further away from the course of the young idealist who is striving to re-establish a medieval monarchy, and to build up a boundless military power, regardless alike of the needs and of the resources of the nation. "Follow Me!" cries the young Emperor, as he demands of his legislators more soldiers, more ships, more arms, more fortresses—but how long, how far will it follow him, this great, slow-moving creature that is day by day awakening to a knowledge of its power, and that has already set its face forward as resolutely as he has turned his toward the darkness of the past?

"HIFALUTIN" HOHENZOLLERN.

Kaiser William.—Follow me, ladies and gentlemen;—my way is the way of universal happiness.

I am the only man who knows it all!

The death of Gambetta is unquestionably a great loss to France. He was the only true democratic conservative statesman that the country possessed, and was a sincere patriot. Although a powerful and flowery orator, with much of the excitability and volatility of all members of the Latin race, he was singularly free from the theatrical mannerism so marked in many great Frenchmen. He did not pose; he was thoroughly honest and terribly sincere in his convictions. He loved liberty, and he loved France, and although the republic may continue to exist without him, it has lost one of its best friends and its strongest pillars of support.

AN UNFINISHED WORK.

Russia is strong geographically and by her weakness. She has no navy to be attacked by a foreign foe; no out-lying dependencies to defend; her scattered population and great area make invasion profitless and indecisive, if not fatal to the successful invader, as in the case of Bonaparte. Her very inertia contributes to her formidableness. She is feared and dreaded by all her neighbors.

England may fear her most of any power because her outlying Indian lots are in Russia's path of expansion, as are the possessions of no other power—a line undefined, remote and inaccessible to England, but one upon which Russia moves from the inside of a circle. Russia, albeit without a navy to meet England, has by far the larger army. England is therefore stronger than Russia on the sea, and in a protracted struggle only excels in the matter of money.

To compensate for this advantage England has a troublesome war on her hands in Soudan, insurection in Manitoba, chronic Irish enmity and a home population honeycombed with Republican ideas and industrial discontent.

In this condition of affairs, with Parliament almost ready to unhorse him, Gladstone was dazzled by the Russian Aurora Borealis. The spectre that haunted Bonaparte's regime and has cast its lurid glare on European politics ever since, is now in one of its brilliant outbursts. What disturbance of the political atmosphere shall result?

THE SPECTRE OF EUROPEAN POLITICS.